D1575457

THE
PROMISE
OF
GREEN
POLITICS

Environmentalism and the Public Sphere

DOUGLAS TORGERSON

DUKE UNIVERSITY PRESS   DURHAM AND LONDON 1999

© 1999 Duke University Press
All rights reserved
Printed in the United States of America
on acid-free paper ∞
Typeset in Trump Mediaeval by
Tseng Information Systems, Inc.
Library of Congress Cataloging-in-Publication Data
appear on the last printed page of this book.

For my mother and the memory of my father

CONTENTS

THIS BOOK IS NOT A GREEN manifesto, nor an attempt to tidy up any of the various manifestos, programs, and blueprints that have been advanced since environmentalism first became notable on the public stage. I take my point of departure from the fact that, over the past three decades, the basic outlines of green concerns have become clear and significant enough that they now frame an environmental discourse that, while diverse and contentious, has sufficient coherence, cohesion, and scope to be significant in public life.

As part of this discourse, green political thought has recently taken shape as a distinctive field of inquiry. In this book, I attempt to rethink green political thought by thinking at the same time both with and against the prevailing concerns and categories of the field. My main point is not to establish final theoretical conclusions or to design a practical program of action, but to explore the promise of green politics. Understanding this promise is important to the process of shaping the green public sphere.

With one foot in the green movement and the other in the domain of political theory, green political thought occupies a point of intersection situated between immediate green concerns and enduring questions that have confronted political theorists over the centuries. This connection clearly raises familiar problems involved in relating theory and practice. However, green political thought is also positioned to inform the identity and direction of the green movement while offering insights into the nature and tasks of political theory.

Against the general backdrop of political theory, the most distinctive feature of green political thought is that it places nature at the center of attention. More precisely, it questions long-cherished presuppositions about human/nature relationships. The primary impetus for this questioning is the perception that the celebrated course of industrialization has rendered modern civilization ecologically irrational, unsustainable in the long run and perhaps even in the short run. Progress, once hailed as the hope and crowning glory of humanity, comes to be portrayed as an enormous fiasco, a self-destructive delusion of grandeur.

Green concerns, however, go beyond human prospects and bring attention to the interests of nonhuman nature. A key feature of green political thought, as of environmental ethics, is the debate between homocentrism and ecocentrism: Should normative deliberations continue to center exclusively or primarily upon human interests, or should the focus of deliberations shift, displacing the traditional centrality of human interests with egalitarian attention to the interests of the natural world?

Questions of identity and strategy are bound up with this debate. What does it mean to be green? Does it mean promoting ecological rationality for the sake of human interests, or does it mean moving beyond homocentric concerns—even sacrificing human interests—in the name of ecocentric egalitarianism? A definitive answer to this question, a clear nod to one alternative or the other, is often thought necessary to establish a coherent green identity, meaningful goals, an effective strategy. What the opposing parties to the debate seem to agree upon is the need for a clear conclusion.

This would mean putting an end to debate, but who would deny that, in a desperate situation, talk must give way to effective action? The green movement in this way confronts an apparent political imperative to push aside questions and banish doubts to move ahead in a concerted manner. The point of political action is success in achieving green goals—particularly, in halting the rampant destruction of nature and the self-destruction of humanity.

But the irony in all this should be obvious. Even though a key element of the green critique of modern culture is to reject instrumentalism as a prevailing orientation, desperate green concerns markedly reinforce an instrumentalist conception of politics. An aura of tragic seriousness prevails. Certainly, there has often been talk of green politics initiating a new politics, a participatory politics at odds with the administrative state, even the whole administrative sphere of advanced industrial society. Green political thought thus contains the potential to think beyond an instrumentalist conception of politics in order to understand more fully the promise of green politics. This potential, however, remains constrained. In this book, I attempt to loosen the constraints by giving explicit attention to the idea that politics is valuable not only in instrumental terms—as a means to ecological rationality, the rights of nature, justice, or a better world—but also in intrinsic terms, as an end in itself. My principal focus is not what it means to be green, but the meaning and value of politics.

The notion of a green state has lately gained attention, with the potential for a green democracy as the key focus (the "green state" was one of the themes at the International Conference on Environmental Justice, University of Melbourne, Australia, October 1–3, 1997). Early calls for authoritarian solutions have been countered by the observation that the narrow instrumentalism of rationalistic management often proves to be glaringly ineffective. At the same time, anarchist prescriptions are taken to neglect problems of coordination in the formulation and administration of legitimate and effective public policy. Only a democratic form, it is argued, can potentially possess the openness, flexibility, coherence, and legitimacy necessary for a fallible humanity to cope with the complexities and uncertainties posed by environmental problems. Of course, this defense of democracy amounts to an argument for enhancing effectiveness rather than a rejection of instrumentalism.

Nonetheless, if a green state is to be democratic, there is the further question of what kind of democracy it is to be. One possibility is some variation on the conventional liberal democratic model, in which democracy is pictured principally as a form of representative government with citizen participation largely limited to voting in elections. Challenges to this conventional model, however, have drawn attention to undemocratic features of the social context of liberal democratic government. Critics have also questioned the model's reliance on a vast administrative apparatus. An alternative, it is argued, would involve active participation, including enhanced deliberation and discourse in a public sphere.

Liberal democracy, in other words, is not simply the opposite of authoritarianism, but in both concept and practice contains its own distinctly authoritarian tendencies. Only a participatory orientation that clearly breaks with authoritarianism would thus seem to provide a green state with that democratic openness and flexibility needed to grapple with environmental problems.

What environmentalism has most significantly created in the prevailing political context is a manner of speaking about the environment that was not previously possible—a range of discursive practices, expressive of green concerns, that allows environmental problems to be recognized, defined, and discussed in meaningful ways. The green movement continues to construct a green discourse and to shape a forum for communication, a green public sphere. Even with its many internal differences and disagreements, the emerging green public sphere poses a challenge to the once comfortable framework of industrialist discourse.

Democratic challenges to the liberal democratic model currently pay particular attention to the promise of the public sphere as an open domain for active communication among citizens. According to this view, democratization must put an end to citizen quiescence, to the sway of mass media propaganda, and to a prevailing faith in the administrative mind. The potential of the public sphere has particularly been acclaimed in regard to the rise of new social movements since the late 1960s. Yet, the diversity of these movements has provoked talk of a plurality of public spheres, differing according to a range of perspectives and identities. Especially with postmodern and feminist interventions, the prospect and desirability of a unitary public sphere, a homogeneous *we* of citizens, have become dubious.

Obviously, any context of meaningful communication depends on the coexistence of identity *and* difference, unity *and* plurality. The capacity to communicate with others does not entail necessary agreement, except to the extent that some minimal agreement on the terms of discussion is needed to understand disagreement. Of course, even this kind of understanding may well be difficult and precarious, and it is surely always bound up with the interplay of power. Nonetheless, unless one maintains that particular identities are fixed and sacrosanct, it is possible to imagine a plurality of public spheres that—although differing within and among themselves—are also part of a larger, dynamic context of meaningful public communication: a public sphere. Here the idea of shared citizenship makes sense. Certainly, this prospect cannot be ruled out in principle, and to argue publicly against its desirability is already to presuppose common terms by which disagreements can be understood.

The green public sphere takes its place amid a plurality of public spheres, promising to undermine the uncritical industrialism that still largely sets the terms of public discourse. Does the green public sphere retain a unique and particular identity? Does it establish alliances with other public spheres that also, in their own ways, challenge the prevailing forms of discourse? Would such alliances open up a communicative space diminishing the differences among these spheres? Is the telos of the green public sphere ultimately to expand and absorb the diversity of public spheres within itself? Or is the green public sphere to lose its own identity while giving to others a green accent? Is the discourse of industrialism to be altogether displaced? Is the green public sphere to remain at a remove from the state and the administrative sphere generally, or is the line of demarcation to be indefinite?

These questions—centered, as they are, on the inescapable ambivalence of identity and difference—could be addressed in terms either of likelihood or desirability. Even to pose them as meaningful questions, however, presupposes the green public sphere as an incipient communicative domain of participants able to understand and discuss shared hopes and prospects. The aim of this book is not to resolve such questions and thereby render further discussion irrelevant. The point, rather, is to encourage meaningful communication by drawing attention to an emerging context that makes it possible.

My interest in the relationship between politics and environment arose during the late 1960s while I was an undergraduate studying political theory at Berkeley. My attention was then captured by a small newspaper story, which reported a biologist's claim that the human species would soon vanish due to environmental deterioration, joining whales and other great mammals in imminent extinction. I asked another undergraduate, a biology major, what he thought of this. I have long forgotten his name, but I still clearly remember his reply. He matter-of-factly told me that an environmental catastrophe leading to human extinction was quite likely. He also said that you had to laugh about it. If you could not see the irony in human self-destruction, he said, if you could not laugh at it, you could well go mad. His recommendation, of course, did not really amount to more than a suggestion of the therapeutic value of gallows humor.

The idea of laughing in the face of environmental catastrophe, nonetheless, not only startled me, but also intrigued me, and I have long wondered about its political significance. Such laughter could well appear outrageous, even disgusting, as inviting politically naïve quiescence if not misanthropic glee. But the laughter may indirectly suggest another message, one that cannot be quickly dismissed and that contains important lessons for green politics.

I was not then fully convinced of an impending environmental catastrophe, but the prospect did appear to me entirely plausible. Despite many efforts to debunk environmentalism with industrialist cheerleading, nothing has happened since to make this prospect seem less likely to me. If anything, events seem to me to have underscored the plausibility of such a scenario. What did strike me as obvious when I first began to think about this prospect was that, if warnings of environmental catastrophe turned out to be at all accurate and convincing to many people, there would be incalculable political consequences. Also, what struck me as remarkable when I initially began focusing attention on this political dimension in the late 1960s was the lack of a more general, concerted concern.

No sooner had I gained this impression, however, than a dramatic transformation occurred. Suddenly, environmental concerns were at the forefront of public attention, and a range of new environmental groups began to spring up. An environmental movement quickly took shape and achieved general recognition with Earth Day in the spring of 1970. With the advent of environmentalism, a green discourse emerged to take a distinctive place in the realm of public debate.

Perhaps because I had signed up in 1969 to do some work with a new ecology group, one day that year I received unsolicited in the mail a set of pamphlets by a certain Murray Bookchin. Though these writings did not turn me into a follower of Bookchin, their sophisticated and insightful quality worked an early and significant effect on my outlook. Emerging green concerns became intimately connected in my view to key problems of political theory.

In the ensuing years, I pursued my studies in political theory and also became involved in environmental activism. Environmental concerns drew my attention as well to problems of environmental policy and administration and ultimately to a good deal of critical work on policy and administration generally.

Early in my education as a political theorist, it was my good fortune to learn from two exceptional teachers—Norman Jacobson at Berkeley and Alkis Kontos at the University of Toronto—the importance of understanding that political theory is not simply concerned with the form and content of arguments. With its textualist dispositions, postmodernism in its own often insightful ways lately has promulgated much the same lesson, but at the risk of exacerbating the disorientations and antipolitical inclinations of modernity. My thinking has by no means remained immune to the influence of such figures as Derrida, Foucault, Deleuze, Rorty, Lyotard, and others, but my focus nonetheless has been much more decisively shaped by a range of thinkers still clearly attracted to the idea of meaningful political life.

Hannah Arendt is the key figure in this regard, and her celebration of politics is pivotal in my effort to understand and assess the promise of green politics. In addition, Sheldon Wolin, Hanna Pitkin, and Henry Kariel also influenced my view of politics. In another vein, the critique of reason and domination developed by the chief figures of early critical theory—Adorno, Horkheimer, and Marcuse—also plays an important role here, as does C. B. Macpherson's critique of possessive individualism.

Obviously, my concern with the public sphere means that Jürgen Habermas is inescapably of central importance, even though I find that his work requires an antidote—particularly supplied here, by the way, through the insights of Mikhail Bakhtin. It is indeed through Bakhtin that we can begin to perceive the full significance of laughter, the comic, and the carnivalesque in green politics and the emergence of a green public sphere.

This book would be impossible in its present form without earlier works that have attempted to delineate the field of green political thought, particularly Andrew Dobson's *Green Political Thought* and Robyn Eckersley's *Environmentalism and Political Theory*. These perceptive, well-informed books deserve attention, and they would prove especially valuable to interested readers lacking a strong background in either political theory or the environmental literature. Both Dobson and Eckersley advance strong ecocentric positions. Although I do not necessarily reject the principle of ecocentrism, I am more inclined to equivocate. My purpose here, at any rate, is not to stake out a moral position but to encourage a political space that invites the consideration and exchange of opinions—a space that would at least take ecocentrism seriously.

Robert Goodin's *Green Political Theory* does not provide an introduction to the field, but prescribes an approach that, Goodin believes, will help to clear up much green confusion. I have learned from Goodin's sophisticated analysis, but I tend to think more against than with him. The work of John Dryzek presents an opposite case. In the areas of green political thought, democratic theory, and public policy, our approaches tend to be complementary, in my view, though there are of course differences. Frank Fischer's work presents a similar case. I have learned much from both of them.

Meeting William Leiss in the Faculty of Environmental Studies at York University during the mid-1970s was important to me because his work helped me to connect my environmental concerns with my interest in critical theory. It was also through Leiss that I first became aware of the remarkable work of John Rodman. I first met Robert Paehlke during the mid-1970s as well, but we became colleagues at Trent University some years later, during the early 1980s. My long association with him at Trent has played a key role in my understanding of environmental matters.

The green public sphere is not something isolated in any single country, but is clearly international in scope. This is a point that can hardly be ignored in a time when the theme of globalization has begun to pervade public discourse. At the same time, the emerging green public sphere increasingly includes voices from the so-called underdeveloped countries. This is the case as well with aboriginal voices, both on an international scale and in those settler nations that have largely displaced first nations from their homelands. These points, although recognized and understood in this book, are not given the kind of systematic attention that their complexity calls for. The focus for my rethinking of green political thought instead proceeds primarily from green perspectives developed in the industrialized countries of the West—an unavoidable point of departure, at least for me. Moving decisively beyond that orientation would involve another rethinking of green political thought.

Anyone seeking simple recipes will not be satisfied by this book. Manifestos, programs, and blueprints can no doubt be worthwhile in gaining an orientation for political practice, but there is a need to think beyond them. Political practice must often be confident and decisive, but an unthinking overconfidence can also mislead, inhibiting that inventive form of action that takes critical account of its context and its purpose.

I am grateful for the advice and encouragement of several people who read portions of the manuscript: Peter Christoff, Frank Fischer, Peter Hay, Robert

Paehlke, Andreas Pickel, and Andrew Wernick. I especially thank the two reviewers who read the full manuscript for Duke University Press, John Dryzek and Robyn Eckersley. Their criticisms were indispensable. Encouragement throughout the project from Valerie Millholland, my editor at Duke, was also of key importance to me in finding the shape of the book. Finally, I would like to thank Mary McLoughlin for insights into the aesthetic and theological dimensions of ecofeminism.

Some portions of this book are drawn from material I have earlier published, though this has been substantially revised and rearranged. The material is used here in accordance with copyright (brackets indicate the chapters in this book where material from the source is mainly to be found): "Policy Professionalism and the Voices of Dissent: The Case of Environmentalism," *Polity* 29 (1997): 345–74 [chapter 4]; "The Uncertain Quest for Sustainability: Public Discourse and the Politics of Environmentalism," in *Greening Environmental Policy: Toward a Politics of Sustainability*, ed. Frank Fischer and Michael Black (London: Paul Chapman Publishers, 1995), 3–20 [chapter 3]; "Strategy and Ideology in Environmentalism: A Decentered Approach to Sustainability," *Industrial and Environmental Crisis Quarterly* 8 (1994): 295–321 [chapters 2, 7]; and "The Paradox of Environmental Ethics," *Alternatives: Perspectives on Society, Technology and Environment* 12, no. 2 (1985): 26–36 [chapter 6].

THE PROMISE OF GREEN POLITICS

THE MEANING OF GREEN POLITICS is obviously bound up with what it means to be *green*. It is a question that pervades the green movement, giving rise to some intense conflicts and an air of tragic seriousness.

This very seriousness can verge on the comic, as in heated controversies over whether certain supermarket products (such as disposable diapers produced in an "environmentally friendly" manner) deserve to be labeled *truly* green.[1] But few greens are inclined to treat the meaning of greenness as a laughing matter.

In green political thought, the question often seems vital and pressing. To address the meaning of green politics in this chapter, however, I do not focus mainly on that question. Instead, I direct attention to the meaning of *politics.*

The meaning of politics has long been a key concern of political theory, but the issue has received scant attention in a green context. The question of what green means threatens to become fairly sterile, though, unless raised along with an effort at understanding the nature of politics as well. It is only with such an effort that we can come to understand the meaning and promise of green politics.

What's in a Name?

Labels like environmental, ecological, and green are bound to be contentious. Conflicting uses point to oppositions within green politics as to its identity, purpose, direction, and boundary. In *Green Political Thought,* for example, Andrew Dobson insists on a sharp demarcation between "environmentalism" and "ecologism." This is a familiar type of distinction, often posed in terms of light and dark green or in terms of reformism and radicalism. The difference for Dobson, however, is not simply one of degree, but also one of kind. There is no question of environmentalism being just a less radical form of ecologism: "environmentalism argues for a managerial approach to environmental problems, secure in the belief that they can be solved without fundamental changes in present values or patterns of production and consumption, while ecologism holds that a sustainable and fulfilling existence presupposes radical changes in our relationship with the non-human natural world and in our mode of social and political life."[2]

For Dobson, this sharp distinction is conceptually important and strategically crucial. Unlike environmentalism, ecologism is a standpoint able both to grasp the limits of the existing order and to help get beyond it. Ecologism, in short, is able to describe, prescribe, and guide in a project of social change.

Dobson is concerned that the ecologism of a radical green politics is in danger of being obscured, confused with an environmentalism that fails to challenge the established order or to proclaim the possibility of a qualitatively different world. Environmentalism is one-dimensional, lacks a clear oppositional stance, and simply acquiesces to the way things are: "Green politics self-consciously confronts dominant paradigms, and my task here is to ensure that it is not swallowed up by them and the interests they often seem to serve."[3]

Dobson is not only describing but also prescribing and constructing—all proper tasks for political thought. Yet his approach also fits the formula typical of strategic thinking: he seeks to identify and consolidate an agency capable of achieving desired goals. Radical thought has long been obsessed with finding the agent of historical change. The search for the agent has now taken inventive twists, but the key assumption remains a strategic posture of uncompromising opposition and resistance to the established social order—a "Great Refusal," as it was prominently heralded in the midst of the 1960s.[4] Along with many others, Dobson reiterates this assumption. Even though it is far from a ridiculous idea, it does require reconsideration in the context of green politics.

I use the terms green and environmental without any sharp distinction, often in an interchangeable way. At the same time, I use environmentalism as an overarching category to capture a range of responses arising in the latter part of the twentieth century to challenge an exuberant industrialism. Even the most minimal environmentalist response reflects at least a recognition of problems in the human/nature relationship that industrialism had once been able to blissfully ignore. In these terms, Dobson's ecologism would be a particular form of environmentalism, though one that may be especially important in its maximal portrayal of the problematic character that the human/nature relationship has assumed under the prevailing order of economy and society.

In its range of minimal to maximal challenges to industrialism,[5] environmentalism informs a green politics that alternates between efforts at incrementally reforming and radically transforming advanced industrial society.
To thus construe environmentalism in terms of a broad range of responses
to industrialism is neither value-free nor without strategic implications for
green politics. One consequence of construing environmentalism broadly—
and viewing ecologism as one of its aspects—is to keep alive a conceptual
tension that testifies to ambivalence, paradox, and irony in green politics.

The Emergence of Green Politics

Green politics arose before it got its name, which did not become prominent until the early 1980s with the official emergence of "green" parties in
various countries, particularly the widely celebrated electoral successes of
die Grünen, the German Greens. As they came to prominence, the German
Greens identified themselves not as a conventional political party, but as
part of a larger movement that involved "multicolored" connections going
well beyond a narrowly construed environmentalism. They saw themselves
as part of a new worldwide movement, both green and democratic, including "groups for the protection of life, nature and environment, citizen's initiatives, the workers' movement, Christian initiatives, peace, human rights,
women's and Third World movements."[6]

The substance of green politics can, nonetheless, be traced to the advent
of contemporary environmentalism, which took a distinctive form in industrially advanced societies during the late 1960s and early 1970s, amid
the emergence of a now familiar range of new social movements.[7] At a time
when countercultural and radical political tendencies fostered the impression among many of impending social transformation—a "greening," as it
was termed in a popular book of the time[8]—the moment was opportune for
previously marginal environmental concerns to take the spotlight on the
political stage.

Worries about environmental degradation—even alarm over the threat of
environmental catastrophe—were increasingly taken for granted in public
discourse. Throughout the industrial world, new environmental groups pro-
liferated while staid conservation organizations were challenged to adopt a
more radical and activist agenda.[9] The traditional focus of the Sierra Club,
for example, prompted David Brower to resign as leader and establish the
Friends of the Earth.[10] Around the same time, in the United States and
Canada, Greenpeace was formed, linking the green theme of environmentalism directly with the peace movement.[11]

From its origins, the distinct identity of the environmental movement
has been attenuated by linkages and overlaps with other social movements.
With the emergence of ecofeminism in the 1980s, an especially important

connection became explicit.[12] Other such connections have clearly emerged more recently as the movement for environmental justice has linked environmental issues to oppression and impoverishment in both the overdeveloped and the underdeveloped worlds.[13] Though the green movement can reasonably be described as having a distinct identity, the homogeneity suggested by a common label tends to obscure internal differences and complex, dynamic relationships with a broader context. And though these diverse and even conflicting elements suggest plurality rather than unity, the green orientation retains significant coherence in its questioning of industrialism and instrumentalism.

A basic green image comes from ecology: greens picture an interdependent and dynamic nature that, with the human species emphatically included, is astonishingly complex and surprising in the fragilities and resiliancies of its systemic relationships. From this perspective, the instrumental orientation of industrialism becomes manifest as a "conscious purpose versus nature" that is unable to comprehend or control its own consequences.[14]

Evidence of environmental damage tends to undermine the exuberant confidence that inspired the advent of the industrial order. Lapses in control—most dramatically evident in famous ecological disasters such as Love Canal, Three Mile Island, Bhopal, Chernobyl, and the Exxon *Valdez*—signal that the rationality of this order is not to be taken for granted. Indeed, its rationality can be challenged in the name of an "ecological rationality" necessary for any viable society.

What is at stake here, as John Dryzek has argued, is the "life-support value of ecosystems": "The preservation of the life-support systems on which human beings depend is a precondition to the continued existence of society itself and its institutional forms."[15] Ecological rationality highlights systemic interdependencies of the natural world with which any sustainable human society must somehow fit. A society becomes "ecologically irrational" when it fails to fit, when its forms of epistemic authority and institutional practice threaten the ecosystemic relations on which it relies.[16]

Means and Ends: Why Democracy?

Green political thought makes no pretense at being a pure theoretical enterprise, but is clearly oriented to problems of practice: to examining and assessing the means and ends of the green movement. Considerations of strategy and outcome are thus intrinsic to the enterprise. As Robert Goodin puts it in *Green Political Theory*, "to advocate environmentalism is to advocate substantive outcomes."[17] Even though it arises largely as a negative response to industrialism, green politics is also clearly *for* something.

The nature of this something, however, has been a matter of considerable debate and disagreement. The concept of ecological rationality would appear to be at least a good candidate as a general idea covering the movement's goals. This concept certainly underlies much of the broad appeal the green movement has generated as well as many of its public policy successes. Fears about ecological catastrophe, even human extinction, gave considerable impetus to the movement in its early years—and continues to do so—provoking concerns that established patterns of industrial development are ecologically irrational and, thus, unsustainable.

Ecological rationality, however, cannot comprehensively cover the goals of the green movement since it addresses only human concerns. A major current running through the green movement is an ethical concern to move beyond a homocentric orientation, to embrace biocentrism or—even more comprehensively—ecocentrism. There is no consensus on whether to make this move, or on what it would mean either conceptually or practically, but it is nonetheless clear that the green movement has thrown homocentrism into question and disturbed its conscience. Questions of the interests, rights, and value of nonhuman nature are as much part of the green agenda as are questions of environmental sustainability.

One way to construe the goals of the green movement is in terms of a sharp conflict between a homocentric ecological rationality and an ecocentric environmental ethics. Ecocentrists tend to accentuate this difference, even to argue that ecocentrism is the distinguishing or essential feature of the green movement and, in particular, of green political thought.[18] On this account, there is nothing very special in a concern for ecological rationality. This is merely a matter of human self-interest, so it is commonly argued, necessarily a concern for any human community and any form of political thought. Obscured by this neatly logical position, however, is historical context and the fluid, dynamic character of human thought and discourse when viewed as part of a process of social change. A social movement does not necessarily have an essential core that can be formed into an unambiguous proposition to serve as a premise in a logical argument.[19]

The green movement, in particular, does not revolve about a well-defined center, but is held together by complex patterns of family resemblance (in the Wittgensteinian sense) arising from various and variable interests, perspectives, ideas, and identities. The coherence of such elements is to be discerned not by focusing on them in detail, or even by trying to map their relationships, but rather by viewing them in contrast to something else. The "something else" in the case of the green movement is a historical pattern of industrialization that—despite continuous innovation and even "postindustrial" features—pervades the modern, or postmodern, world. Against the backdrop of industrialization, the green movement betokens less a conclusion than a questioning of what is taken for granted by the industrial world. Throwing into question the arrogant assumptions of industrialism, the green movement provokes a reconsideration of the entire human/nature relationship. The promotion of ecological rationality no less than ecocentrism arises from this reconsideration, which holds out the promise of change in the terms and conditions of public discourse.

In *Green Political Theory*, Goodin's basic point is to underscore the distinction between means and ends in the green movement. In positing a "green theory of value" about nature that expresses the essential aim of the movement—a goal that greens either do promote or ought to promote if they are to be consistent with the supposed logic of their position—Goodin seeks to disentangle this aim from political and personal values that greens often happen to espouse as well.[20] The disentanglement is achieved, however, by diverting attention from the green movement as a cultural and historical phenomenon and focusing on merely one of its aspects.

By distinguishing and disentangling an essential green aim from contingent aspects of the green movement, Goodin seeks to put democracy in its place, particularly "green support for grassroots democracy." "To advocate democracy," he argues, "is to advocate procedures," not "substantive outcomes," and certainly not the outcomes that are essential to environmentalism (168). In an inventive response to Goodin, Robyn Eckersley has argued that green values concerning nature are bound together with the green espousal of democracy not by happenstance but "at the level of principle." They are essentially rather than contingently related, in other words, wedded through a common idea. The linking concept for Eckersley is "autonomy,"[21] which in this context applies to nonhuman as well as human beings. Although it might appear peculiar from a standpoint outside environmentalism, an application of the idea of autonomy to nonhuman nature can make sense if one accepts something like John Rodman's view that the natural world, nonhuman as well as human, exhibits unfolding structures and potentialities that demand human care and respect.[22] Advocating democracy as an essential green value—necessary because human autonomy also demands care and respect—Eckersley can thus block at a conceptual level authoritarian impulses that have at times emerged from environmentalism: "authoritarianism," she concludes, "would have to be ruled out at the level of green principle."[23]

Debates over authoritarianism and democracy in green political thought generally proceed in instrumental terms. The big question is what governmental form offers the most effective response to environmental crisis. Against the authoritarian claim that the crisis demands the urgent and concerted action that only concentrated power can bring, democrats answer that the crisis demands the diffusion of power necessary for flexible and creative action.[24] This instrumental response to authoritarianism does not satisfy Eckersley. She wants to address the question on the grounds of principle, as staked out by Goodin.[25] Both the instrumental argument for democracy and Eckersely's argument in principle do seem largely persuasive, but the two arguments suffer from a common weakness in their shared ahistorical character.

The argument in principle risks becoming another footnote to Plato, attached to the purity of a concept that has been enshrined as an idealized end. Eckersley's invocation of the concept of autonomy cannot simply serve as a conclusion—a fixed principle for green political thought—but at most serves to set the agenda for a discussion. We need to ask what autonomy can reasonably mean short of an idealism that would deny the radically contingent character of either nature or humanity. Assuming we are able to clarify the meaning of autonomy as a reasonable end—as a critique of domination implies—how are we to proceed in a historical context of power that systematically denies autonomy, in a world marked by the human domination of nature and human nature? To act in such a context to promote autonomy is to exert power against prevailing alignments of power, whether or not one employs such means as lies and deception, or coercion, force, and violence.

Surely, one might argue that means and ends have to be consistent, that the means must somehow contain or anticipate the ends. But unless one holds to the impossible—to the idea that means and ends could just suddenly be collapsed together—then the principle of autonomy cannot by itself tell what is to be done. We are faced with having to consider whether the principle of autonomy should, at times, be compromised or sacrificed for the sake of later realizing the principle more fully. Would any authoritarian means ever be permissible to this end? This conundrum is part of an old story in emancipatory theory and practice, but it still bears repeating.[26]

It might seem strange to suggest that the instrumental argument for democracy is ahistorical. After all, if environmentalism is a response to problems generated in the course of industrialization, then the need for democracy to solve these problems clearly arises in a definite historical context. Nonetheless, the instrumental argument proceeds by contrasting democratic and authoritarian systems as two abstract models, two items out of a tool kit, so to speak. By examining the properties of these tools in light of the problem to be fixed, we supposedly will see which one we need to use. This focus, however, leaves out of consideration the historical struggles for power through which present problems have emerged, along with any concrete possibilities of addressing them effectively.

The Historical Context of Power:
Understanding the Administrative Sphere

What is the relevant historical context of power? An answer best begins in the negative, by saying what it is not. Arising during the 1960s in industrially advanced countries, most prominently the United States, environmentalism and related social movements offered a rude awakening to professional students of government. After the relative quiescence of the post–World War II period, the disruption and turbulence generated by movements for social transformation did not fit with the neat models of the mature democratic system crafted by political scientists who, especially in America, exhibited an abiding faith that the free, equal, orderly, prosperous, and secure world of liberal democracy was the best of all possible worlds. In retrospect, it is clear that these models not only left out the environmental problems that were emerging under the impact of industrialization, but also systematically obscured obvious oppression by race, class, and gender as well as the continuing domination of whole peoples in a supposedly post-colonial world.[27] The historical context of power was largely obscured by the benign images of liberal democracy promulgated at that time—images that have shown remarkable staying power in popular discourse and have recently, with the end of the Soviet Union, been reinvigorated in terms of a triumphant victory of democracy and free markets.[28]

The democracy actually achieved under liberal democracy has largely come as a result of struggles over the past two centuries or so by subordinated peoples who have sought to gain some measure of power against starkly authoritarian and oligarchical institutions. With the rise of representative government, the gradual extension of suffrage to people who had been formally and informally excluded by class, race, and gender serves as a marker of these historical struggles. But the advent of universal adult suffrage in liberal democracies has by no means eliminated the significance of authoritarian and oligarchical patterns in social, economic, and state institutions.

Liberal democracy never pretended to do away with the dramatic economic and social inequalities of capitalism; these were conceived as necessary and legitimate. There was, of course, the supposed equality of the market. All were proclaimed formally equal in the sphere of the market—capitalists and workers, rich and poor alike—whether or not they had anything more to sell than their skins. Demands for social justice were in part eventually (and rather grudgingly) accommodated with welfare-state policies that bolstered consumer demand and promoted mass acquiescence. Still, liberal democracy singles out government as an island of democracy in an undemocratic sea of economic and social relations. The effect is to render democracy largely a governmental formality, something of a symbol that fosters the legitimacy of the established order while helping to rationalize or obscure actual power relations.[29]

One of the great ironies of liberal democracy is that, just as democracy seemed to be achieved by extension of citizenship rights to the entire adult population, the functional significance of citizenship declined. The public sphere, of roughly the late–seventeenth to mid–nineteenth centuries, was an active domain of civil society devoted to communication that shaped a public opinion significant to the legitimacy of the state. Although participation in the public sphere was generally limited to educated, propertied men, those who did participate enjoyed significant independence and collectively influenced affairs of state.[30] With the citizenry expanding to encompass a mass population in the late nineteenth and early twentieth centuries, however, the significance of public opinion was largely inverted. Associated less with active discussion, public opinion became more a product of the propaganda techniques and disciplinary practices employed and refined by administrative organizations throughout the domains of state, economy, and society.[31]

No sooner had the liberal democratic consensus of the mid–twentieth century seemingly smoothed over all potential difficulties, however, than a range of new social movements (including environmentalism) suddenly burst onto the scene, renewing the potential for active democratic citizenship. The disruptions so disturbed some academic guardians of liberal democracy that a "crisis of democracy" was declared. Democracy was threatened by too much democracy: the demands of new social movements were beginning to overload the liberal democratic system.[32] It was vital to block moves toward participatory democracy by reaffirming the legitimacy of liberal democracy as a form of representative government, in which official parliamentary assemblies provide a forum for the authorized voices of the citizenry.[33]

Those who endorsed the potential for active democratic citizenship looked instead to civil society as the key source of vitality: to the realm of a public sphere outside the established institutions of both state and economy. Jürgen Habermas has especially maintained the importance of discourse in the public sphere, but has also stressed a sharp demarcation between the realm of public discourse and state institutions that possess decision-making authority: "Discourses," he has bluntly declared, "do not govern."[34] Questions of interconnection and overlap have arisen, however, along with a distinction between "weak" and "strong" public spheres.[35]

Following a conceptual innovation by Dryzek, Habermas has referred to "discursive designs" as open and egalitarian sites of communication that provide "the organizational substratum of the general public of citizens."[36]

Whereas Habermas characteristically locates these sites exclusively in the domain of civil society, Dryzek has had no difficulty locating at least a potential for discursive designs in the state as well as in civil society.

A deliberate policy orientation is possible both in advancing "discursive democracy" and in the particular cause of "ecological democratization."[37] However, it is also possible—and likely advisable, Dryzek suggests—to reject direct participation and instead to constitute "public spheres defined in terms of their opposition to the state and its imperatives." Preferring to speak of a plurality of public spheres instead of a single public sphere, he fears that public spheres risk a loss of critical capacity when associated with the state. Two complementary green paths might thus be possible: "one within the state to take advantage of every bit of flexibility in the liberal democratic system, another outside, more democratic and vital."[38]

Although Dryzek comes down mainly on the side of an oppositional posture, it is noteworthy that he still pictures this opposition—"oriented towards, but separate from, state institutions"[39]—as part of an expanded policy process, an opposition working its influence on policy outcomes through largely unofficial channels. There is thus a note of some ambivalence in Dryzek's position; indeed, he indicates that his stance is provisional, subject to change with a changing context.

Can the main issue be conceptualized adequately, however, simply in terms of the relationship between public sphere(s) and the state? No single model—for example, class, elite, or pluralist—could convey the historical context of power in its relevant complexity.[40] However, the idea of the *administrative sphere* is conceptually important in understanding this context.[41] The administrative sphere extends beyond the state to encompass that fragmented, yet somehow also coherent, complex of public and private administrative organizations that, with varying modes of conflict and coalescence, largely shapes the pace and character of development in industrially advanced societies. Claus Offe, for example, has drawn attention to a typical pattern of public policy formation whereby state officials join with representatives of powerful private organizations, building a policy "consensus" through informal consultations and negotiations shielded from public view.[42]

There is thus a communicative context—a quiet, most imperfect kind of discursive design—that already pervades the administrative sphere, shaping the institutions and outcomes of public policy. If the door to this domain sometimes opens to greens, they seldom get much of a voice or even access to particularly important encounters. Withdrawal into separate public spheres is one reasonable response, especially if this withdrawal draws attention to the generally closed character of the administrative sphere. Banging loudly and insistently on the door, however, can be another reasonable possibility, especially if there is a chance of access to information that will expose the inner workings of the administrative sphere. There is no general rule to decide what to do; judgments and dispositions arise in particular contexts such that numerous options (and combinations of options) must be counted as reasonable.

To think in terms of an administrative sphere potentially open to discursive designs helps to focus attention on a crucial aspect of context that confronts green politics. The concept is meant to avoid any view that would assimilate administrative practice to systemic functioning. The concept of an administrative *sphere*—in contrast to a concept of "administrative system"—draws attention to the complexity of communication that, though often obscured, pervades administrative organizations.[43] The communicative practices of the administrative sphere particularly betray the often implicit icon of an *administrative mind*.[44] This image significantly influences administrative communication while obscuring its complexity and significance: a monological image of administration reinforces the legitimacy of prevailing practice.

The image of the administrative mind suggests an impartial reason, which exercises a supreme, unquestionable authority in pursuit of the universal well-being of humanity. In its contemporary technocratic form, the administrative mind gestures to the functional operations of a multifaceted system, monitored and regulated through depersonalized analytic techniques. Yet technocratic images still mingle with more traditional ones, suggesting command and obedience in an organizational hierarchy subordinated to a single head.[45] These traditional images have still deeper connections with monarchial and even theocratic ideas. Detached from mundane conflict and error, the administrative mind casts a benign aura of assured order. Under the unified direction of this mind, an otherwise confusing and uncertain world becomes calculable and controllable.

Understanding the historical context of power depends on understanding the administrative sphere. For, with the emergence of modern bureaucracy and its panoply of technocratic devices, the public discourse of citizens and debates by citizen representatives in parliamentary assemblies came to be displaced in significance by administrative operations. In the emerging administrative sphere, officials of government agencies and business corporations especially played key roles in formulating and implementing policies to promote an orderly course of industrialization.[46] To ask whether a democratic or authoritarian model of government best promises ecological rationality is an exercise that borders on irrelevancy if one ignores this context of power.

The quest to dominate nature is not a project of humanity in general. It is a historically specific project of modernity. The domination of nature is part of a larger pattern of domination that includes systematic domination by human beings over other human beings and, indeed, over human nature itself. During the early emergence of environmentalism, William Leiss drew upon the insights of critical theory to argue this case and to draw a pointed conclusion: "a concern with ecology necessarily becomes part of a *social* movement" that, in facing the environmental destruction wrought by established power, is unable to avoid "challenging the authoritarian decision-making powers vested in corporate and governmental institutions."[47]

There can thus be no question of simply taking an existing democracy, as if it were some shining ideal, and then exchanging it for authoritarian rule to address an ecological crisis. Significant authoritarian elements already pervade actual democracy. Proposals for an authoritarian response to environmental problems make sense only if one assumes a successful challenge to *established* authoritarian power. Where could such a challenge possibly come from, apart from democratic social movements? Of course, it is not inconceivable—or without historical precedent—that democratic forces could foster a new authoritarianism. As strategies for change, however, neither authoritarian prescriptions nor democratic responses to them make much sense in a historical vacuum. Admittedly, no strategic perplexities are resolved by simply pointing to an array of new social movements, environmentalism prominent among them, and suggesting that these will somehow produce a grand ecological solution. Yet, by indicating the inescapably democratic dimension of any such solution within the existing framework of power, this focus nonetheless allows strategic perplexities to become visible.

What Is Green Political Thought?

Green political thought faces a problem of identity. The question is partly rooted in the internal differences of the green movement and in disputes over the movement's boundaries—in the issue, that is, of what green means. But the question also involves the nature of political thought itself. There is a nice ambiguity to the term political thought, convenient in providing a big tent to cover a diverse range of intellectual activities. However, the ambiguity also obscures a distinction between *theory* and *ideology*. Is green political thought merely the explicit ideological dimension of a social movement, entirely devoted to the outlook and problems of that movement? Or is green political thought an effort to engage and contribute to political theory?

Although tensions and conflicting loyalties seem inescapable, these two identities are not of necessity mutually exclusive. Even the narrower task of serving the green movement may depend on attention to wider theoretical concerns. One reason for this lies in the internal diversity of the movement itself, which introduces interests and perspectives that cannot be comfortably contained within any fixed ideological framework and which guarantees contention over the orientation of theory and practice. There is little risk that green political thought could long rest comfortably with ideological rigidity.

Nonetheless, green political thought exhibits some characteristic features indicating that ideological constraints can be a problem. In particular, the moralistic tendency often evident in the green movement carries over at times into green political thought. Although perhaps refreshing amid the frequent cynicism of modern society, this tendency risks a rigidity that could inhibit both self-criticism and insights into practical possibilities.

To appeal to political theory rather than ideology is not to invoke some rationalistic fantasy that political ideas or principles are innocent of interests and perspectives, nor is it to suggest that explicit rational argumentation is the only—or even always the most effective—means by which to pursue self-criticism or practical insight. A dystopian satire like Zamyatin's novel, *We,* for example, is merely one of innumerable artistic works that, through diverse genres, exercise critically insightful political thought but do not take the directly expository form generally associated with political theory.[48]

Ideologies, especially as they are newly emerging in anticipation of historical change (when they are "utopias," in Karl Mannheim's terminology[49]), can be sources of critical insight and innovative practical orientation. Yet, such insight and innovation, even when expressed in universalistic terms, typically depend on the standpoint of quite particular interests and perspectives. Thought tends to become blocked—ideologically constrained—at the horizon of that standpoint; the interests and perspectives of the ideology do not by themselves make for a breakthrough.

Yet, in political theorizing—as in artistic innovation—one does presuppose a particular combination of detachment and commitment that imaginatively seeks out, questions, and presses against boundaries. This is not to say that the practice of political theory can escape its context or the constraints of ideology, only that it attempts "to break out of the context from within."[50] It is obvious that actual theoretical practices are ideologically constrained. The point is that such constraint poses a problem for a theoretical project but it presents no difficulty for a frankly ideological position. Political theory is guided by an outlook that, while acutely sensitive to context, does not just accept but quite deliberately seeks to get beyond contextual constraints through an exercise of political imagination. Even if this effort seems ultimately in vain, it is rich in consequences for the quality of political thought.[51]

The main reason green political thought requires some serious theoretical commitment is that, without it, we can expect an erosion of intellectual vitality and flexibility in its orientation. Theoretical commitment, of course, is not without risk. There is a particular risk in the theoretically necessary task of challenging one's own assumptions and exposing these to the criticism of others. In a political context, it would be foolish to ignore this risk. But can the green movement adequately address its own concerns if it does not somehow take the risk?

Rethinking Green Political Thought:
Three Faces of Politics

The question of what it means to be green becomes pressing if we want to determine the precise identity and purpose of the green movement. But why is it important to do this? Analytic reason, preoccupied with the importance and necessity of clear definitions, might respond that unless we precisely determine the identity and purpose of the green movement, we just cannot know what we are talking about. This is what Goodin seems to believe. For Dobson and many others, the key consideration is strategic: a coherent green identity needs to be constructed and protected from pseudo-greens who would lead the movement astray. It is in this vein that Rudolph Bahro has proclaimed the importance of "building the green movement."[52]

In common political terms, what is implicit in asking the meaning of green is a distinction between us and them, friend and foe. The pressing job becomes one of constructing and maintaining a *we* able to deal with the historical challenges and struggles of transformative politics. What is also implicit is a particular notion of politics; a view of political action as strategic, as an instrument, a means to an end.

To rethink green political thought and understand the promise of green politics, this notion of politics must be questioned. The thinker who clearly stands out as most relevant to this task is Hannah Arendt, for she accomplished what has been called—without exaggeration—"the most radical rethinking of political action" in the twentieth century.[53] Indeed, Arendt's conception of politics is radically nonstrategic and noninstrumental, to the extent of provoking protests that she empties politics of all that we can reasonably understand as political. Arendt maintains that politics is an art, but not just in order to distinguish her image of politics from the fantasies of scientism. For she crucially insists that politics is not just any kind of art. Distinguishing it from arts that culminate in a finished, lasting product (such as sculpture, painting, and architecture), she proclaims that politics is one of the performing arts.

Like playing a musical instrument or enacting a drama, politics is sheer performance and possesses value in its performance. The chief political virtue she thus maintains through a unique translation of Machiavelli's *virtù*, is not just political skill or prowess, but *virtuosity*. In a remarkable departure from conventional thinking, Arendt urges us to appreciate that the value of politics is not extrinsic—does not lie in its outcomes—but is intrinsic: the value of politics is manifest in political action itself.[54]

By insisting that politics has intrinsic value, Arendt reinforced an important thrust of the social movements that emerged from the 1960s. In these movements, environmentalism included, there was not only an aim of creating social change, but also "a positive concept of politics" coupled with the goal of rehabilitating and extending "the practice of citizenship."[55] This was "the promise of politics" that Henry Kariel celebrated in the 1960s.[56]

These movements, of course, also had more pressing aims—for example, equality, justice, community, survival, natural harmony—which could easily override an impulse for political vitality. Indeed, the prospect that such objectives might be administratively imposed through authoritarian governance continually haunts such movements, and sometimes offers a temptation. A positive concept of politics, nonetheless, runs against the prevailing form of modern governance. From this posture, democracy is no mere means. To advocate democracy is not just to advocate procedures, as the stock-in-trade of much liberal democratic theory would have it,[57] but is also to advocate space for political action.

Already implicit in green politics, as in other movements, is thus a rethinking of politics that challenges the authoritarian and oligarchical features of modern government. A rethinking of politics is not something that needs to be imposed on green political thought from without, but it is something that needs to be developed further, made conceptually explicit and considered with a systematic focus.

Among social movements, feminism has pressed this rethinking furthest, guided by its key slogan, "The personal is political." The upshot of the idea, carried but a bit further, is that politics is *everywhere*.[58] Yet the notion of politics here tends to merge with the notion of power relationships: Since power is omnipresent, so too is politics. Indeed, politics is reduced to an interplay of power that collapses back into a ubiquitous instrumentality.

With this conception of politics, challenges to technocratic administration or to other kinds of authoritarian power are left with nothing to offer but another form of instrumentality, simply a different pattern of power relationships.[59] That the challenge so faithfully mirrors what it opposes is no mere accident, nor is it simply a product of the largely instrumentalist character of modern thought. The insight that power is everywhere reflects actual developments in the emergence of modern society, as noted by numerous critics from Max Weber to Michel Foucault.[60]

How can the circle of instrumentality be broken? That question haunts critics of modern institutions, even when they employ a conceptual framework ultimately caught within that very circle. Habermas thus has hopes for the public sphere because it provides an institution at least oriented by a principle of open and unconstrained communication. This principle breaks out of the circle of instrumentality because it requires communicative practices that cannot be reduced to force or manipulation. The premise here is that the principle of open and unconstrained communication, though never fully realized in practice, is at least assumed and may not always be a total mirage.[61]

People do sometimes talk to one another with the shared belief that everyone has something to say and that, to hear what is said, one must not seek to control, but must let be, listen, and understand. For Habermas, this principle—together with historical practices at least partially guided by it—raises the prospect of a public sphere in which modern development is treated not as a matter of necessity nor as a matter to be determined by the technocratic administrators of a mass society, but as a matter for public discussion.[62]

Concerned about the constraining character of a unitary public sphere, some writers have sought to reformulate the idea in terms of a plurality of public spheres that would allow spaces for difference, as this idea has been promoted from postmodern and feminist standpoints.[63] The underlying goal nonetheless remains a collective disposition reached through open communication. In Habermas's terms, this would be in principle a discursive formation of opinion and will that would perform a political function by providing legitimate direction to modern society.

Conceptually, though, Habermas's public sphere in the end rejoins the circle of instrumentality. While allowing space for open discussion unconstrained by decision-making imperatives, the public sphere retains a quite specific purpose: to work an influence on authoritative decisions.[64] The ultimate instrumentalism of this approach may not be immediately apparent, but becomes visible in contrast to Arendt's celebration of the public as a realm of action.

In proposing a radically noninstrumental understanding of politics, Arendt also developed in *The Human Condition* a threefold conception of the "active life." Her key mission in this, her central work, was to counter the philosophical disposition, dominant since Plato, to demean the active life while exalting the contemplative life. As she clearly testified with her last (and unfinished) major work, *The Life of the Mind*, her point was not to reject the contemplative life, but to put it in its place, so as to reclaim a space for the "lost treasure" of action, particularly for the public life of political action. By promoting action in a common world that relates people to one another, Arendt sought to counter the rise of instrumentalized behavior in the context of a mass society that makes possible the uniquely modern phenomenon of totalitarianism. The totalitarian nightmare looms over Arendt's thought, in fact, and underscores the significance of her overriding insistence on promoting the plurality of political life in contrast to the homogeneity of a comprehensively administered society.[65]

In delineating her three forms of the active life, Arendt employs the labels "labor," "work," and "action." She of course especially prizes action, which must be singled out and honored in the context of the pervasive instrumentalism that diminishes it. Of the three forms, labor and work share an instrumental character yet are to be distinguished from one another. *Labor* pertains to economic activity, to human beings as natural beings laboring in their interchange with nature: what Marx termed, in a formulation Arendt repeats, the human "metabolism" with nature.[66] *Work* pertains to the construction of enduring artifacts, most broadly the artifice of civilization (chap. 4). Both labor and work are thus oriented to the achievement of extrinsic ends.

Action, however, is self-contained; its ends are intrinsic. It is that meaningful, inventive conduct (taking the quintessential form of speech) through which human beings enact and reveal both the plurality of their distinct identities and the commonality of the human condition with its frailty and unpredictability. In the course of action, human beings become recognizable to one another as distinct individuals: "This revelatory quality of speech and action," Arendt explains, "comes to the fore where people are *with* others and neither for nor against them—that is, in sheer human togetherness."[67] A public "space of appearance" (199) offers the potential for action, and it is thus that Arendt advocates a performative, indeed theatrical, concept of politics that is startling in its noninstrumental character.

For predictable reasons, some readers of Arendt simply reject her position outright. Others, attracted by her sympathy for political participation, try to assimilate her thinking in service to participatory schemes that nonetheless retain an overarching instrumentalism. As Dana Villa has argued, the latter approach threatens to obscure what is distinctive about Arendt.[68] My approach in this book insists upon the distinctiveness of Arendt's conception of the political, particularly because the very strangeness of her idea not only makes it stand out, but also makes it vulnerable to misunderstanding, liable to be blurred and absorbed by more familiar notions. To grasp the import and distinctiveness of Arendt's concept of politics, though, it is not necessary to suppose that the phenomenon she reveals and promotes actually encompasses all that we can reasonably mean by politics.

Arendt discloses the potential of action as an aspect of politics that, without her concept, would at best be barely perceptible. Yet, her conceptual scheme for understanding the active life is not grounded metaphysically. Arendt's are not necessary concepts corresponding to transcendent essences, but matters of judgment, considered opinions that take account of other opinions and at least anticipate an exchange of opinions in a common space of appearance.[69] In fact, she suggests an interconnection between thought and action by describing political thought as "representative": it is a form of dialogical thinking, in which one imagines and anticipates one's presence with others in an open exchange of opinions.[70] In this sense, her thinking is political in form as well as content.

Arendt may open the door for another configuration of politics when she says that its "essence"—in an obviously nonmetaphysical sense of that word —is "debate" (241). This is of course quite different from arguing that the essence of politics is, say, power relationships or policymaking, though both can also reasonably be considered inextricable from politics. Without losing sight of Arendt's noninstrumental, performative sense of political action, it remains possible to examine the idea of politics-as-debate in terms of its significance for more common, instrumental understandings of politics.

Two aspects of the instrumental dimension of politics can, in fact, be distinguished by drawing upon Arendt's tripartite scheme of the active life: the aspect of functional politics (corresponding to the category of labor) and the aspect of constitutive politics (corresponding to the category of work). In brief, functional politics is concerned with the maintenance and operation of a socioeconomic system, particularly as it effects an interchange with nonhuman nature. Constitutive politics is concerned with constructing or transforming the cultural artifice of a civilization. These two aspects of instrumental politics together stand in stark contrast to the noninstrumental politics that Arendt celebrates: a politics that is performative, oriented to theatricality. Performative politics is concerned, in a word, with itself—with the sheer, intrinsic value of politics as a form of action. Debate is obviously at the center of performative politics, but debate is also significant for both functional and constitutive politics.

Arendt's striking opinions on the nature of politics can thus be fully acknowledged yet also turned against her thinking to reveal three different aspects, or faces, of politics. All of the three faces of politics—functional, constitutive, and performative—are central in my effort to rethink green political thought and understand the promise of green politics. They will appear in various guises throughout the book, but the distinctions will become particularly explicit and systematic at the end (in chapters 7 and 8) as I attempt to work through the idea and implications of a green public sphere.[71]

What Are We? The Idea of a Green Public Sphere

Green political thought often seems obsessed with trying to bring unity to the green movement. In *Toward Unity among Environmentalists*, Bryan

Norton has offered an intriguing variant on this effort. He begins with a commonplace observation on the lack of overall coherence: "There has emerged within the movement no single, coherent consensus regarding positive values, no widely shared vision of a future and better world in which human populations live in harmony with the natural world they inhabit."[72] The typical response to this situation is to make it the task of green political thought somehow to identify or construct such a shared vision. Yet, unlike others who seek coherence in terms of the movement's ultimate ends—as with Dobson's ecologism and Goodin's green theory of value—Norton draws attention to a significant agreement among environmentalists on policy goals. Although there are "diverging worldviews," he says, there are "converging policies" (187). This means that environmentalists can join in a common cause to work for similar policies. Norton's path, of course, depends on actual agreements on policy, of which there is no guarantee (witness, e.g., Bahro's dramatic departure from the German Green Party over its "compromise" on the issue of animal experimentation[73]).

There is, in any case, a difficulty in all these proposals for unity. In contrast to the suggestion of Norton and to the suggestions of Dobson and Goodin, the idea of a green public sphere answers the call for overall agreement in the green movement by questioning its possibility and even its desirability. The big question is whether it is possible or desirable to speak of the green movement as a *we*—and, if so, in what sense.

The formation and protection of a *we* as a common, coherent identity is clearly what many contributors to green political thought have had in mind, notably Bahro in his proposal to build the green movement. The idea of a *we* is here that of a collective subject (an *I* writ large) performing its historical mission as the agent of social change.[74] This instrumentalist conception of the historical subject has long been key to Marxian revolutionary thought—"Workers of the world, unite!"—and exerts a continuing influence on transformative social movements, particularly environmentalism.[75]

Is it possible or desirable to conceive the green movement as a *we?* The answer may depend on whether this *we* can be understood in anything other than instrumental terms. The very idea of building the green movement has distinctly instrumentalist overtones, suggesting the construction of a device strategically designed to effect social change. The irony of building a green movement after this image is that the principle of construction becomes one of coherence and cohesion, a narrowing and sharpening of the movement into a finely honed instrument. The logic of this approach—despite all talk of diversity and inclusiveness—is that elements that cannot merge with the movement's essential identity must be pruned away and, in effect, excommunicated.

The potential to escape the totalizing logic of instrumentalism in a green context depends (conceptually at least) on thinking not *only* in terms of a green movement, but also in terms of a *green public sphere*. Here the *we* would not be an instrument, but a space of appearance, a common world. The point would not be to achieve overall agreement—some final settlement of issues—but to make meaningful disagreement possible. Concerns to promote unity and coherence in green politics often overlook the obvious: a discourse is emerging as the basis for a green public sphere.[76]

The significance of the green public sphere resides not merely in reaching conclusions and resolving issues, but in sustaining a process of ecologically informed discourse that through its agenda, presuppositions, and cultural images challenges the monological administrative mind and the prevailing discourse of industrialism. For now, it is obvious that the green public sphere is only partially formed and is continually threatened by a hostile context of power. Still incomplete and open to incessant challenge, this sphere cannot be an arena of pure performativity—just a theater appreciated for its own sake—but must also be concerned with outcomes relevant to its own construction and protection: to the project of building and shaping a green public sphere. The point, then, is not to dispense altogether with instrumentality in the green movement, but to recognize clearly that instrumentality is not everything, especially in the best of causes.

THE SPECTER OF THE ADMINISTRATIVE mind haunts strategic thinking, creating *and* obscuring many perplexities. Strategy is serious business. We must be constantly vigilant, heroically tragic in our outlook. Comedy is out of the question. This seems to be so even if an appreciation for the comic may be needed for revealing strategic perplexities and for fostering a practical orientation to context able to take them seriously into account.

Ritualized patterns of instrumentalist thought pervade the modern project of industrialism and are common in various efforts not only to promote, but also to redirect, block, or transform it. The basic pattern of thinking was largely fixed as faith in rational governance gained sway during the Enlightenment and, anticipating today's technocratic propensities, began to shape the character of state policy.

Although it should not need saying, the greatest innovation in the development of social technology emerged in that earlier time—the product of a nascent economic science—with the notion of a naturally self-regulating market mechanism. State policies were to recognize and promote the operation of the market mechanism, harmonizing society with the natural order. This was the cause that Adam Smith advanced with his quasi-theological metaphor of the "invisible hand."[1]

Instrumentalist patterns of thought remain widely repeated today, either explicitly or implicitly, in state management of capitalist economies, in corporate strategy making, in revolutionary theory and practice, in socialist planning, in the planned creation of "free" markets, in many environmental organizations, even—nota bene—in much green political thought.

The administrative mind has dethroned Fortuna, Machiavelli's Renaissance goddess. Today strategic thought typically bears the imprint of mechanism, the metaphor that has been central to the understanding of both nature and human society ever since the early modern era: "The rationalization of administration and of the natural order was occurring simultaneously. Rational management in the social and economic spheres helps to explain the appeal of mechanism as a rational order created by a powerful sovereign deity. As Descartes wrote . . . in 1630, 'God sets up mathematical laws in nature as the king sets up laws in his kingdom.'"[2] The image of the administrative mind, while a figure of intelligent guidance for a rationalized cosmos, also retains significant theological roots as well as associations with the magical and the miraculous. It thus did not seem strange when physicist Alvin Weinberg once implicitly invoked the mind of the magus to promote the widespread adoption of nuclear power as a "Faustian bargain."[3] Clichés about the "magic of the market," however, remain the most obvious example of this tendency.

A peculiar mixture of rationalism with elements of the magical and the miraculous not only guides the march of industrial progress, but also informs efforts that would redefine, redirect, or stop it. David W. Orr helps to underscore this point with a touch of the comic: "A cartoon that once appeared in *American Scientist* showed a white-frocked scientist standing before a chalkboard with the equation $[x] + [y] +$ [then a miracle occurs] $= z$." "Most strategies of social change," Orr adds, "have similar dependence on the miraculous." This particularly is the case, he suggests, with green strategies.[4]

There is a simple notion that, in one form or another, underlies much green strategic thought: Environmental problems are sure to get worse, to increase in scope and severity, and when they do, more and more people will be moved to join the green cause, thus enhancing its power and its chance of making a real difference for the well-being of all (with the meaning of "all" varying in terms of ecocentric and homocentric views).[5] Sometimes this general idea is formulated in a "materialist" way, to suggest that people will be led to effect change through compelling need; at other times, the scenario is "idealist," with change coming through a transformation of consciousness. These two variations on a theme, even when vaguely formulated, obviously repeat the basic frameworks—set, respectively, by Marxian materialism and Hegelian idealism—of historical development through dialectical movement.

Although Marx and Hegel may each be open to the charge of relying overmuch on something miraculous, both of their historical narratives had the virtue of clear central characters—the proletariat for Marx, a publicly spirited civil service for Hegel—carrying out their historical missions in service to the universal. The green narrative, in contrast, tends to portray a vague humanity confronting a limit and somehow collectively overcoming it. The riddle this story presents is how to identify in more precise terms a central character as the agent of the action: a historical subject capable of enacting the scenario. A coherent strategy for the green movement awaits the birth of this hero. In the hero's absence, however, one might begin to question the very idea of coherent strategy and, even, the very idea of a green movement.

Green Practices and Strategic Questions

If there is a keynote among green strategies, it is expressed in the slogan "Think globally, act locally."[6] As is usual with slogans, the words are suggestive but do not define themselves. The words most obviously draw attention to ecological interdependencies on the planet Earth as a physical location in the natural universe. But the phrase also suggests a larger problem, that of relating the general and the particular, and a need for greater sensitivity to the complex interdependencies of an uncertain context.

To the habits of the administrative mind, the notion of thinking globally simply indicates the need for a comprehensive conceptual scheme into which all particulars can be fit and properly located. In strategic terms, the scheme is needed in systematically determining the specific means necessary to achieve clearly defined ends. This approach is most evident in mainstream planning for ecological rationality (e.g., sustainable development programs), but many habits of the administrative mind reappear in radical thinking as well.

Insights gained from practice often challenge the administrative mind and have, in fact, provoked alternative modes of strategic thinking, both reformist and radical. In a reformist vein, incrementalism—as it arises from the tradition of Deweyan pragmatism—has long been an irritant to the administrative mind, particularly in its home domain of policy and management.[7] In a radical mode, post-Marxist and postmodern thinking about social change also makes for significant departures.[8]

More important to practice than final clarity on means and ends is a process of contextual orientation, a continuous mapping of self-in-context that, although always to a large extent tacit, can also be refined and enhanced through deliberate inquiry.[9] But the orientation always remains in part allusive and suggestive, never reducible to a final, explicit definition.[10] It is by acting as much as by setting out goals in advance that the limits and opportunities of new situations emerge, providing a context in which means and ends play off one another and are revised in an ongoing process of multiple outcomes. Unexpected results and opportune moments become more important than anything one might imagine in advance.

Green political practices are strikingly diverse, marked by often bewildering interconnections, strange bedfellows, mixed motives, and variegated contexts that keep changing. Many mapmakers have attempted to chart this terrain, and such mapping is needed to gain a meaningful orientation. If we are to avoid mistaking our maps for the terrain, however, we also need to take the risk of proliferating, questioning, and complicating our maps.

The distinction between radical and reformist tendencies, between dark green and light green, is a commonplace of green strategic thinking. It is a cliché that has its truth—and is certainly vital in getting our bearings—but it also threatens to become a moralistic duality obscuring differences and relationships vital to practical insight. In *The Political Practice of Environmental Organizations,* Ulf Hjelmar begins with this basic contrast, but probes in a nuanced manner the differences between a radical "practice of problematization" and a reformist "practice of effectiveness." Radical practice seeks to problematize environmental issues in a way that challenges established institutions. Reformist practice seeks pathways through established institutions to achieve limited successes. However, Hjelmar stresses the "analytical"—that is to say, fictionally exaggerated—character of this contrast: "In concrete events a practice of problematization can only with difficulty be separated from other forms of political action, such as a practice of political effectiveness."[11] Elements of the two mingle together.

Noting a lack of serious green strategic thought, Andrew Dobson insists that a "central strategic issue" of the green movement is the question of "whether light-green politics . . . makes dark-green politics more or less likely."[12] The crux of the matter for Dobson is whether the two shades of green politics aim for substantially the same goal, with one simply in more of a hurry than the other, or instead work at cross purposes.

What does it mean, however, to claim this as a central issue? It first of all assumes a clear distinction between two forms of green politics: "Discussion of any aspect of green politics," as Dobson puts it, "is dogged by the necessity to distinguish between its dark-green and light-green . . . manifestations" (164). Such a sharp distinction, although offering a clear and convenient map, also obscures much. Dobson constructs stable ideological identities—and avoids "dilution of radical green principles" (130)—by assuming away much of the confusing, chaotic diversity that makes up political reality. In broader terms, what he ultimately assumes is the possibility for a theory of history that would illuminate particulars and allow them to make sense in a larger pattern. Despite heroic efforts in the past, no such theory is available; indeed, the heroic theoretical quest seems to have reached a dead end.

An alternative approach to inquiry would not focus directly on unanswerable questions of ultimate historical consequences, but would instead ask about tendencies in emerging green practices. In this regard, Hjelmar maintains that the split between reform and radical wings in the green movement, sharply accentuated in the 1970s and 1980s, is becoming a thing of

the past in much actual green practice: "Today . . . environmental organizations are not so easy to place on a scale ranging from mainstream to radical
types of political action." In an increasingly complex context, "the tradition
of acting in a particular and one-sided way is vanishing."[13]

The case of Greenpeace helps to illustrate Hjelmar's point. Begun in
1969 as a small alliance of environmentalists and peace movement activists opposed to nuclear testing on Alaska's Amchitca Island, Greenpeace
has grown to become the largest environmental organization in the world.
It has also responded to a highly professionalized policy context in the
United States, as Hjelmar points out, by developing a professional team of
congressional lobbyists. Greenpeace has thus taken on a feature of more
mainstream environmental organizations while quite deliberately retaining
the features that have made it distinctive. Hjelmar here quotes a striking
statement from Greenpeace's executive director: "We are multimedia in the
sense that we are not a lobbying group or a research organization or a litigation house or a grassroots activist movement, but we are a bit of all those
things. So when we formulate campaigns or projects, we combine all those
things in what we do."[14]

Hjelmar also shows how radical activists at times overcome dualistic
thinking and consider the consequences of their approach in the context of
reform-oriented initiatives. Pursuing a practice of problematization, these
activists help prepare the ground for a practice of effectiveness by deliberately "pushing the edge of acceptable environmental action further out
than before."[15] Of course, this is a knife that can cut both ways, and these
observations offer no compelling general answer to Dobson's question.

Dobson wisely equivocates in giving an overall answer to his question,
explicitly indicating that there is room for debate.[16] And perhaps that is the
appropriate conclusion: it is a matter for debate, for an exchange of opinion,
in which differing opinions will serve not necessarily to provide a direct
answer to the question but to illuminate the conceptual and practical complexities involved.

Viewed in that regard, the strategic point of the question becomes less
pressing. What difference could an overall answer make anyway? It is not
as if some Great Leader will rely on the answer to mandate a uniform direction for the green movement. Once one *accepts* the inescapably broad and
diverse nature of the green movement, the question offers an opportunity
for discussion, for partially enacting a green public sphere.

The green public sphere, as a space for discussion, is not governed by a
single direction but by an interest in a plurality of opinions that, even if inconvenient and troubling, help illuminate whatever is being discussed. Instrumentality, on the other hand, is the watchword for a movement with a
clear direction and a goal in view. The green public sphere cannot be imagined as boundless—some limits and coherence are necessary even for mean-

ingful disagreements—but its inclination is toward inclusion. The thrust of Dobson's question, however, anticipates an end to discussion, closing the green public sphere and subordinating it to the coherent strategic direction of a radical green movement.

Systematic Strategy? Radical Negation and Reformist Affirmation

Insisting on theoretical and practical coherence, Alan Carter has advanced a "radical green political theory" in terms of a basic contrast between two dynamics: one that takes us "to the brink of ecological catastrophe" and an alternative that would be "environmentally benign." Each dynamic, the "hazardous" and the "benign," forms a highly interdependent and coherent whole. Consequently, he argues, opposition "on all fronts" to the hazardous dynamic would be "an appropriate political strategy."[17] Carter's picture of things is not implausible, but its neat and orderly appearance might lead one to question it. What he clearly assumes is a confident view of the scope and capacity of human rationality. Not only is it deemed possible in this view to perceive the hazards of an established socioeconomic dynamic, but it is also deemed possible to lay out in advance the design of a dynamic that would be benign.

Carter's idea of a strategic posture opposing the hazardous dynamic "on all fronts" also presupposes a collective agent with sufficient cohesion and knowledge to serve as a point of unity for theory and practice, a cohesive historical subject, that is, capable of sizing up the situation in a comprehensive manner and acting appropriately in a coordinated manner. Carter can accordingly describe the practical upshot of radical green political theory as a systematic strategy of "negation": "what links together theoretically the various aspects of radical green political theory—decentralization, participatory democracy, self-sufficiency, egalitarianism, alternative technology, pacifism and internationalism—is the need to inhibit the environmentally hazardous dynamic that we are presently imprisoned within. Hence, the various elements of radical green political thought consist in the systematic negation of every element of this dynamic" (53; italics deleted). Although he invokes the jargon of negation and its distinctly dialectical overtones, Carter's version of theoretical-practical coherence seems to omit dialectical process in favor of an opposition between two abstract totalities. Indeed, posing a clear duality of hazardous and benign dynamics neglects the potential for historical contingencies that could well belie the idealized neatness of any such model.

Green reformism may appear, at first glance, to avoid the kind of totalizing logic that underpins Carter's radical negation. In *Green Delusions*, for example, Martin Lewis has called for "a new alliance of moderates" to shift the environmental movement away from radical green excess, redirecting it along explicitly reformist lines: "the movement must devise realistic plans and concrete strategies"—a task, he adds, that will require "working with, not against, society at large."[18]

This reform orientation suggests the heritage of progressive, liberal pragmatism that Dewey fostered early in the twentieth century and that Charles Lindblom's concept of incrementalism later translated into terms of an explicit approach to strategy. Yet, Lindblom's disjointed, piecemeal "science of muddling through" does not simply stand by itself, but appeals to a larger sense of order, an "intelligence" of liberal democracy.[19]

To the extent that it is determined to work "with, not against" the established society, a green incremental reformism adopts a strategic posture that is simply the mirror image of systematic negation. It is a strategy of systematic affirmation that, though it may well call for significant change, assumes a socioeconomic order that is fundamentally adequate to green concerns, particularly for seeing that catastrophic scenarios are not played out. As Dobson aptly puts it, such green reformism assumes that "the liberal-democratic decision-making process and the economic structures with which it is engaged are sufficiently open to allow the green agenda to be fulfilled through them."[20] For the sake of this assumption, incremental reformism forfeits critical insight into the powers and the irrationalities that structure its context.

Radical Differences and the Administrative Mind

Radical environmentalism is composed of diverse, often conflicting, approaches—most prominently, social ecology, deep ecology, and ecofeminism. What these particular approaches tend to share is a clear opposition to industrialism; they often challenge the administrative mind, but they also still often find themselves under its shadow.

This happens in different ways. In social ecology, a consistent rejection of hierarchy and centralization is combined with demands for strategic coherence, along with a reassuring promise of unity in diversity—of a natural harmony that humans are naturally inclined to seek to fulfill themselves as social and natural beings. With deep ecology, an ecocentric critique of technocracy mixes with an astonishing reliance on intensified management according to "objective" criteria. In ecofeminism, hope for change is often maintained by implicitly recalling the theological origins of the administrative mind: strategic perplexities become less pressing when change is to proceed from the level of spirit. Alternatively, hope depends on privileging an ecofeminist *we* as the agent of social transformation.

Moving decisively from Marxism to anarchism in developing his concept of social ecology, Murray Bookchin has nonetheless taken very seriously Marx's view that human beings, as natural beings, live in a continuing interchange, or metabolism, with nature. Where Marx saw unrelenting struggle culminating in human control over nature in a rationally administered industrial civilization, Bookchin perceives an interchange that carries the potential for an organic, ecological society. In a context of nonhierarchical relationships, humanity and nature become harmoniously integrated as diverse human and natural potentials develop through a "dynamic stability of the whole."[21] Bookchin's social ecology involves forms of rationality and technology that develop as part of this emerging whole: ecologically knowledgeable human beings—acutely aware of themselves as natural beings—come to "re-enter natural evolution as conscious social beings" (217).

While drawing critically upon Hegel as well as Marx and Engels, Bookchin combines ecological and evolutionary concepts to fashion a philosophy of "dialectical naturalism."[22] Within an open-ended process of natural development, the human mind emerges as a distinctive aspect of a dynamic pattern of evolving forms. Bookchin sees human reason as part of "a broader 'mentality,' or subjectivity, that inheres in nature as a whole," developing "from the seemingly 'passive' interactivity of the inorganic to the highly cerebral processes of human intellect and volition."[23] By celebrating the importance of critically reflexive human rationality in natural development, however, he perplexes ecocentrists, who view this stance as all-too-homocentric.[24] Nonetheless, he offers a potent reminder that humans are not alien from nature, but fully part of it—a point ecocentrists sometimes seem nearly as prone to forget as homocentrists.

Bookchin is intent to do more, however, than merely offer helpful suggestions to the green movement. His aim is to create, or at least decisively promote, a coherent structuring of theoretical and programmatic ideas adequate to the historical task of realizing the potential for an ecological society: "more than ever, we desperately need coherence . . . a real *structure* of ideas" to provide "a coherent outlook and program."[25] Indeed, despite the distance he moves away from Marx, Bookchin's assumptions about theory and practice echo the basic pattern set by the young Marx, who, in his critique of Hegel's *Philosophy of Right*, spoke of "the lightning of thought" penetrating the "soil of the people": "Just as philosophy finds its *material* weapons in the proletariat, so the proletariat finds its *intellectual* weapons in philosophy."[26] Though a particular class, the proletariat embodied a universal emancipatory interest that could be realized only in the creation of a classless society.

In moving to anarchism, Bookchin sharply rejected Marx's reliance on the proletariat as the agency of revolutionary change and in the mid-1960s called upon Marxists to pay attention to a more broadly based potential for a revolutionary movement. With the "post-scarcity" conditions emerging with "a technology of abundance," a process of "class decomposition" ensues, creating the potential to move beyond the insecurities imposed by the organization of scarcity in a repressive society. With the advent of a "non-class" agent of social change, anarchism—as "a libidinal movement of humanity against coercion in any form"—gains the ability to build human communities through a "basic sense of decency, sympathy, and mutual aid" that is "innate" to human beings.[27]

Ecology provided the key insight for what has remained in Bookchin, over the years, a consistent hope for an ecological society. The ecological destructiveness of advanced industrial society, especially when driven by a capitalist imperative to grow at all costs, suggests to Bookchin the necessity for liberation and the potential for an ecology movement to advance "a general human interest that can unify humanity as a whole." This would, at a minimum, mean creating "a harmonious balance with nature."[28] The ecology movement, as Bookchin conceives it, thus has the capacity to avoid the particularism that has deformed past revolutionary movements: "The present ecological crisis is potentially capable of mobilizing a degree of public support and involvement that is more transclass and wider than any issue that humanity has faced in the past. And with the passing of time, this crisis will become starker and more all-embracing than it is today" (172).

Bookchin emphasizes the anarchist sensitivity to historical spontaneity and choice. Yet precisely because the course of things is not set, a coherent theory seems needed to provide overall direction to a movement that, pulled in different directions, is threatening to come apart: "The ecology movement has divided into several questionable tendencies that often directly contradict each other" (160). Reformist environmentalism and a mystifying, misanthropic deep ecology are two key tendencies that bring us to a point of crisis in the movement: "We stand at a crossroads of conflicting pathways" (204).

Bookchin insists upon a radical opposition to hierarchy, to "domination and subjugation" (8) that would counter both reformist moves tending to reinforce the prevailing form of oppression and the authoritarian impulses of deep ecology that promise merely another form of oppression. As conceived by Bookchin, the ecology movement finds common cause with other social movements opposed to oppression, particularly with feminism's opposition to patriarchy. The key question for Bookchin is whether present social movements can meet their "historical challenge"—"whether the ecological and feminist movements" in particular "can be broadened into a sweeping *social movement*."[29]

Broadening, however, is only part of the story: "Although ecology advances a message of diversity, it does so as *unity* in diversity."[30] A coherent movement for social change also demands a narrowing, the removal of inconsistent elements. Bookchin clearly indicates that his purpose is both to broaden and to restrict. He is determined "to peel away the fungus that has accumulated around the movement and look at the promising fruit ecology can yield for the future"; for "ecology alone, firmly rooted in *social* criticism and a vision of *social* reconstruction, can provide us with the means for remaking society in a way that will benefit nature *and* humanity" (13).

DEEP ECOLOGY

The opposition Arne Naess has posed between "deep ecology" and "shallow ecology" makes for an especially catchy version of the contrast between radical and reform approaches. Though clearly ecocentric in orientation, deep ecology does not affirm a clear position. Naess, a professional philosopher influenced by ancient skepticism, seems reluctant to specify a comprehensive doctrine or to try to justify one philosophically. He suggests that deep ecology is an orientation that digs deeply "into the premises of our thinking," and he encourages individuals to work out their own ecocentric belief systems.[31] Deep ecology indeed displays eclectic samplings from a broad range of religions, philosophies, and cultures, and has no overarching outlook of the kind Bookchin's dialectical naturalism supplies for social ecology.

Human domination, domestication, and destruction of nature constitute deep ecology's central concern. What this concern tends to overshadow, however, is the problem of the human domination, domestication, and destruction of human beings and human nature. There is certainly nothing in deep ecology to match the comprehensive critique of hierarchy that Bookchin offers. Authoritarian, moralistic, and misanthropic views have, in fact, all found expression among deep ecologists. Even though it may have no necessary connection to these views, deep ecology—at best naïve about political power and human history—hardly rules them out.

The difficulty becomes especially clear when deep ecology asks strategic questions, as in Devall and Sessions's book *Deep Ecology*. These authors are sharply critical of scientistic and technocratic features of environmental management, but they still assert a hope in "wise" management. Though stressing the importance of decentralization, they expose their deeper inclinations when they suggest "the need for land-use agencies to move away from policy decisions based on subjective criteria such as 'public opinion' to more objective criteria based upon sound ecological principles."[32] Looking forward to wise management in the long term, they acknowledge a need for something short of this ideal in an "interim" period. Here they exhibit reluctant awareness of a problem: "when interim proposals are made to protect the biosphere from destructive individuals and groups, these proposals are seen by many as a form of ecological fascism and totalitarianism. This is *a very real danger* as more intensive management restrictions are instituted to lessen the impact of people on the environment. We believe that genuine freedom for humans and nonhumans lies in deep ecology futures, but totalitarian dangers lurk in the interim period." Devall and Sessions's admirably frank admission of totalitarian dangers—their keenest political insight—appeared, however, only in a scholarly journal.[33] The passage was dropped when the journal article was revised and published as a chapter of their book.[34] In the book, things are much cosier, with strategy comfortably formulated in clichéd terms of ecological consciousness potentially affecting management practices: "If enough citizens cultivate their own ecological consciousness and act through the political process to inform managers and government agencies of deep ecology, some significant changes in the direction of wise long-term management policies can be achieved" (158).

ECOFEMINISM

Despite considerable diversity in ecofeminism, two tendencies are particularly prominent. There is, first, a cultural tendency closely associated with a concern for feminist spiritual imagery. There is also a more concrete social focus, usually concerned with grassroots activism in particular contexts of both affluent and impoverished countries.[35]

The spiritual tendency in ecofeminism can easily be ridiculed, rejected as simply naïve and quiescent or as starkly dangerous—as recalling the frightful deployment of pagan mythology in the Nazi celebration of "blood and soil." It seems hardly necessary to say more than this to dismiss the irrationality of spiritual indulgence and to scare everyone back to the security of reason. Yet, by invoking images of an archaic earth-based spirituality—particularly variations on the figure of an early earth goddess—ecofeminist spirituality at least creates a sharp contrast to expose the normally implicit spiritual dimension of industrialist rationalism, the faith in a phallocentric administrative mind.[36]

Though ecofeminist spirituality has been denounced as a decline into superstition, such criticism may often miss the mark by taking literally a metaphorical use of mythic and mystical imagery meant to evoke elusive dimensions of identity and experience. By Charlene Spretnak's "working definition of spirituality," at least, the spiritual dimension of green politics assumes an aesthetic character: "the focusing of human awareness on the subtle aspects of existence, a practice that reveals to us profound interconnectedness." According to Spretnak, "a 'spiritual infrastructure' is essential for a successful transformation of our society," but she notably does not argue that this is by itself sufficient.[37]

The vague strategic posture of ecofeminist spirituality nonetheless re-inforces a decided inclination to see change in terms of consciousness rais-ing. Faith in the promise of earth-based spirituality thereby tends to mirror the notion—central to Western theology and metaphysics and translated into historical terms by Hegel—that the phenomenal world expresses the creativity and movement of spiritual reality. The upshot of this orientation, in the context of ecofeminist spirituality, is to divert attention from the analysis of power.

Ecofeminists, of course, often do mount determined resistance to the actualities of power. Yet, the focus of action generally centers on the local and the particular, and larger strategic questions tend to be neglected. Lee Quinby's "Ecofeminism and the Politics of Resistance," however, offers a notable exception. Following Foucault, she argues against coherent theory as a guide to practice. The demand for a coherent unity of theory and prac-tice follows a logic of exclusion serving "to limit political creativity." By avoiding "the totalizing impulses of masculinist politics," ecofeminism pro-motes "decentered political struggle" as an effective counter to "decentered power": "the strength thus far of ecofeminism has been to target abuses of power at the local level, in a multiplicity of places."[38]

In a critique of ecofeminism from a feminist position deeply indebted to Bookchin, Janet Biehl has, not surprisingly, rejected ecofeminist spirituality as incoherent and irrational. Without any hesitation, however, Biehl also ex-plicitly encompasses in her critique Quinby's "postmodernism": "to abjure coherence . . . is to abjure reason itself, and its project of attempting to give a coherent explanation of the social world."[39] A postmodern ecofeminism, however, can hardly be criticized in the same breath as an ecofeminist spiri-tuality that hearkens back to archaic traditions.

Postmodernism does not really abandon modern rationality, but turns it on its ear by showing how the demand for rational coherence gets tripped up by the only thing that can separate rationality from dogma: the de-mand for persistent questioning. Biehl too lightly dismisses as a postmod-ern affectation Quinby's accent on persistent questioning. To quote Quinby: "Ecofeminism as resistance politics . . . suggests that theory in the inter-rogative mode—as opposed to theory in the prescriptive mode—asks diffi-cult questions; that is, it asks questions that pose difficulties, even, perhaps especially, for one's own practices. In fact, the we of ecofeminism is most formidable in its opposition to power when it challenges its own assump-tions."[40] In her response to Quinby, Biehl implicitly indicates how much social ecology and dialectical naturalism retain presuppositions of the ad-ministrative mind and how far Quinby's Foucauldian questioning of coher-ence goes in escaping them.

Yet, in advocating diverse struggles "against power," Quinby unavoidably lends her position an implicit coherence, even comprehensiveness: "struggling against specific sites of power not only weakens the junctures of power's networks but also empowers those who do the struggling" (124). Quinby thereby enters into the well-known perplexities that beset Foucault's account of power whenever it explicitly ventures beyond interrogation and endorses a clearly prescriptive stance.[41] The very complexity and pervasiveness of power, as conceived by Foucault, obscure the clear lines of demarcation that could provide a rationale for taking sides in particular struggles.

At the moment of prescription in Quinby's discussion, "power" suddenly looms as an alien and illegitimate thing unto itself. In particular struggles, a line between contending *powers* is normally drawn between us and them, friend and foe. Quinby, however, stakes out such a line at a level of generality. Although implicit, a reified opponent thus becomes the key fixture of Quinby's argument. Questioning this fixture would not only challenge particular assumptions of an ecofeminist *we*, but would also throw into question the very meaning and possibility of such a *we*.

Karen Warren affirms an ecofeminist *we*, but denies it any sharp delineation by reconceptualizing feminism as "a movement to end all forms of oppression."[42] In a largely complementary effort to promote ecofeminism, Ynestra King supplies the obvious corollary by pointing to the need for feminists to create "an ideal of freedom."[43] Ecofeminism thus confronts the key problem ultimately facing any critique of domination: conceptualizing an affirmative notion of liberation.[44]

In what is perhaps the most sophisticated statement of an ecofeminist strategy, Ariel Salleh does not take up the task of fashioning an ideal of freedom. In affirming an ecofeminist *we*, she instead rather paradoxically invokes the principle of "nonidentity" from Theodor Adorno's negative dialectics.[45] In strategic terms, she deploys this principle to enhance and preserve ecofeminist identity while blocking "premature theoretical closure in any new totalization" that would incorporate and subordinate ecofeminist voices.[46] Salleh especially objects to the way the proletariat has been privileged as a historical agent, arguing that "it makes sense to strategically prioritize ecofeminist voices at this point in time" (117).

Promoting an ecofeminist identity, Salleh thus gives a curiously affirmative reading to negative dialectics. She advocates a new historical privilege for ecofeminism, a strategic posture "privileging women temporarily as historical agents par excellence" (120). Given the historical propensity for temporary privilege to become rather long-lasting, however, it would be relevant—if one grants Salleh her point—to ask what temporary might mean. Perhaps jokingly in a somewhat similar context, Warren interestingly suggests something like two millennia.[47]

How should this privileged historical agency be oriented to action? Although Salleh recommends a "dialectical zigzag course," she also attempts to define a clear focus for political practice: "The most urgent and fundamental political task is to dismantle ideological attitudes that have severed men's sense of embeddedness in nature; and this, in turn, can only happen once nature is no longer fixated, commodified as an object, outside of and separate from humans."[60] Entwined in this formulation are the traditional Marxian categories of economic base—the human interchange with nature—and ideological superstructure. What is most urgent, says Salleh, is action at the ideological level to undo the distortions of patriarchy; yet this task can be accomplished only once the economic practice of commodifying nature is ended. The apparent chicken-and-egg paradox of this formulation may well be appropriate to a dialectical zigzag course, but the scope of the zig and the extent of the zag might in practice also tend to undermine any privileged historical agency.

To speak in terms of privileged historical agency recalls the old notion of a revolutionary vanguard, an idea clearly bound up with the metaphor of a rationally coordinated movement. In regard to a green public sphere, such talk is immediately problematic. It is one thing to recognize the distinctiveness and importance of a voice, quite another to exalt an agent of history.

The Dialectics of Ecological Resistance

The spiritual dimension of green politics often seems at odds with practical politics, having, by the account of critics, a politically naïve obsession about the potential of ecological consciousness. This criticism recalls Marx's critique of Hegelian idealism, as summed up in his more general dictum against traditional philosophers: the point is not just to interpret the world, but to change it.

John Rodman's influential treatment of ecological consciousness is explicitly formulated along dialectical lines. None of his four forms—resource conservation, moral extensionism, wilderness preservation, ecological sensibility—is independent of the rest. The culminating form, ecological sensibility, arises historically through a process in which various forms reveal their limits and new forms arise.[49]

There is an ambivalence in Rodman, however, regarding the source of dialectical tension and change. At times, the limits overcome by dialectical movement appear to be conceptual—the insufficiency of an idea—with change seemingly internal to the development of ideas in critical thought. At other times, Rodman's discussion clearly points to practical struggles. The ambivalence stems from the old opposition of Hegel and Marx, and Rodman can hardly be unaware of this. At one point, indeed, he clearly formulates the idealist postulate that provides "the basic principle of Hegelian metaphysics": "This postulate made it possible to interpret life teleologically in terms of a two-fold process of 'realization,' whereby the spiritual principle, existing as a potency, achieved through the practical activity of [human beings] an objective embodiment in the world of institutions, and achieved through the intellectual activity of [human beings] a consciousness of itself as the fundamental principle structuring the universe."[50] Here Rodman indicates how Hegelian idealism portrayed the relationship between human intellectual and practical activity or, in other words, between theory and practice.

The ambivalence in his dialectical treatment of ecological consciousness suggests a sympathy for idealism, but he does not stake out a metaphysical position. His repeated invocation of metaphor and analogy, indeed, indicates a deliberate "as if" quality to his thinking.[51] He is not disclosing some ultimate reality, but offering a mode of orientation within an ultimately indeterminate world.

The forms of ecological consciousness in Rodman are connected to forms of practice. Ecological sensibility, in particular, is a mode of experience expressed by the practice of "ecological resistance."[52] Within an ecologically informed, metaphoric mirroring of psyche, polis, and cosmos, ecological resistance expresses "a felt need to resist the repression, censorship, or liquidation of potentialities that lie within both human and nonhuman nature, and to liberate suppressed potentialities from the yoke of domestication and threatened extinction."[53]

Rodman suggests that the phrase "liberation of nature," although profoundly misleading if taken literally, may yet offer an appropriate metaphor to guide the practice of green politics.[54] For the cause of ecological resistance, Rodman adopts the maxim of Thoreau's essay on "Civil Disobedience": "Let your life be a counter friction to stop the machine."[55] "The resistance of a single person," Rodman maintains, ". . . has . . . a multi-dimensional depth of meaning"[56]: "An act of Ecological Resistance," he adds, ". . . is an affirmation of the integrity of a naturally diverse self-and-world. Its meaning is not exhausted by its success or failure in the linear sequence of events, since its meaning lies also in the multi-dimensional depth of an act in one realm that simultaneously affirms a principle valid in many realms."[57] Ecological resistance is "holistic" in character, involving the individual as a participant in a kind of "ritual action whereby one aligns the self with the ultimate order of things." "By making the principle of diversity central," ecological resistance is able to "incorporate" the other forms of ecological consciousness and action "as moments within the dialectic of a larger whole" (54–56).

Yet, the culmination of any dialectical process in an apparently self-sufficient whole always poses an unsettling question: What next? What has been left outside the whole as a potentially unsettling other? What, in a dialectical sense, are the limits of ecological resistance?

Clearly, the development of ecological consciousness, in Rodman's view, does not assume for consciousness the kind of role that it has in the scenarios of Hegelian Marxism. Far from identifying in collective terms an effective liberatory agent, Rodman's account tends conceptually to individualize resistance while instrumental effectiveness is subordinated to a celebration of ecological experience and expression.

The fact that Rodman does not discover the missing agent of historical change could be regarded as just another failure of idealism. However, it might be recognized that Rodman seems to do no worse than many neo-Marxists who, despairing of the proletariat, have exhausted themselves in vain quests for this holy grail. Marcuse's emancipatory hopes, for example, could never be as convincing as his proclamation of the "Great Refusal."[58] Rodman's depiction of ecological resistance, promising no historical transformation, may suggest an assessment of prevailing social institutions that is far from naïve.

The account of theory and practice in Rodman is thus strikingly similar to other dialectical efforts that would link theory and practice through a concept of consciousness.[59] Hope for a historical agent capable of transforming the whole cannot be sustained and gives way to a celebration of resistance. Yet, for someone of Marcuse's Marxian propensities, the hope, though frustrated, nonetheless keeps clearly in view the historical goal of qualitative social change. For someone with Rodman's idealist sympathies, the hope itself becomes vague. Without either an idealist metaphysics or a definite role for a collective agency of historical transformation, Rodman is left with a form of consciousness involving the experience and expression of an individual subject who yearns for the whole but is ultimately unable to complete it, either intellectually or practically.

Rodman presents the image of the self standing in resistance to the monocultural juggernaut of industrialism. But by conceiving resistance ultimately in terms of individual consciousness, he offers a political orientation that is actually antipolitical at its core. Ecological resistance, as he says, is a kind of ritual action that orients the individual in terms of a metaphoric mirroring of psyche, polis, and cosmos. Action culminates in multidimensional meaning, but not in a diversity of opinions exchanged in political debate. Conceiving political action on *that* model of diversity would mean shifting from the paradigm of consciousness to the paradigm of communication and raising the prospect of a green public sphere.

"We represent a total concept," say die Grünen, "as opposed to the one-dimensional . . . brand of politics." Here, implicitly aligning themselves with Marcuse's critique of "one-dimensional society," the German Greens declare their radical character: "Our policies are guided by long-term visions for the future and are founded on four basic principles: ecology, social responsibility, grass roots democracy, and nonviolence."[70] Even though claiming to be "in front" rather than "left or right," the Greens emerged from a specifically German conjunction of environmental concern and radical politics. The cleavage between radical and reform orientations, so obvious in the United States and elsewhere, was not characteristic of die Grünen. Despite the diversity among the Greens, what they have generally shared is a radical orientation: "all currents adhere to a *radical* vision of the future."[61]

The well-known dispute between green fundamentalists and green realists (Fundis vs. Realos) is misconstrued if seen in terms of a tension between radical and reformist ends.[62] The main difference, in Hjelmar's terms, was whether to emphasize practices of problematization or practices of effectiveness. Party organization and success did not fit well with the practice of problematization favored by fundamentalists, as Ruldolph Bahro stressed in 1985 when leaving the Greens to concentrate on building a fundamentalist green movement. Party organization had, in his view, become "a counterproductive tool."[63] The realist practice of effectiveness, although oriented by what Helmut Wiesenthal has called a "practical reform discourse,"[64] also takes a critical posture toward established institutions. The reforms are deliberately conceived and promoted as part of a project of *radical* reformism.[65]

RUDOLPH BAHRO: GREEN FUNDAMENTALIST

Bahro, once a Marxist heretic in the former East Germany, over the years has exhibited different approaches to green strategy.[66] What nonetheless remains constant in Bahro is an affinity to the "utopian socialism" that Marx and Engels criticized for creating "castles in the air."[67] Especially as he has promoted ecomonasticism, Bahro has sought a position outside and opposed to the industrial order in its totality, rejecting the Marxian idea that necessary conditions for social transformation—including the historical agent—are somehow to emerge from the dynamics of the established order. A "Total Alternative" must confront the industrial system.[68]

In institutional terms, Bahro calls for a "new Benedictine order," a network of communes in which to promote spiritual and lifestyle changes, at once individual and collective, that can exert a transformative influence on the whole: "The accumulation of spiritual forces . . . will at a particular point in time which can't be foreseen exceed a threshold size. Such a 'critical mass' . . . then acquires under certain circumstances a transformative influence over the whole society" (98).

Despite the central role that spirituality obviously plays in Bahro's thinking, he has indicated that his "mentality" remains significantly Marxist (73, 28). It is thus that he demands a theoretically coherent radical program that is not watered down by reformism: "Anyone who still has a trace of Marxist training in them as far as method is concerned, can never be satisfied with . . . eclecticism, that is with the mixing of positions instead of integration on one particular position" (46). For Bahro, the industrial system faces a dire crisis not, as Marx had expected of capitalism, primarily because of its internal dynamics, but because of the external threats imposed by natural limits (25).

Bahro calls for the creation of "areas liberated from the industrial system" (29), but his program here finds itself in something of a quandary, for he remains enough of a Marxist to recognize that the creation of opportunities for livelihood outside the industrial system will require a diversion capital (26, 47, 20). He nonetheless insists that a change in consciousness is the first priority: "there will be no zones liberated from the industrial system if we don't liberate the consciousness for them in advance."[69]

Although Bahro may well have some dialectical process in mind, his strategic priority is clear enough. The question of timing cannot be regarded as a side issue, for Bahro displays a sense of urgency, demanding radical change in the face of catastrophe. "Even faced with the most stringent proofs," he nonetheless says at one point, "the only thing that remains for us is to rely on the possibility of error in the analysis and deliberately try something like the famous planting of a tree in the face of the announcement that the end of the world is coming."[70] What is intriguing about this statement is that his strategy here becomes a posture—a gesture—in the face of almost impossible odds. But are not gestures other than tree planting—or ecomonasticism—also possible? One alternative would be cultivating a green public sphere.

HELMUT WIESENTHAL: GREEN REALIST

While promoting reforms within the established system, Helmut Wiesenthal seeks levers that would advance change at a structural level. His orientation has been aptly summed up by John Ferris: "Central to Wiesenthal's strategy for ecological reform is the idea that there must be societal structural reforms to make it possible for people to live in ecologically responsible ways. Both current values and structural mechanisms 'lock' people into unsustainable 'lifestyles.'"[71]

Interestingly, Wiesenthal's approach here, quite at odds with Bahro's spiritualism, exhibits a significant similarity with Marxian materialism. There is no moralizing; attention turns instead to the way systemic incentive structures shape the choices and interactions of individuals and groups. According to Ferris, this focus results in a strategic orientation that, in marked contrast to Bahro, opposes green achievements if they are gained at the cost of increased social insecurity (22).

Wiesenthal warns against the fundamentalist propensity to rely on "some noble guiding principle": "Reality, in its principle-less complexity, would only strike back all the harder."[72] The value of a policy alternative, he stresses, is not enhanced by appealing "for greater individual sacrifice" (216). Such an appeal, in his view, simply amounts to a moralistic indulgence that is bound to be ineffective, except perhaps as a way of masking strategic confusion and enhancing the cohesive identity of a movement (204, 217).

Wiesenthal's key question is formulated by Ferris in the following terms: "How would it be feasible for the populations of highly urbanized regions like Europe to live lives of 'self-reliant independence' without radical changes in housing, transportation, employment, health and many other areas of public policy?"[73] Attuned to a complex and ambiguous context, Wiesenthal's green realism thus does not focus either narrowly on reform policies for environmental protection or broadly on a blanket rejection of the industrial system, but calls for a tolerance of ambiguity.[74]

In the terrain of green politics, one finds no single dividing line at the center of things, such as the Marxian opposition between capital and labor, but "an unclear and fluctuating conflictual structure." In strategic terms, this context calls for "well-considered decisions that take account of reciprocal relations and learning processes" (204). Theory, disciplined by attention to the details and nuances of practical situations, comes to guide a practice of effectiveness concerned not simply with issues of environmental policy, as these are commonly understood, but also with questions of social policy (e.g., proposals on shorter working time and a guaranteed minimum income [187]) that involve the larger operations of the industrial system and have the potential to alter its dynamics.

As a theorist and practitioner, Wiesenthal's key point of reference remains die Grünen as "a party of reform" acting "as the agent of new issues and as the promoter of comprehensive democratisation" (219). Party organization thus provides a "collective actor" able to make "judicious" moves in the strategic realities of the political world. Wiesenthal's position thereby anticipates theoretical coherence and a cohesive, purposeful party organization. Despite a measured tone and an explicit disavowal of emotionalism, he reveals an air of desperation. In the face of environmental destruction, he has little time for radical posturing or principled withdrawal, or for "the kind of patience suited to a philosophy seminar" (219). He wants coherent organization and decisive, realistic action.

The problem with green realism, from Bahro's fundamentalist perspective, is that it amounts merely to tinkering with a mechanism that needs to be scrapped. From an ecosocialist viewpoint, there is a parallel though quite different difficulty. Wiesenthal's realism is not realistic enough, Werner Hülsberg has argued, because its approach to reform, neglecting realities of power in a capitalist society, is inclined toward proposals that are "ultimately naive." For Hülsberg, it is obvious that any serious move in the direction of radical reform at a structural level would meet "fierce" resistance by capitalists, backed by the threat of "an investment strike and flight of capital." Given the realities of a capitalist society, to focus on "achieving the achievable" is to risk such a shrinkage in the scope of reform proposals that no radicalism is left.[75]

The main weakness of green realism from an ecosocialist perspective is that the focus on reform initiatives within a context of party organization neglects the need for a larger mobilization of social forces and tends to lose sight of radical goals. Hülsberg thus envisions a potential reform bloc, involving the Greens and the much more popular and powerful Social Democratic Party, but insists that an alliance is out of the question without a dramatic shift of forces in favor of the Greens. Changing the relation of forces between the parties thus rises to the top of his ecosocialist agenda, and to this end, he advocates "a combination of parliamentary initiative and extraparliamentary mobilization." With a "decisive shift" in favor of the Greens and "growing self-mobilization" among social movements, Hülsberg argues, there could be "a government coalition . . . capable of making a qualitative breakthrough": this would mean "radical reform in the literal sense of the term" (216–18).

Even with the kind of red-green governing coalition Hülsberg imagines, the viability of such a breakthrough would still be questionable. Decisive, on the ecosocialist premises he employs, would be the power of capital in the underlying socioeconomic structure. How to revolutionize the alignment of power at this level was the question Marx addressed. He did not look merely at machinations at an overt level of political action—whether of the kind recommended by a Bahro, a Wiesenthal, or a Hülsberg—but focused attention on how socioeconomic dynamics immanent to capitalism prepared the way for a historical transformation. This is where eco-Marxists continue to look.

Capitalism, Nature, Socialism: Eco-Marxist Contradictions

The category of nature is central to Marx, the key to his materialism. As natural beings, humans are necessarily part of a continuous interchange with nature as a whole—a "metabolism with nature."[76] This metabolism, for Marx, takes the constant form of struggle (3:958), but the struggle assumes different forms, changing historically with differing modes of production. The various economic forms, in turn, generate their own characteristic struggles among human beings, particularly according to class divisions rooted in differing relationships to the means of production.[77]

In Marxian historical materialism, the "central contradiction" that makes a mode of production capitalistic is an incompatibility between socialized production and individualized appropriation.[78] A socializing tendency, in other words, is intrinsic to capitalist development and becomes particularly manifest in its industrial phase. The rise of the factory system, the concentration of ownership, the emergence of joint stock companies, the management of firms by salaried employees—these developments, according to Marx and Engels, show how capitalist production tends to become socialized: how the germ of socialism emerges as part of the capitalist dynamic and has nothing initially to do with state economic management, even though the state already begins under capitalism to take on significant roles in the promotion and coordination of economic activity.[79]

Capitalism is ultimately driven, however, by the acquisitive calculations of individuals who invest with the motive of profit within the opportunities and constraints of the system. If the system does not promise profit to the "possessive individual,"[80] in other words, it malfunctions—hence economic crisis and persistent efforts both by capitalist enterprises and by the state to enhance conditions for profitability. The malfunctioning of the system disrupts the socially organized metabolism with nature, a disruption that places the vast majority of the population in a desperate situation since their livelihood depends on opportunities to sell their labor power to capitalist enterprise.[81]

The vast potential for human benefit harbored in the forces of production becomes constrained by the social relations of production. Thus the incompatibility between increasingly socialized production and continuingly individualized appropriation emerges as a contradiction between the forces and relations of production. Especially during periods of economic crisis, the contradiction manifests itself through obvious irrationalities, creating open social conflict between the bourgeoisie and the proletariat. In traditional Marxism, this development sets the stage for social revolution and a new role for the state. The state becomes decisive in the revolutionary process, no longer seeking to maintain individualistic appropriation as the driving force of the system, but determining a planned course of development, guided directly by considerations of human need, and thereby bringing to completion the socializing process that capitalism began.[82]

The environmentalist idea that ecological scarcity portends dramatic social change[83] has been pictured in eco-Marxist terms as creating the potential for another, perhaps parallel, path to socialism. Attempting to follow as closely as possible the language and logic of Marx, James O'Connor argues that capitalism encounters limits not only from its own internal dynamics (as when productive forces are constrained by class-divided social relationships), but also from external conditions that the capitalist mode of production requires in order to function.[84]

A greening of Marxism begins with the recognition that nature, ecologically conceived, is obviously such a condition, yet is systematically threatened by capitalist development: hence the trajectory of dialectical movement suggested in the title of the leading eco-Marxist journal, *Capitalism, Nature, Socialism*. According to O'Connor, "In ecological Marxism, economic crisis is the cauldron in which capital restructures the conditions of production . . . in ways that make them more transparently social in form and content, for example, permanent-yield forests, land reclamation, regional land use and/or resource planning, population policy, health policy, labor market regulation, toxic waste disposal planning, and so on."[85] The socializing tendency of capitalist development here manifests itself again. Capitalism, through both private enterprise and the state, "switches to more social forms of the provision of production conditions"; but by taking this step, "capitalism tends to self-destruct or subvert itself," thereby "making socialism at least more imaginable" (210).

Introducing a vague but suggestive notion of "ecological exploitation," O'Connor further indicates that just as the exploitation of labor gave rise to a social movement to challenge capitalism, so the exploitation of nature gives rise to a socially diverse environmental movement that carries another challenge. In terms of Marxian crisis theory, O'Connor thus speaks of these developments as arising, in turn, from "first" and "second" contradictions of capitalism (211).

While many radical green positions either strongly question or explicitly oppose capitalism on ecological grounds, the project of abolishing the capitalist system is the central priority of eco-Marxism. Indeed, the "eco" has been appended to Marxism slowly and, at times, reluctantly. As early as 1974, however, Hans Magnus Enzensberger argued that Marxists should take seriously the possibility that there might be something to the environmentalist idea that pressing ahead with the established pattern of industrialization risks "catastrophic results."[86]

From a Marxist perspective, the problem would not be industrialization per se, but its capitalist form. "Socialism," Enzensberger indicated, would then be "a question of survival" (48). *If* it could be shown that the capitalist mode of production is inherently incompatible with ecological rationality, then the eco-Marxist project of abolishing the system could not be regarded as an add-on to the green movement, but would emerge as necessarily central to it. This, however, is a troublesome "if."

"Is an ecologically sustainable capitalism possible?" O'Connor thus puts the question in quite clear and direct terms.[87] However, his answer is not so clear. Although David Pepper takes him as "demonstrating how there is no hope" for such a possibility,[88] O'Connor actually equivocates. "The evidence," he says, "favors the judgment that capitalism is not ecologically sustainable."[89] This is hardly a definitive statement, but O'Connor is further well aware that even an emphatic declaration based on evidence alone falls short of a systematic conclusion based both on evidence and a clearly conceptualized model of the mode of production. Indeed, his explicit "systematic answer to the question" superficially appears to be a no, but is actually a highly qualified yes: "Not *unless and until*," he says, "capital changes its face in ways that would make it unrecognizable to bankers, money managers, venture capitalists, and CEOs, looking at themselves in the mirror today" (158; emphasis added). Possible, that is, but not very likely. O'Connor's words may suggest a reductio ad absurdum, but he is also reluctantly acknowledging that the answer depends on what "capitalism" means.

The case against ecologically sustainable capitalism would seem to be simple and overwhelming if one accepts two apparently obvious points: (1) there is a persistent growth dynamic intrinsic to capitalism, and (2) endless growth is impossible in an ecologically finite world. Yet, the conclusion would also assume that the growth dynamic intrinsic to capitalism depended on some definite relationship to "ecological exploitation." Marx, of course, tried to show something quite different: that capitalist profitability depended on exploiting the labor power of human beings.

Capitalist development certainly remains a form of the human struggle with nature, and its competitive features can especially be shown to generate all sorts of ecological irrationalities. However, it is precisely O'Connor's point that these irrationalities call forth socializing tendencies already immanent to capitalism. It is a "foregone conclusion" that both private capitalist enterprises and the capitalist state will respond to "the crisis of nature" through attempts at more coherent planning and development, including a "technology-led restructuring of production conditions."[90]

But the outcome is uncertain. The changes may or may not prove helpful to capitalism as a whole or to particular enterprises. For the result depends on things that are unpredictable: the specific measures adopted, their interrelationships, and their actual effects in the ongoing interchange with nature (212). Because of capitalist competition and pressing incentives for individual firms to externalize costs, moreover, there is a clear propensity for continuing ecological irrationality. But there is no way to tell in advance how far socializing tendencies toward rational coordination can proceed under capitalism (or, indeed, exactly how to mark the point of moving beyond that system).

With his equivocation on the question of ecologically sustainable capitalism, O'Connor resists the Marxist temptation to celebrate the inevitable downfall of capitalism and the imminent rise of socialism. The unexpected flexibility and adaptability demonstrated by the capitalist system since Marx, particularly with the advent of the welfare state, has, indeed, exhausted the credibility of all talk along these lines. O'Connor speaks instead not only of the system's contradictions, but also of the "quite loose and flexible" character of key relationships within the system (205, 210). "The telos of crisis" under capitalism, he says, "is . . . to create the possibility of imagining more clearly a transition to socialism" (209; cf. 210). Actually transforming the system remains an even more uncertain prospect.

Capitalism is thus not only dynamic, but also ambiguous—an ambiguity that socialism shares.[91] What capitalism and socialism have in common historically is an institutional and ideological commitment to industrialism, particularly through the rise of their administrative spheres and an allegiance, in one form or another, to the administrative mind. The green movement generally anticipates an economy—a metabolism with nature— that is somehow qualitatively different from industrial capitalism or socialism. But there is no clear and unequivocal economic form for the green movement necessarily to pursue, apart from that form's being somehow ecologically sustainable. Certainly, there is no economic blueprint ready for the administrative mind to follow.

With its current economic irrationalities, O'Connor maintains, capitalism "must sooner or later lead to a 'rebellion of nature,' that is, to powerful social movements demanding an end to ecological exploitation."[92] Whatever it might mean exactly to stop exploiting nature, it is not clear that these social movements would necessarily pursue an agenda of blocking capitalism and promoting socialism. The problem of revolutionary agency thus arises in a particularly pointed form for eco-Marxism.

For Marx the proletariat was both a product of capitalism and its dialectical gravedigger due to the particular location of workers in class relationships. Once faith in the proletariat wanes and reliance begins to shift to diverse sources of potential opposition, however, dialectical coherence verges on a confused eclecticism. This clearly concerns O'Connor. He disparagingly suggests that, under the influence of postmodernism, the post-Marxist displacement of class opposition in favor of multiple, decentered sites of resistance amounts to little more than "recycled anarchism" (220). O'Connor wishes to maintain some coherent class identity for oppositional social movements. These movements do, indeed, tend to share a common class position in the broad sense that they are generally made up of people who lack control over the means of production. However, this does not erase the great diversity and tension existing among social movements, even within the green movement itself.

The Very Idea of a Green Movement

In one of his most famous lines, Hegel likened truth to "a bacchanalian revel" in which everyone is drunk with self-importance.[93] Debates over green strategies are often, like Hegel's bacchanalian revel, filled with a bewildering array of positions with each ultimately convinced that it offers the only right, possible, or sufficient way.

What unites green strategies of various stripes and hues, however, is the very idea of social *movement*. In discussing the German Greens, Werner Hülsberg indeed explicitly bases his argument on this metaphor: "Now every movement, as the name suggests, has to do with 'movement': it has to remain in motion, otherwise it comes to an end. There are, however, objective and subjective limits to this 'movement' which have to do with the general stage of awareness and development of class conflict. There are limits to the expansion of a social movement which, if the movement fails to break through them, bring about a decline and a search for new forms."[94] What clearly lingers in the background of this idea is the Hegelian concept of world-historical process as the dialectical movement of mind, particularly as reconceptualized in terms of Marxian historical materialism: not as a logical "movement of pure reason," as Marx put it, but as "a practical movement, a *revolution.*"[95]

Whereas Marx took the revolutionary potential of the working class to be central in moving beyond the capitalist mode of production, much twentieth-century theory sympathetic to Marx raised doubts about this potential and began a rather desperate effort to find or create new sources of revolutionary agency. When the new social movements of today began to emerge in the 1960s and 1970s, they were often portrayed as "*the* movement"—a single oppositional movement of the new left—and they thus restored hope to the great refusal in Marcuse's version of critical theory.[96] More recently, Marcuse's Hegelian Marxism has been displaced by a post-Marxist orientation, particularly as developed by Ernesto Laclau and Chantal Mouffe.[97] Influenced by postmodern thinking, they take an interplay of diverse social movements as key to a transformative politics of radical democracy.

The green movement has often been pictured as part of an ensemble of new social movements that collectively announce the advent of a new age, a social transformation that may be irresistible and inevitable.[98] Though these social movements may well bear a family resemblance in a common opposition to the established order, they do not constitute a common front. There is much diversity and disagreement.

Even environmentalists are not necessarily allies in all situations. Differences arise over what kinds of organization are desirable (e.g., political parties or antiparties, professionalized organizations, decentralized networks, communes, grassroots groups) and over tactical questions of what is to be done (e.g., lobbying, electoral campaigning, civil disobedience, "monkey wrenching" or ecosabotage, public hearing interventions, protest marches, green consumerism, alternative lifestyles, consumer boycotts, environmental litigation).

In its early heyday, environmentalism could announce that we are all in the same boat. If so, left-wing critics responded, we are not all traveling in the same class. This insight draws attention to inequities that underscore differences in the green movement. The focus on class helps reveal that workers in their workplaces and homes are more vulnerable to environmental hazards than the affluent. Ecofeminism focuses on inequities of gender, and the environmental justice movement has a special concern about racial inequality. A green anticolonialism has also arisen to challenge international inequalities. Yet the focus on class, however, also draws attention as well to the fact that much of the impetus for the green movement (and other new social movements) arose among those centered in the advanced industrial countries who, well educated and enjoying relative socioeconomic security, came to count the costs of industrialization and to embrace nonacquisitive values.[99]

What is the green movement? Can these differences somehow be resolved? Can the various elements be brought into a complementary relationship, or at least worked up into a plausible scenario that can give hope and direction to the green movement and new social movements generally?

Laclau and Mouffe's post-Marxist strategy takes its point of departure from Marx's materialist inversion of Hegel's dialectic, yet dialectical movement is itself supplanted by an open-ended interplay of differences. Under the influence of Foucault, they turn to a diversity of social movements as constituting new sites of social antagonism arising in resistance to oppressive power. However, a Foucauldian manner of resistance, focused on the local and the particular, would be insufficient for a post-Marxist strategy of transformative change to radical democracy. The transformative hope depends on retaining a link to Marxism through the Gramscian theme of hegemonic struggle.

Among Marxist theorists, Antonio Gramsci focused perhaps the most clearly on historical ironies and paradoxes as he stressed the need for a revolutionary movement to establish alliances and tactical compromises among diverse social interests. Almost as much as Marx, Machiavelli provides a key point of reference for Gramsci, who is particularly drawn to Machiavelli's account of the relationship between fortune and *virtù*.[100] The contingencies of fortune—with all their "bizarre combinations"[101]—arise as a political reality that challenges the *virtù*, the will and prowess, of the prince. Of course, Gramsci has in mind not Machiavelli's Renaissance prince, nor an individual hero, but a "modern prince," which takes the form of the revolutionary Marxist party (147, 188–89).

Unlike Machiavelli's premodern prince, Gramsci's modern prince does not depend simply on clever insights and adaptability within a shifting, surprising field of contingency. The dynamics of the mode of production remain identifiable and measurable, the indirect basis of historical conjunctures—the passing irrationalities of fortune (177–78, 180–81). The modern prince arises as a rational organization that, through a flexible unity of theory and practice at multiple levels of historical movement, brings order and coherent direction, as well as "moral and intellectual unity" (181; cf. 365). In the end, the rationality of the administrative mind overshadows the contingent domain of hegemonic struggle (180–95).

From a postmodern posture, Laclau and Mouffe emphatically proclaim an antiessentialism that Gramsci intimates but ultimately resists. Indeed, they elaborate a "logic of the contingent,"[102] which recalls, at least implicitly, the premodern world of fortune's reign. They do not, however, celebrate either Machiavelli's Renaissance prince or Gramsci's modern prince, but suggest a postmodern prince (186–87).

The project of radical democracy dispenses altogether with a centralizing move à la Gramsci: "There is no unique privileged position." The key to Laclau and Mouffe's strategy, rather, is "a plurality of social logics" constituted in "a plurality of spaces" (190). What becomes necessary for the project, moreover, is "the construction of a new 'common sense' which changes the identity of the different groups" so that their differing practices are able to complement one another (183). Radical democratic politics, they argue, should institutionalize openness by constructing a "space" of "contradictory tension" that invites plurality (189). Diverse social forces are thus to be included.

Yet, even with the explicit encouragement of openness, there would appear to be an at least provisional identity—hence a principle of exclusion—already implicit in the very notions of antagonism and transformation.[103] Just as Gramsci repeatedly invokes the imagery of warfare, so the coherence of a decentered hegemony would seem to require a sharp, even if implicit, distinction between potential enemies and allies. Laclau and Mouffe refuse to disavow the need for an oppositional posture that totalizes "as negativity" the established order of society. This extreme posture is needed to avoid the other extreme of a reformism "without a project."[104] As part of a precarious, "unstable equilibrium," they suggest, the oppositional posture is necessary but not ultimate (97–98).

A striking metaphorical ambivalence, or shift, occurs in Laclau and Mouffe's work. Just as Jean-François Lyotard has emphasized that postmodernity exposes and breaks up the grand narratives of modernity,[105] Laclau and Mouffe shift away from the pervasive metaphor of movement. A point of equilibrium, however tense and unstable, suggests not movement, but a certain cessation or containment of movement. And it cannot be part of the radical democratic project to get beyond the space of contradictory tension because this would require a closure shutting out the practice of radical democratic politics itself. They imagine not a "unified public space," but "a proliferation of radically new and different political spaces."[106] An underlying metaphor of space is thus retained, but there is no longer a journey that traverses space toward a receding horizon. The political spaces of radical democratic politics retain their differences, yet also open onto one another; as spaces for creating and contesting meanings, they provide room for debate and disagreement.

Laclau and Mouffe's concept of a decentered hegemony depends on the idea that separate identities are maintained, but the concept also serves to heighten the perplexities posed by lines of conflict within and among different movements. Although they would disavow a privileged perspective, Laclau and Mouffe maintain an oppositional posture that demands the key distinction between allies and enemies. This distinction obviously is of prime importance as a movement becomes mobilized and sets out on a course to achieve its goals. Coupled with the sense that urgent and decisive action is necessary, however, the distinction carries the risk of turning potential allies into unnecessary enemies precisely at the moment that solidarity is deemed crucial.

The question of where, when, and how to draw the line is not one that answers itself. Laclau and Mouffe certainly make no suggestion that the right answer is bound to emerge from the exigencies of practice. This distinction between friends and foes, the implicit key to a radical democratic strategy, thus threatens to undermine the very openness of radical democratic practice. In terms of the green movement, the distinction anticipates the vantage point of an administrative mind capable of giving sound guidance, of authoritatively answering all the normative and strategic issues bound up with the question of what it means to be green.

The Virtue of Mixing Metaphors

Maintaining a consistency of means and ends is often deemed the hall-mark of coherent green political practice.[107] However, the very metaphor of a green *movement* accentuates the separation of means and ends by sug-gesting the distance that must be traversed to reach the destination.[108] It is a long and serious journey, clearly suggesting the grand narrative of a tragically heroic quest. Green theory and practice often implicitly invoke a tragic narrative, taking on an air of desperation because there is no one to assume the hero's role and because the quest is, in any case, too uncertain.

The metaphor of the green movement may be inescapable simply because green ends are so doubtful of achievement. However, another metaphor is available, that of activity emerging within a place. It is not the path of a movement but the space of a discourse. This metaphor does not suggest that theoretical and practical coherence is required so that an idealized *we* can prepare for the journey ahead, but instead draws attention to a partially existing *we*, capable of shared meaning, that needs disagreement as well as agreement to nurture its discourse.

Mixing metaphors in this manner may not eliminate perplexities, but it also does not mask them. There surely is a vast distance for the green movement to traverse, but there is a precious discursive space as well— an emerging green public sphere—that does not travel well. Recognition of this perplexity disrupts the cliché of narrative movement along tragic lines. Movement may yet continue, but the competing metaphor encourages an ironic look at self-in-context that deflates heroic pretensions and adds a comic touch to the story line.

Upon entering the public scene, environmentalism disturbed the established discourse of advanced industrial society. Technocratic discourse has usually overwhelmed concerns about the morality of dominating nature, but doubts about the human *ability* to dominate nature have proven more worrisome. As the future has been thrown into question, there has been a significant, albeit highly equivocal, greening of public discourse. According to John Dryzek, "*the* enduring legacy" of environmental activism may be a reframing of discourse. Contemporary public discourse indeed exhibits a "language of environment" that makes possible new forms of argument and contention.[1]

While constitutive of the green public sphere, the environmental focus also has a broader reach. The green impact on public discourse has not been homogeneous, however, and over the decades has exhibited a striking shift in focus. In the late 1960s and early 1970s, as environmentalism initially raised the question of "limits," there was obviously an implicit concern with sustainability. But "sustainability" did not enter the focus of public discourse as a key term until the late 1980s, when "sustainable development" became the watchword of environmentalism. The change from a focus on limits to a focus on sustainability occurred in a vacuum, but within a larger, shifting context of public discourse.

From "Limits" to "Sustainability"

The perception of environmental crisis animating the dramatic rise of environmentalism in the late 1960s and early 1970s was announced in various ways and with different emphases. By far the most dramatic announcement, however, was *The Limits to Growth*, which attracted attention both because it employed a computer-oriented method and because its sponsor, the Club of Rome, drew its members from the international elites of science, business, and government. With its technocratic source and style, *The Limits to Growth* provoked concern and attracted enormous publicity, but its message was ultimately too blunt and dismal, too at odds with the industrialist ideology, for it to be acceptable.

The centerpiece of *The Limits to Growth* was a computer model of the "world system," portraying the prospect of "overshoot and collapse" if trends of exponential growth were not significantly curtailed. The study sought an alternative that, while providing for "the basic material requirements" of the population, would be "sustainable" (166, 158). This possibility—termed "the state of global equilibrium"—was based on the idea of "the stationary state," particularly as adapted by Herman E. Daly from John Stuart Mill's mid-nineteenth-century work, *Principles of Political Economy*.[3]

In considering an end of growth—a prospect that had haunted classical political economy since Adam Smith—Mill raised the question of the purpose of growth: "Towards what ultimate point is society tending by its industrial progress?"[4] Unlike Smith, Mill was not averse to the prospect of a stationary state, but actually saw in it an improvement of the human condition. Once productive capacity became advanced, the chief question was how to enhance distribution rather than production. Disaffected with "struggling to get on" as an "ideal of life," Mill decisively revised the myth of progress by, in effect, identifying the stationary state as the goal of growth: "There would be as much scope as ever for all kinds of mental culture, and moral and social progress; as much room for improving the Art of Living, and much more likelihood of its being improved, when minds ceased to be engrossed by the art of getting on" (756–57).

Mill's vision gave the authors of *The Limits to Growth* an enticing image with which to affirm the equilibrium state as a desirable goal.[5] By invoking Mill's images of vitality and dynamism, they sought to avoid the connotation of stagnation often surrounding the notion of stability. Nonetheless, they clearly subordinated the attractive prospect of a progressive future without growth to the distinctly more modest aim of avoiding global catastrophe.

The Limits to Growth possessed an ironic, rhetorical power: industrialist ideology was thrown into doubt through the very technocratic imagery that normally sustains it. Supported by such imagery, the "doom-and-gloom" focus on limits captured the popular imagination, but was too threatening to the ideology of industrialism. *The Limits to Growth* thus provoked a vociferous reaction from many academics, journalists, business leaders, and politicians—sometimes in the form of carefully considered criticism and sometimes in the form of an angry response to the study's apparent lack of *faith* in technology and progress.[6]

By directly challenging the confident expectations of industrialism, the environmentalist focus on limits during the late 1960s and early 1970s came eventually to pay the price of declining credibility. Environmentalists began to recognize that, to be taken seriously amid the prevailing industrialism of public discourse, a change was necessary in the focus of their message. The revival of environmentalism in the late 1980s[7] placed the environment on the agenda of public discourse without directly violating the reigning myth.

A "win-win" solution to the environmental crisis was formulated in terms of "sustainable development," particularly as defined under the auspices of the United Nations by the Brundtland Commission: "development that meets the needs of the present without compromising the ability of future generations to meet their own needs." "The concept of sustainable development," according to the Commission, "provides a framework for the integration of environmental policies and development strategies—the term 'development' being used here in its *broadest* sense."[8]

Whatever sustainable development may have meant to the Brundtland Commission and to the many who have since used the term, the significant rhetorical impact arose from a smooth coordination and reconciliation of what, in the previous discourse of limits, had appeared as opposites: sustainability and development. Environmentalism could thus advance with a motto that escaped the stigma of "limits to growth," countering the claim that environmentalism was a doctrine of hopelessness that would deny progress and consign most of humanity, particularly the underdeveloped nations, to impoverished stagnation. Though the Brundtland Commission presented a familiar litany of environmental problems, its tone was strikingly upbeat: "We also found grounds for hope: that people can cooperate to build a future that is more prosperous, more just, and more secure; that a new era of economic growth can be attained, one based on policies that sustain and expand the Earth's resource base; and that the progress that some have known over the last century can be experienced by all in the years ahead" (28).

There is a vagueness to the term "development"; in a broad sense, the term can mean a process of change involving distinct alternatives to the established pattern. The Brundtland Commission in fact seems to play on this vagueness by saying that it intends development in "its broadest sense." However, the text repeatedly suggests that this broadest sense is actually rather narrow, amounting to no more that a fairly conventional notion of "progress" (27–28, 37, 43). What the Commission's concept of sustainable development thus lacks is a vision of alternative historical possibilities, such as the dramatic redefinition of progress advanced by Mill and repeated by contemporary environmentalists, including the authors of *The Limits to Growth*.

The term sustainable development suggests a comfortable reconciliation with the presuppositions of industrialist ideology. Indeed, the discourse on sustainable development includes ambiguities and associations that make for two crucial equations that appear in a more or less explicit manner:

sustainable = sustained

development = growth

In the discourse of sustainable development, there is an explicit appearance of phrases such as "sustained development" and "sustainable economic growth." Not only are these phrases more in keeping with industrialist ideology than "sustainable development," but sustainability is thus implicitly put at ease with what had appeared to be its opposite: sustained economic growth.[9] With such associations, the rhetoric of sustainable development helps to render plausible such notions as the "greening" of business and sets the stage for a significant change in the tone, and even substance, of environmental politics.

Environmental Politics and "Sustainable Development"

Early reports of environmental crisis tended to cast politics of the environment in terms of a stark opposition between environmentalists and industrialists. At the time of Earth Day 1970, there were disagreements among environmentalists about whether to promote the reform of established institutions or to adopt a posture of radical opposition. Yet the possibility of falling prey to co-optation by industrial interests loomed over the debate and was a widely recognized danger. Proponents of environmentalism generally took it for granted that the existing pattern of industrial development was deeply flawed. The very controversy reinforced a cultural dimension of green politics at the time—a festive, unruly, carnival atmosphere at odds with the severe tone of advanced industrial society and its administrative sphere.

As the 1970s advanced, however, there came a period of institutionalization, in which many of the sharply oppositional features of environmentalism were at least partially smoothed over. According to Samuel Hays's description of this change in the American context, green politics tended to be eclipsed by "environmental management"; broad "public debate" gave way to a discourse that was oriented to "centralized direction by technical experts" and guided by "the terminology and conceptual focus of management."[10] The institutionalization of environmental concern meant an entry of environmentalism into the world of administration, but entry into this world also meant adaptation to it: "Environmental management linked private and public agencies in reinforcing and supportive relationships of common perception, purpose, and choice. Such relationships were influenced heavily by tendencies from all sides toward stability and predictability in system management."[11]

In this world, the antagonism between environmentalist and industrialist was attenuated by the emergence of "a middle ground" of environmental professionals who, though environmentally informed and concerned, came increasingly under the influence of a concerted corporate attempt to control the focus of the discourse. Given what they viewed as an inescapable "conflict between economics and environmental objectives," corporate advocates maintained that environmental initiatives should carry a heavy burden of proof—waiting always upon indisputable scientific conclusions and, with cost-benefit analysis instituted as "the central language of public discourse over environmental policy," following technocratic decision-making procedures. In the administrative world of the environmental professional, controversy came to be seen as a problem leading to irrationality and policy stalemate. A contentious environmental politics should give way to reason, to discussions largely limited to calm, deliberate administrative settings.[12]

Despite this call to administrative reason, a sharp political polarization remained between environmentalist and industrialist camps. In response to a growing movement that for a time enjoyed wide popular support, business interests mobilized both to resist environmental regulation and to reclaim public opinion. By 1980, for example, a business-sponsored National Coalition for Growth was in place in the United States to challenge green views advanced in connection with the tenth anniversary of Earth Day (413). Protagonists in both the environmentalist and industrialist camps could readily assume that the interests of the two sides were diametrically opposed. If environmentalists tended to view business—perhaps, indeed, the entire system of corporate capitalism—as the problem, as being necessarily antienvironmentalist, business proponents in turn tended to assume an antienvironmentalist role, viewing environmentalism as a direct threat to business legitimacy.

Caught between opposing environmentalist and industrialist forces, environmental professionalism influenced both, reducing the conflict to some extent. By the twentieth anniversary of Earth Day, indeed, both environmentalist and industrialist figures could voice enthusiasm for business as at least a partial solution to environmental problems. This enthusiasm pictured business—in contrast to the state—as an innovative, flexible, adaptive institution, able to respond quickly to the signals of the market. Business responsiveness included the creation of lines of "green" products to meet consumer concerns. More significantly, this responsiveness involved new technologies and productive processes designed in a context that combined environmentalist influence with intense international competition. The new technologies often proved to be both profitable and environmentally friendly, enhancing efficiency while reducing the through-put of resources and the generation of pollutants.[13]

Despite continuing conflicts, discussion was now possible among environmentalists, environmental professionals, business leaders, and government officials. "Sustainable development" provided a focus for discussion[14]: it was a term that, unlike "limits to growth," seemed consistent with the ideology of industrialism. In praising the Brundtland Commission, one corporate executive clearly indicated the importance of shifting from limits to sustainability. By accenting sustainable development, the Brundtland Commission helped to create "an intellectual climate in which industry could move": "It was a total change from the Club of Rome talking about the world running out of resources. Industry simply didn't believe it because it's simply not true."[15] A Business Council on Sustainable Development, formed in 1990, became involved in a preliminary process that led up to the 1992 United Nations Conference on Environment and Development (UNCED) in Rio de Janiero, which also became known as the Rio Conference or the Earth Summit. After Rio, a World Business Council on Sustainable Development would by 1995 include 130 of the largest corporations in the world.[16] As a book on the "greening" of business indicates, "sustainable development accentuates the positive."[17] Nonetheless, even with this positive accent, the idea of sustainable development can, without much difficulty, be construed in ways that challenge industrialism.

By dramatically bringing the governmental leaders of the world together at a conference under the rubric of sustainable development, the Earth Summit marked the culminating moment of Brundtland's initiative. Rio also provided a venue for a Global Forum of nongovernmental organizations and an Earth Parliament of indigenous peoples. The conference thus created an opportunity for some radical proposals to be pressed onto the agenda of the world's governmental leaders, at least momentarily. In an address on behalf of nongovernmental organizations to the plenary of the Earth Summit, Kenyan activist Wanagari Matthai argued that the creation of "environmentally sound and equitable societies" would require extraordinary changes: from ending poverty and creating fair relations among nations, to enhancing democracy at all levels, local to global.[18] The final agreements of the Earth Summit, of course, avoided any such thing.

Despite the spectacle of the world's leaders gathering together in the name of environmental concern—something unimaginable two decades or so earlier—there were widespread doubts about the sincerity of many of these leaders, especially as the American delegation launched determined initiatives to eliminate or weaken the environmentalist thrust of provisions to final agreements.[19] Greenpeace countered with a little drama of its own on the day following the address of U.S. President George Bush. Eluding security at night, members of the group were ready the next morning to unfurl a giant banner on a prominent mountain cliff: it simply showed an image of the earth marked SOLD.[20]

Was the official conference anything but a mere propaganda exercise for a group of national leaders with industrialist rather than environmentalist priorities? Obviously, the official conference was, for the most part, precisely such an exercise, and many governmental leaders would have preferred simply to get through the ritual and then forget it.[21] However, it is still remarkable that green politics had become significant enough in the realm of public discourse to make the world's leaders go through such an exercise.

The Uncertain Quest

Since the term sustainable development was propelled into public discourse in 1987 by the report of the Brundtland Commission, a plethora of definitions has emerged—by one count just a few years after the Brundtland report, at least forty significant efforts.[22] Early in the 1990s in the United States, the National Academy of Sciences embarked on an effort to develop a definition, but the result was a collection of various concerns rather than a "concise definition." The explicit task of clarifying the meaning of the concept so that it could be used scientifically was undertaken by the United Nations Educational, Scientific and Cultural Organization (UNESCO) in 1996.[23]

In technocratic management terms, such a scientifically usable definition is necessary, but of course not nearly sufficient. The goal of sustainable development requires a precisely specified objective, an operational definition, but also enormously enhanced administrative capacity. Even if agreement could be reached on an operational definition, the scope of the remaining administrative task would surely overwhelm the capacities of any existing or imaginable administrative apparatus. Keeping track of quantifiable flows of energy and materials is a task so vast that it would threaten, as Richard Norgaard has ironically pointed out, to exhaust the capabilities of all available labor. Even this information would be far short of what would be necessary: knowledge of both quantifiable and unquantifiable flows through the systematic integration of the measurements in a comprehensive model.[24] In light of the scope of knowledge needed to pursue sustainable development in a rationalistic manner, a staggering human ignorance is evident.[25]

The quest for sustainability cannot help but be uncertain: events always join an array of variables that is both inexhaustible and ambiguous. Even if one takes for granted many conventional assumptions concerning the conceptualization and categorization of phenomena, there are always more variables than can be identified, much less measured with any precision, or even counted. This inexhaustibility and ambiguity, possibly obscured through precise operationalizations and measurements in narrowly defined contexts, nonetheless become obvious when one tries to imagine the sum of all innovations and their relationships.

The quest for sustainability thus challenges the administrative mind. At the least, it seems, a rationalistic orientation must be displaced by a more adaptive strategy, one less concerned with the problem of definition and tolerant of diverse, even conflicting and contradictory approaches. This is, in effect, what David Brooks suggests as he recommends abandoning the search for a definition: "What is needed now is not more discussion about sustainable development but more experimentation with it. We must try different development strategies, and keep trying until they find the best fit for particular times, particular places and particular peoples. Some policies will get us closer; others will turn out to be inefficient, destructive, or inequitable. But the experiments must continue until each community finds a set that works economically, ecologically and politically."[26] Thus Brooks is consistent when he endorses the recommendations of the Brundtland report, although he finds that it does not fully meet the challenge of sustainability. Even if the approach initiated by Brundtland "is inadequate to get us onto a fully sustainable path," he says, "there is little if anything in its recommendations that would be inappropriate in our search for that path" (407).

Strategy based on the unitary order of the administrative mind here gives way to an adaptive strategy, to the incrementalism depicted in Charles Lindblom's famous phrase "the science of 'muddling through.'" Although such incrementalism has mistakenly been viewed as being necessarily inconsistent with major socioeconomic change, it still is an approach that tends to be at ease with established institutions and with the comfortable assumption that "mutual adjustments" in a pluralistic political process give rise to a larger "intelligence" promoting order and progress.[27] Though departing from the administrative mind, this orientation still remains in its shadow.

In *Compass and Gyroscope*, Kai Lee has made a sophisticated case for an incremental approach that takes a bolder step away from this shadow. The quest for sustainability, in Lee's view, involves "social learning," conceived as a "combination of adaptive management and political change."[38] He stresses the many troubles of the quest "in a world of complexity and uncertainty" (199) and rejects efforts to reduce sustainable development to a precise definition or formula, conceiving it instead as an orienting vision: "Sustainable development is not a policy objective so much as it is a vision of appropriate human endeavor on the planet we inhabit" (198). His approach is thus a kind of "planning without goals": proceeding without a comprehensive strategy while promoting a general direction through trial and error and a piecemeal search for opportunities.[29] There is also no clear need for "central control," in Lee's view: "What no one knows," he says, "is whether central governance is possible, or necessary, or sufficient."[30]

At odds with the administrative mind, Lee's social learning approach to sustainability offers no guarantees, no comprehensive plan to relieve uncertainty, but a general orientation to policy along with the effort to specify necessary, but not necessarily sufficient, steps. What he thus offers is an incrementally adaptive environmentalist strategy that largely escapes the shadow of the administrative mind. Nonetheless, Lee's approach does presuppose significant accommodation with established institutions in a manner that separates his orientation from radical forms of environmentalism. He assumes a vision of sustainable development that does not venture into such radical territory; his reformist orientation thus does not challenge, indeed implicitly reaffirms, the framework of the prevailing institutional world.

Sustainable Development in Context

Any sustainable development vision is obviously open to dispute. Indeed, uncertainty, combined with differing interests and perspectives, ensures that the quest for sustainability cannot comfortably be contained by the terms of technical discourse but is pressed into a political context where the meaning of key terms is vigorously contested. Much room is thus left for debate. Still, the prevailing focus on sustainable development reflects the kind of background consensus often needed to mobilize support for limited policy initiatives.

Sustainable development operates much like other objectives in public discourse: it has meanings that are "multiple," "conflicting," and "vague." The meanings are multiple and conflicting because political actors want many, different things. The meanings are vague because the vagueness allows for a coalescence of potentially opposed actors to work together for an apparently common end. They can do this without generating the antagonisms that would be sure to arise from an effort to establish a comprehensive strategy for a precisely defined objective.[31]

In the world of environmental politics, the ambiguity of sustainable development often seems attractive because it fosters enhanced cooperation among one-time opponents, the proverbial strange bedfellows of political life. In contrast to the acrimony of earlier environmental politics, environmentalists and industrialists gain at least the appearance of a common ground. The vagueness of "sustainable development," a weakness in terms of technical discourse, has the political virtue of allowing political actors "to proceed without having to agree also on exactly what to do."[32] Of course, this political virtue is more attractive to environmentalists focused on the prospect of reform than to environmentalists advocating radical social transformation. But the focus on sustainable development allows at least some green perspectives to enter established circles of policy debate.

Despite efforts to reduce the notion of sustainable development to technical terms, the discourse of sustainability contains ambiguities and uncertainties that, in a public context of differing interests and perspectives, makes the discourse politically unpredictable. Both the conceptual and practical meaning of sustainable development depend on context, and apparently limited incremental reforms may have consequences that set in motion or converge with larger changes.[33]

When the meaning of the term is debated at a conceptual level, potential practical consequences for different interests loom in the background. It is one thing to ask in the abstract what sustainable development means. It is quite another to ask who is to define the meaning of the term in a concrete policy dispute. This is the question that really points to the ambivalence of the term and its potential impact.

The twists and turns in the case of Clayoquot Sound offer an illuminating illustration. Here an old growth temperate rainforest under threat of clear-cut logging became something of an international cause célèbre, described by Environmental Defense Fund representative Robert Kennedy Jr. as "the flashpoint in one of the defining environmental battles of our time."[34] Located on the west coast of Vancouver Island in Canada, Clayoquot Sound became a place of remarkable contention over the meaning of sustainable development.

As logging companies decided in the 1980s to exercise their rights to "tree license farms" in areas of Clayoquot Sound, an alliance of environmentalists, town residents, and aboriginal groups responded with public protest and civil disobedience, including actions to block existing logging roads and the construction of new ones. The various elements of the alliance had differences over goals and tactics, but they were united in opposition to the pace and method of timber extraction the logging industry was pursuing with support from the provincial government.[35]

When the notion of sustainable development came to prominence in Canada and throughout the world, a coalition of environmentalists and area residents calling itself the Friends of Clayoquot Sound (FOCS) saw promise in the idea. In the context of a campaign attempting to halt the construction of a new logging road, FOCS proposed a moratorium of six months that would allow "time for the preparation of a sustainable development plan for the region." "The Friends," according to one observer, "saw the issue as not whether the area should have logging but where and how logging should take place." The logging industry objected to the FOCS proposal as "mere subterfuge," and the idea was rejected by the provincial government of British Columbia.[36]

Even if the industry was right in viewing FOCS's proposed moratorium for planning as insincere, the group's call for sustainable development is significant in suggesting a radical potential in the idea, at least at the level of practical maneuver. The notion of sustainable development framed much of the ensuing debate. The initiative on this front initially remained with the forces opposing the plans of the logging industry. Particularly for residents of the small Clayoquot town of Tofino, the idea seemed to have potential, and a community steering committee was organized to formulate a strategy for sustainable development.

The process involved public meetings and drew on the involvement of area residents, but the steering committee rejected a proposal from the logging industry that the committee be expanded to include industry representatives. Instead, the steering committee presented a proposal to the provincial government in 1989 for "community based sustainable development." Advocating an approach "in which economic and environmental planning and management would be fully integrated," the steering committee put itself in opposition to the single-use approach of the timber industry.[37] The key to sustainable development under the plan was compatible multiple use: "Land that should be managed for timber, tourism, fisheries, and several other uses, is effectively being managed only for timber production. Although, with proper planning and management, timber production, tourism and fish habitat maintenance are potentially compatible, recent logging rates and practices in Clayoquot Sound are incompatible with tourism and are likely to cause its demise. Indeed, they raise questions about the sustainability of forestry in the region."[38]

The logging industry quickly responded, entering the discourse on sustainability with its own proposal for "a sustainable integrated forest management plan," but the Tofino steering committee rejected it as simply another single-use approach, focused on logging at an uninterrupted pace. The provincial government then intervened with an effort, which eventually failed, to reach "consensus" on a sustainable development plan for the area.[39]

Throughout all the talk of sustainable development, there was no government moratorium or slowdown, and logging went on as before. When the government made it clear that logging would continue during the work of the Clayoquot Sound Sustainable Development Strategy Steering Committee, the environmentalist representative resigned in protest, claiming that the government lacked a serious commitment to sustainable development. Denouncing what they portrayed as a strategy by government and industry to "talk and log," environmentalists renewed their stance of public protest and civil disobedience. The FOCS, as one member recounts, had sought "to lobby for greater public control over the fate of our ancient forests, but everything we said was co-opted by either government or industry. All of a sudden industry was calling itself environmentalist and government was giving lip service to sustainable development."[40]

Although the final committee report indicated a failure to reach consensus among the remaining parties, the provincial government issued a definitive decision. The government action enraged environmentalists, sparking major protests and acts of civil disobedience that drew international attention and culminated in the summer of 1993 with the largest mass arrest in Canadian history. A few months later, the government backed away from its decision and established a Scientific Panel for Sustainable Forest Practices in Clayoquot Sound as "an impartial panel of recognized experts" capable of "providing a sustainable future for Clayoquot, and ensuring that forestry activities in the Sound stand up to world scrutiny."[41]

Through its various twists and turns, the Clayoquot controversy illustrates how contention over what sustainable development means also involves disputes over who is to give meaning to the term. A wide range of actors sought to give meaning to sustainable development. By taking the initiative, the community-based alliance injected a key idea into the public discourse: an accent on sustainability was tied to a redefinition of development. Especially thrown into question was the notion that a single use of the forest—timber extraction through clear-cutting—was sustainable.

Development in that peculiarly industrialist sense was rejected in favor of development defined in terms of multiple use. What sustainable development came to imply was a change in power relations, in which influence over the character and path of development would shift from the industry-government alliance to an alliance at the grassroots. It is not surprising that the ensuing discourse over sustainability, framed increasingly by government, did not satisfy this alliance or the environmentalists within it. That those opposed to the established path of industrialist development could have any appreciable effect on the pattern of events was certainly due less to the force of their argument than to a willingness to take dramatic public action. However, this action was not simply something apart from the discourse but also constituted a discursive intervention: it had a meaning, and the meaning was that the laudable goal of sustainable development in Clayoquot Sound had been perverted at the hands of industry and government.[42]

It is striking, though not surprising, that the provincial government reverted to an apparent technocratic ritual. Yet it is also striking that public opposition to industrialist initiatives can obviously no longer be quelled by such a move. Environmentalists were highly suspicious of the scientific panel and the way its work might be used by the government.[43] What informs this suspicion is the view that, if sustainability is to be taken seriously, sustainable development cannot be made compatible with the established path of industrialism in the forest. Despite all rhetorical ploys, all the efforts to cast the connection between sustainability and development in terms compatible with industrialist interests, the notion of sustainable development retains a critical edge in this context and harbors radical potential.

It is also possible that things will not play out as expected. The mandate and orientation of the scientific panel actually held some surprises. Set up in the name of sustainability, the panel came to reflect an increased recognition of the proprietary interest in the land that aboriginal people had staked through successful court actions. Most strikingly, the scientific panel did not adhere to a scientistic notion of knowledge, but explicitly sought to combine scientific knowledge with the "traditional knowledge" of the aboriginal people. As it turned out, the panel endorsed aboriginal perspectives and the potential for multiple use of the forest, against the single-use championed by the logging industry.[44]

Conclusion

In contrast to the disturbing specter of the limits to growth, the advent of sustainable development has heralded the ascent of a reform strategy involving deliberate accommodation with established institutions. This can be a cause for concern among many radical environmentalists, who remain suspicious both of the notion of sustainable development and of any move toward compromise. The concern is that sustainable development may end up as little more than a dishonest platitude inhibiting "the profound transformation of our industrial society that is so urgently required."[45]

Is the apparently happy conjunction of sustainability and development not simply a slick way of dodging the really significant challenges that the goal of ecological rationality presents to industrialism? Is the idea of sustainable development not just an implicit reaffirmation of faith in industrialism, particularly the confident expectation that development, in any conventional meaning of the term, can actually be sustained? Much depends on whether one accents development or sustainability. An accent on development retains an attachment to conventional conceptions of progress while deflecting attention from the challenge of ecological rationality. But an accent on sustainability suggests that the concept of development must be adjusted accordingly. Placing the accent on sustainability makes sustainable development a green challenge to industrialism.

The opposition between environmentalism and industrialism, though diminished, has by no means vanished. When the idea of sustainable development is pressed forward in a manner that reveals troubling implications for particular interests and industrialism generally—as was done by some in the context of the Earth Summit—powerful resistance quickly arises. Concerted opposition to environmentalism also remains salient in powerful right-wing circles. The radical environmentalist rejection of industrial interests comes at times to be mirrored, in antienvironmentalist circles, by an equally sharp condemnation of business "appeasement" of environmentalism: "sustainable development" is denounced as a term that serves "to mask an anti-industrial agenda"[46] because the idea is "so vague that it can be stretched to suit anyone's purpose to restrain capitalist development."[47]

The industrialist faith in progress offered a mode of closure to the world of public discourse: a form of "uncertainty absorption"[48] that inhibited the serious consideration of alternatives to the conventional path of development. By advancing a discourse of sustainability, environmentalism has provoked uncertainties. Although the dominant accent of sustainability discourse appears to fit comfortably with a technical administrative focus, with a cautious reformism, and with the steady advance of industrialization, this discourse has the potential to disrupt the prevailing contours of public debate.

Central to the concern with sustainability, after all, are doubts about the very possibility of maintaining the conventional path of progress. Even if the critical edge of green radicalism can be dulled in this discursive context, there still remains room to question the meaning of sustainable development. The term cannot be contained within the conventional technocratic framework of policy debate but emerges as a disputed symbol. Seemingly at ease with reformist discourse, the term also opens a space for a critique of industrialism.

Attempts to assimilate the discourse of sustainability to prior expectations, to rehabilitate conventional notions of progress under the heading of sustainable development, are undercut from the outset because the discourse itself has arisen from doubts about the possibility of fulfilling those very expectations. Such doubts also provoke questions of desirability, for uncertainty about the direction of development suggests an element of choice. Not only do environmental issues become increasingly salient, but there is room to reconsider the purpose and direction of development,[49] along with the entire human/nature relationship. No longer ruled out of consideration by a supposed imperative of progress,[50] this range of environmental issues not only animates the green public sphere but also enters the larger agenda of public discourse.

A T FIRST GLANCE, policy professionalism and dissenting social movements appear to be two irreconcilably opposed worlds. Usually situated within the administrative sphere, policy professionalism finds itself confronted by voices of dissent opposed to established power.[1] Yet neither of these two worlds exists outside the influence of the other. Theory and practice in the professional policy world itself now actually contain antitechnocratic and antiscientistic tendencies. There have been serious calls for expanded participation in policy deliberations as part of a larger project of enhancing democracy.[2]

Green politics plays its particular dissenting role by throwing into question the faith in progress that sustains the advanced industrial order. At the same time, green politics has clearly made a mark on the world of policy professionalism, affecting both the terms of public discourse and particular features of the policy process. Green influence on policy professionalism and the administrative sphere is evident in three related, though distinguishable, ways: through agenda setting, problem definition, and epistemology.[3]

In terms of agenda setting, environmentalism brought to attention general concerns, specific issues, and particular elements of evidence that had been ignored or neglected by policy professionalism and industrialism generally. Defining environmental problems, moreover, is a matter of contention that exhibits a dynamic of power and insight.[4] Industrialist and managerialist assumptions tend to shape conventional formulations, focusing attention on discrete problems viewed in terms of strictly delimited contexts. Environmentalism, in contrast, offers insights into inconvenient connections, suggesting the redefinition of problems in terms of a richer context. Green discourse has thus introduced distinctive ways of framing and defining policy problems. The environmental movement has also provoked epistemological controversy, questioning established conventions and suggesting new, or at least revised, standards as to what can legitimately count as knowledge or evidence relevant to the policy process—mounting a challenge, in short, to the administrative mind.

There is no single voice of green dissent, of course, but multiple voices—differences of opinion and differences as well of perspective, interest, and identity. Viewed historically, nonetheless, the emergence of green dissent lends itself to a fairly straightforward account. As early as 1962, Rachel Carson's *Silent Spring* foreshadowed the rise of the environmental movement and set something of a pattern, mixing the voices of science, populism, and poetry in a manner that challenged the tight-lipped professionalism of the administrative sphere.[5] With deep roots in the early conservation movement, environmentalism clearly emerged in the late 1960s and early 1970s speaking with different voices, conspicuously those of both naturalist and resource manager. There was also a significantly new tone, for environmentalism expressed an identity shaped in the context of an emerging array of dissenting social movements. The voices of green dissent soon came to include voices from feminism and the peace movement. Grassroots green dissent especially arose during the 1980s, with the issue of toxic wastes in the United States. Around the same period, the voice of environmental justice emerged to speak of the inequitable distribution of environmental risk: how this inequity amounts to a form of racism, how it threatens workers in the workplace and the poor in their homes, and how internationally it is but an extension of colonialist practice.[6]

Green dissent has thus been expressed through different voices over the course of the decades since the 1960s, new voices rising as old ones fade. But the story line can, of course, hardly be so simple. The differing voices of green dissent are not altogether distinct. They converge as well as diverge, and they tend to shape one another both through their similarities and contrasts. It can also be argued that an apparent latecomer like environmental justice has actually been around a long time, particularly in early concerns about the urban environment in America.[7]

With the emergence of these various voices, it is in any case obvious that they combine in the dynamic of a nascent green public sphere that has as much diversity as unity and is by no means fixed in its contours. The differences give rise to internal tensions and controversies, but they also mean that the green public sphere has no homogeneous influence on policy professionalism or the administrative sphere generally.

Professionalism and Dissent

Convinced that the direction of advanced industrial society was significantly flawed, environmentalists in the early 1970s debated the options of radical action or reform, but generally shared a concern that their efforts could be co-opted by the prevailing institutions of government and industry. Many sharply oppositional features of environmentalism were, indeed, smoothed over as the 1970s advanced.

Government confidently portrayed new rules and agencies as the solution to the environmental crisis, industry vigorously defended itself against disturbing demands, and the largely quiescent domain of environmental professionalism grew significantly. Yet, the core of the institutional response to environmentalism was, as the previous chapter suggested, a call to reason. Contentious environmental politics was a source of irrationality and policy stalemate, in the professional view, and should give way to direction by experts able to speak a rational policy language.[8]

Professional policy discourse provides an adjunct to the established order, facing its problems and speaking its language. The professional orientation thus tends to constrain those elements of environmentalism that would draw attention to new problems and would speak a new language. The professional world of environmental policy has expanded and become institutionalized, though, in a manner that both reflects and resists the influence of environmentalist dissent. Green dissent has not simply been constrained by policy professionalism but has worked its own influence on the world of the policy professional.

Environment Becomes an Issue

Although the modern state has consistently adopted policies to advance the cause of industrialization, relatively little attention was given to the environmental consequences of these policies until the emerging environmental movement dramatically entered the public spotlight in the late 1960s.[9] The environment was then high on the public policy agenda, but there remained the question of how long this prominence would last.[10]

From a green perspective, the environment constituted an enormous blindspot for industrialization. Putting the environment securely on the policy agenda meant somehow institutionalizing a focus on the environment. Changes in the state administrative apparatus helped to serve this purpose by placing the "environmental" symbol prominently in the titles and mandates of agencies that were either entirely new or created by a realignment of previously existing administrative units. Another chief means to the end of keeping a focus on the environment was environmental impact assessment, the most visible influence of environmentalism on procedures in public policy.

Though environmental impact assessment—and related innovations such as technology assessment and social impact assessment—have often been aptly criticized for a propensity to become little more than technocratic rituals, these practices are not always easily contained. They bring attention in a routine way to matters that before would have remained invisible, and this altered focus has the potential to influence the flow of policy considerations while promoting entry into the process of interests and perspectives that would previously have been excluded.[11] Environmental impact assessment has thus been described as a "worm in the brain," as possessing the "subversive" potential of "making bureaucracies think."[12]

Once the environment became an issue, there remained the question of which particular problems ought to be addressed. By the time of the first Earth Day, concern was primarily focused on air and water pollution issues. The next two decades, though, were to witness a burgeoning of the range of environmental issues, often related to new industrial processes and consumer products emerging in the postwar era:[13] issues such as toxic waste, acid rain, and ozone depletion.

Early environmentalist moves, both in terms of popular agitation and public policy, remained marked by an industrialist tendency toward linear thinking and narrowly conceived solutions, dealing with one pollution problem at a time. Attention was focused on the "end of the pipe," on installing filters on existing equipment or finding ways of diluting pollution. Little focus yet was directed to the redesign of techniques and activities in light of wider patterns and cycles of ecosystemic relationships. Greater attention turned in this direction as new environmental issues began to crowd onto the policy agenda.

The early response to environmental problems, according to Albert Weale, had as its "underlying logic" the identification of "a distinct area of public policy requiring its own specialist expertise and its own institutions for the conduct of policy discussion." In Weale's analysis, a "new politics of pollution" emerged to displace the old orientation with a discourse of *ecological modernization*.[14]

The new politics, according to Weale, especially challenges the widely held initial assumption that the goals of environmental protection and economic development are fundamentally incompatible. In advancing the idea of sustainable development, the Brundtland Commission provided impetus to the view that protecting environmental quality was a necessary condition for long-term economic development.[15] The notion of ecological modernization now draws attention to the potential for an environmentally sensitive technology to be developed in response to consumer and governmental demands. More broadly, the new politics of pollution promotes an integrated response to environmental problems.

Proposals for an integrated approach focus on "the holistic nature of the environment" in prescribing "rational environmental management."[16] An integrated approach thus appeals to a comprehensive rationality at odds with incrementalism and seems to anticipate a reign of technical experts housed in an overarching administrative apparatus. The idea of ecological modernization particularly suggests that, for all its technological sophistication, industrialism so far has not been technologically sophisticated enough.

Ecological irrationalities can thus be taken as pointing to the need for enhanced rationality and expertise, with ecological rationality being promised by such innovations as "industrial ecology," the idea of redesigning the industrial system on a "straight-forward analogy with natural ecological systems" so that waste is integrated "fully into the web of industrial relationships."[17] Obviously, a significant enhancement of technical expertise would be necessary to reorient the industrial system along such lines. However, the very nature and scope of the project also raises big questions about how to develop, organize, and apply the relevant expertise.

The new politics of the environment remains ambivalent in regard to the question of expertise. As the scope and complexity of environmental concerns increase, they go well beyond the competence of narrow specialists, and there is no obvious organizational design to use in integrating the necessary specialties for rational environmental management. Even if the right kind of organization were obvious, there would be no ready recipe for gaining the power to carry out the changes.

The expansion of environmental concerns beyond narrowly conceived issues such as air and water pollution has not happened simply because of the contributions of expert knowledge, but because a diverse green movement has helped to press these concerns onto the public agenda. There has been a move beyond specialists to a wider and more diverse policy community. Green activists have been able to use openings in the political processes of liberal democracies and have often demonstrated a technical competence that rivals or excels that of the established experts.[18] With a new politics addressing new issues, an appeal to rational environmental management can no longer simply rely on the technocratic model but suggests a politics of expertise in open arenas of public discourse.[19]

Defining the Toxic Waste Problem

Toxic waste was the first of the new environmental issues to enter the public agenda.[20] The matter had largely remained a nonissue throughout the early rise of the environmental movement and the institutionalization of an environmental focus in public policy: "Early air- and water-pollution laws were debated and enacted without awareness or consideration of what to do with the waste materials once we stopped dumping them in the air and water."[21] Nonetheless, hardly more than a decade after the first Earth Day, then-Senator Al Gore could call the toxic waste problem "the centerpiece of the environmental movement."[22]

The disposal of toxic wastes did not become a major concern until after 1978 when, especially with the citizen activism and publicity surrounding the case of Love Canal, past practices of toxic waste storage and disposal were sharply questioned. The toxic waste problem dramatically entered the public agenda, as a grassroots antitoxics movement emerged as a new voice of green dissent and public officials began to respond.[23] There remained a question, however, of how the toxic waste problem was to be defined. Focusing attention on toxic wastes was, by itself, a significant reframing of environmental problems. Still, the characteristic policy response largely amounted to an extension of past practice. The problem remained defined primarily in terms of disposal.

As toxic wastes came onto the public policy agenda, it became apparent that past disposal practices had generated a massive problem, a lapse in control that ran against rationalistic expectations of the industrial world. Reestablishing a smooth pattern of industrial development meant a massive, expensive project of finding and cleaning up past mistakes[24] while making sure that future disposal practices would be methodically planned and controlled. The difference between past and future, however, was to be simple: disposal would receive much more careful attention and would be handled with more effective techniques.

With this form of problem definition, a major difficulty has emerged to confront policy professionals, who typically encounter great resistance when attempting to site improved hazardous waste treatment and disposal facilities. The situation has spawned a vast policy literature on the NIMBY (not-in-my-backyard) syndrome and related administrative frustrations: "From a managerial perspective . . . protestors are simply incapable of appreciating the information they are being given . . . The typical remedy . . . is the injection of greater expertise into the policy process."[25]

Opponents to the siting of new facilities can, however, lay claim to a rationality of their own. Because the past record of toxic waste management shows a glaring ineffectiveness, residents can offer good reasons for doubting the competence and commitment of policy professionals who propose a disposal site in their area. The difficulty for these professionals is exacerbated by the fact that they can no longer simply rely on unchallengeable claims that they know best, for they have no monopoly on the relevant knowledge. The members of effectively organized and sophisticated environmental groups now have the capacity to uncover errors and weaknesses in site plans. Indeed, they "have frequently shown that the industry has simply not done its technical homework."[26] Moreover, environmentalists can readily point to a preoccupation with disposal as evidence of an industrialist blind spot that helped to turn toxic waste into a major problem in the first place.

How might the problem of toxic waste—and its costs and dangers—have been avoided? Asking this question not only throws into doubt the past rationality of the administrative organizations that presided over the process of industrialization, but suggests a new problem orientation: how to restructure the industrial system to minimize the generation of toxic waste.[27]

The supposedly emotional NIMBY syndrome may actually help in promoting a more ecologically rational response to the toxic waste problem than professionalism could achieve if left to its own devices. Noting that the idea, if not the practice, of toxic waste reduction has now begun to overcome resistance and gain consideration in powerful circles of industry and government, Andrew Szasz indicates the importance of citizen action: "The hazardous waste movement did not invent the idea of source reduction; it was, however, the historical agent that created the conditions that finally forced the idea to the center of environmental policy."[28]

Defining Environmental Problems

Early efforts to treat environmental problems one at a time gave rise to difficulties of problem displacement,[29] perhaps most notoriously evident when taller smokestacks to dilute air pollution contributed to distant problems of acid rain. Problems can be displaced through space or time or, as an Environmental Protection Agency (EPA) administrator observed in 1985, across media: "somewhere in the country, toxic metals are being removed from the air, transferred to the waste water stream, removed again via water pollution controls, converted to sludge, shipped to an incinerator and returned to the air."[30] Problem displacement bears witness to the complex interdependencies of environmental problems, but the flip side is that these very interdependencies carry a promise of ecological rationality. The trick is for problems to be defined so that actions to resolve one problem help to resolve, rather than to exacerbate, other problems.

The case of toxic wastes shows concretely how environmentalism contains a propensity not only to recognize but to define problems in ways that depart from policy professionalism. A focus on the interdependencies of natural cycles and systems leads beyond neatly circumscribed contexts toward complexities that both demand comprehensive rationality and elude analysis and management modeled on the image of the administrative mind. The redefinition of environmental problems also often suggests potential solutions that appear elegant in terms of design yet probably are disruptive of existing social and institutional arrangements.

The problem of waste disposal, toxic or not, can be redefined in terms of waste reduction and recycling. Controlling pesticide pollution becomes a problem of changing agriculture to require fewer pesticides while putting to use organic nutrients that would otherwise end up in the waste stream. Health care is to shift its focus from cure to prevention, promoting reduced pollution in the workplace and the wider environment while encouraging healthful dietary patterns—which, in turn, also happen to reinforce changing agricultural practices. Air pollution control devices on vehicles are seen as being no more than part of the solution to a problem that also requires vehicle redesign to lower fuel consumption, maybe new fuels, and even a restructuring of the entire transportation system that would reconsider work and settlement patterns to reduce transportation needs. The energy problem is redefined as meeting energy needs primarily through greater reliance on conservation and efficiency measures that complement and reinforce efforts concerning waste, health, pollution, and so on.

A dramatic instance of environmental problem redefinition was advanced by Amory Lovins in response to energy concerns during the mid-1970s.[31] Imagine the energy problem as one of trying to fill a fuel can, he suggested. For some reason, you never seem able to fill it up, no matter how much you increase the flow into the can; then you realize that there are holes in the can. Lovins's basic solution to the energy problem—filling the holes—depended on redefining the problem as not being one of insufficient supply. Against the "hard path" of increasing energy supply to keep up with rapidly escalating demand, Lovins formulated his well-known "soft path": to control demand by enhancing efficiency and matching energy supply to end uses. He pressed his point home by indicating that large amounts of energy are required to produce energy and that other environmental problems are closely tied to expanding energy consumption. Lovins's intervention unsettled the dominant view that took increased energy use for granted as a measure of progress. In fact, Lovins maintained that the soft path ran so much against the prevailing cultural, institutional, and political orientation of industrial society that its full adoption would require major changes in the established order.

As an example of environmental problem redefinition, Lovins's promotion of a soft energy path reveals what the perspective of the administrative mind often obscures. Conventional problem definition follows well-worn patterns and pathways, clichéd habits of thought sanctioned by scientism and industrialism. By posing the energy problem in terms of two divergent pathways, Lovins has helped draw attention to a dynamic of power and insight.

Problem definition is by no means merely a task of analysis but is, more broadly, a political process that involves different interests, perspectives, and identities. Power is not merely evident in the outcome of open contention among clearly posed alternatives, but enters into the formulation of the alternatives themselves.[32] Lovins's promotion of a soft energy path is thus both an intellectual and political achievement, a matter of insight *and* power. The idea of a soft energy path challenged an institutional and ideological context—an established framework of interests, perspectives, and identities—that discouraged the very formulation and expression of the idea.

Environmental problem redefinition generally involves a reversal of key relationships in the initial formulation of a problem, a kind of reversal typical of creative problem solving. Defining the energy problem in terms of decreasing demand rather than increasing supply—and invoking Robert Frost's "The Road Not Taken"[33]—Lovins's promotion of a soft energy path offers a prototype of problem redefinition that has been (implicitly and explicitly) followed in other environmentally significant policy areas. In health policy, for example, a focus on prevention, including protection from environmental contaminants, can displace a focus centered on costly, high-tech cures. Similarly, in the field of transportation, Christopher J. Bosso has cited a paradigmatic evolution among policy intellectuals to argue that "traffic congestion . . . is perhaps the best example of how evolving human practices may slowly be leading to the kinds of cultural change that will alter significantly the social construction of a public problem."[34] An industrialist approach concerned with increasing the supply of roads contrasts sharply with a green focus on transportation system changes to keep the demand for roads in check.

The metaphorical contrast between hard and soft orientations suggests a key difference between industrialist and environmental forms of problem definition. This contrast was present as early as when Rachel Carson, denouncing the "current vogue for poisons," also invoked Frost's "other road" to call for a "biological" rather than a "chemical" approach to insect control. She wanted techniques designed with an "understanding of the living organisms they seek to control, and of the whole fabric of life to which these organisms belong."[35] Environmental problem redefinition involves "softness" in the particular sense of a flexibility and openness that contrasts with the hardness, the rigor mortis, of analytic conventions sanctioned by the administrative mind.

The discourse of ecological modernization is inclined to portray environmental difficulties as problems of design that can ultimately be overcome with ecologically sophisticated technology. In this respect, as Maarten Hajer has argued, ecological modernization fits a "techno-administrative" mold.[36] Yet the whole notion of ecological modernization, including related ideas like industrial ecology, has emerged as a departure from industrialism. By expanding the understanding of environmental problems and drawing attention to a broader context of ecosystemic and socioeconomic relationships, ecological modernization can be viewed as a "soft path" writ large. Can such a path be followed simply as a large-scale technological fix? Saying yes would mean that, once environmental problems had been appropriately redefined, there would be no more need to listen to the voices of green dissent.

Against such ecomodernist naïveté, Hajer advances a "reflexive model": "ecological modernization . . . ceases to be a primarily techno-administrative affair in which . . . solutions are selected that respect the implicit social order of expert discourse." Instead, "ecological modernization fosters a public domain" as a locus of social choice. This difference initiates a form of discursive practice that breaks with the techo-administrative drive "to find one universal language to facilitate the search for the most effective and most efficient solutions to unequivocal problems." Rather than creating "new expert organizations" insulated from the public domain, reflexive ecological modernization promotes "new institutional arrangements in which different discourses (and concerns) can be . . . related to one another." In effect, the approach seeks ways of correcting the bias of the administrative mind and breaking the scientistic "monopoly on knowledge claims": "Reflexive ecological modernization emphasizes the importance of the mobilization of independent opinions versus the respected power of authorities."[37]

The key problem in conventional ecomodernist discourse, Hajer maintains, is a "lack of debate on what an ecological modernization should mean."[38] Is it to be a new departure in the human/nature relationship, or just a new way of maintaining what Herman E. Daly has called "growthmania"? In the early 1970s, Daly followed John Stuart Mill's nineteenth-century idea of a desirable stationary-state to anticipate much of ecological modernization. Daly defined the key problem of a "steady-state economy" not in terms of limiting productive output, but in terms of limiting energy and material throughput. In promoting a steady state economy, however, he did not believe that design changes could adequately limit the throughput of physical resources. He instead called for broader social, economic, and political changes, for "citizens to find the moral resources necessary to overcome the vested interests and . . . compulsions of growthmania."[39]

The key, in Mill's earlier perspective, was changing the distribution of wealth and decreasing inequality. However threatening to entrenched and privileged interests, this idea raises the prospect of ecological modernization that, while transforming the shape of the industrial system, is not tied to growth and has the capacity to reduce human toil and strife, the "struggling to get on" that Mill viewed as a regrettable, temporary phase of industrial progress.[40] Ecomodernist discourse is reluctant to take this step, indeed seems virtually designed to avoid reckoning with the implications of limiting growth. Certainly, Brundtland's promotion of sustainable development, for all its talk of improving the lot of impoverished countries, resists any such reckoning and draws much of its rhetorical impact, as we saw in the previous chapter, from what the phrase often seems to suggest: the prospect of sustaining economic growth.

Key interests and identities are bound up with economic expansion, and a challenge to growth seems to carry the risk of increasing social insecurity. "The continued dependency of social security upon economic growth," Claus Offe has further argued, "conditions the immediate interests of employees in ways which will favour growth even at the expense of environmentally and ecologically sound policies."[41] Despite efforts to ally labor and environmentalism—for example, on the issue of health and safety in the workplace[42]—this difference carries with it the propensity for division, at times outright hostility.

Much of the industrialist reaction against environmentalism repeatedly raises alarms about the threat that environmental measures pose to jobs. There have been efforts to defend environmentalism by demonstrating that environmental measures increase employment through the creation of environmental protection industries and the promotion of labor intensity in production.[43] The industrialist position is surely disingenuous, though, because what primarily threatens job security is a dynamic that arises from economic competition: the persistent drive to lower production costs by substituting increasingly sophisticated—indeed, "intelligent"—machinery for human labor power. Scoring this point against industrialism is of questionable help to environmentalism, however, for it suggests that the environmentalist claim to promote employment is tied to the maintenance of increasingly inefficient production methods. The need thus appears for a more thoroughgoing redefinition of the problem of jobs and environment, one that would loosen the tight connection between employment and economic security.

A key question of social policy here can be recast as an environmental problem. Over the past several decades, there have been numerous proposals that would see a radical reform of the welfare state through the institution of a guaranteed basic income, and this idea has become so prominent in environmental circles that it has been called "the flagship" of green economic policy.[44] Already in the early 1970s, indeed, Warren A. Johnson explicitly proposed such a guaranteed income "as an environmental measure." By contributing to a desperate, yet senseless, spiral of overproduction and consumption, he argued, work is becoming less socially useful and has indeed begun to threaten the future: "We work too much."[45] The guaranteed income as an environmental measure aims "to remove the necessity of maintaining continuous economic growth," to "discourage economic growth while still providing a flexible device" for maintaining economic stability.[46]

In green realist terms, as proposed by Helmut Wiesenthal and others, the guaranteed basic income, or social minimum, appears as a key step in reforming the industrial world so that people on a wide scale are offered concrete opportunities—and not just presented with moralistic demands—to adopt more environmentally friendly living patterns. Significantly, the move is designed to accomplish this change in private life choices not by increasing social insecurity, but instead by taking the opposite path: decreasing the basis of economic insecurity and desperation in a way that promises at least to slow down the rat race of the workaday world. If it diminished anxious attachments to particular jobs, such a trend would also enhance social flexibility and, by reducing a key source of resistance, would tend to provide an expanded ground of public support for green change.[47] The case for a guaranteed basic income is more typically made in terms of social justice than in terms of ecological rationality,[48] but it is notable that ecological concern here intersects with the agenda of social justice. With the idea of basic income as an environmental measure, what seems primarily a matter of socioeconomic policy is turned around and recast in terms of environmental policy. This twist puts the idea in a different context and gives it new significance.

Environmental problem definition is of course not a monological or univocal affair. The voices of green dissent are multiple and dynamic, often differing among themselves, but not always or in all respects. As we have seen, for example, green economic alternatives involve questions of social justice, and these intersect with concerns of the environmental justice movement. Although differing green voices carry the potential to divide, they also have much in common. They have the potential for an interplay of opinions, a green discourse generating insights that challenge the administrative mind.

Challenging the Administrative Mind

Inspired by images of the administrative mind, policy professionalism takes its cue from scientism, the celebration of science as the only source of legitimate knowledge. Challenges to scientism often begin by pointing to a striking paradox: *Faith* in science is not itself a form of scientific knowledge.[49] Modern culture, convinced that problems have solutions,[50] has granted the scientific enterprise an authority and prestige that it could not claim for itself without violating its own epistemological premises.

The impressive technological achievements supporting this faith have typically depended on a narrow focus, attention to a strictly delimited set of variables. Success has thus come from systematic inattention to the complexities and ambiguities of a broader context. The administrative organizations of advanced industrial society, moreover, have exhibited a "bounded rationality" secure in the belief that the world is "mostly empty"—that contextual interdependencies and uncertainties are largely irrelevant to administrative decisions.[51] Problems can thus be rationally isolated, addressed, and solved through highly selective attention by administrative organizations, aided by scientific experts.

By directing attention to neglected contexts, environmentalism poses a challenge to a long cultural tradition. From an environmentalist perspective, technological development based on narrowly focused analysis exhibits an enormous blind spot: technology worked to the extent that one could ignore its side effects, but environmentalism announced a crisis that consisted precisely in an accumulation and interaction of neglected side effects. The simplifying assumptions and reductive moves of technocratically oriented policy professionalism become less convincing as the vagaries of an uncertain context are exposed. When the administrative mind is made to think outside its conventional boxes, the fragility of its bounded rationality is exposed: administrative organizations are faced with a "gross increase in . . . *relevant uncertainty.*"[52]

Experience with environmental problems shows scientific investigation to be insufficient. Attention to "trans-scientific" issues, for example, reveals questions of key policy relevance that can be framed in conventional scientific terms but—due to constraints of time, expense, and ethics—are entirely impractical to answer through scientific investigation.[53] The overall problem, as Robert Gibson has argued, is not only one of uncertainty, but of enormous *ignorance.*

Gibson suggests that ecological rationality is inseparable from "an attitude of environmental humility," an orientation attuned to problems that arise when humans fail "to respect the complexity and vulnerability of the environment, and to appreciate the limits of human knowledge and understanding."[54] He argues against the common notion that we are "near the point at which properly supervised and directed scientists and administrators, assisted by specialized experts, could identify the right responses to most policy problems." This and similar beliefs are exposed as "dangerous fictions" when one considers such complex issues as acid rain, the greenhouse effect, and holes in the ozone layer.[55]

To return to an earlier example, the toxic waste problem poses a clear challenge to the administrative mind at an epistemological level. Effectively managing these toxic wastes came as an afterthought to the industrial world and the administrative sphere. It became strikingly obvious that very little was known about the problem during, to use Sylvia Tesh's term, a "pre-environmentalist" period.[56] Grasping the epistemological challenge means focusing on pre-environmentalist assumptions about what makes knowledge legitimate and relevant.

The antitoxics movement has pointed to clear evidence of public and private mismanagement of toxic wastes. No one was really in control or knew what was happening: "government knew very little about the magnitude of the hazardous waste problem as it embarked upon regulating it."[57] At the same time, the movement has loudly protested dangers arising from exposure to hazardous chemicals in the environment. Here, however, the grounds for protest have not been so clear-cut. Indeed, the dangers claimed by these groups have not generally been supported by scientific research based on conventional presuppositions.[58]

One possible response to the situation would be for the antitoxic movement to fold its tent and admit it has been wrong, just as many policy professionals might like to think. Another response would be to exalt the role of common sense and community-based experience, to hold that these—not scientifically grounded expertise—possess the ultimate wisdom.[59] Tesh, however, does not draw the conclusion that environmental concerns have failed the test of science, or that direct experiential knowledge can lay claim to the final word. She instead reexamines science from an environmentalist perspective. Her point is that commonsense understandings of the world actually permeate scientific practice.[60]

In assessing environmentalist concerns, Tesh maintains that epidemiology has been marked by the pre-environmentalist assumptions of industrialism: "In standard epidemiological practice the questions one asks, the studies one designs, the rules of evidence one obeys, and the interpretation one gives to results all start from the pre-environmentalist premise that the ambient environment is healthful and the scientist's task is to look for evidence to the contrary" (9). This pre-environmentalist premise, however, is itself not a scientific finding but a matter of common sense—precisely the type of common sense that has supported the advance of industrialization. Environmentalism challenges this common sense with a perspective suitable for an "environmentalist epidemiology" that would shift the burden of proof: "Instead of presuming that nature is clean and looking for evidence to the contrary, as the null hypothesis requires, investigators might start from the assumption that nature is *polluted* and look for evidence to the contrary. Such a tack would shift the burden of proof from those who would clean up the environment to those who would endanger it" (13–14).

As Tesh poses the issue, the key difference between employing pre-environmentalist and environmentalist assumptions is one of shifting "the burden of proof." The further issue that arises is, of course, how to decide where the burden of proof ought to be placed. Tesh claims that environmentalist assumptions are better suited to a science that seeks the prevention of disease (14). What her argument reveals, in any case, is that the choice of assumptions is not one for which scientific expertise possesses ultimate authority: nonexperts also have a legitimate say. The epistemological orientation of policy professionalism here confronts a challenge from within, from issues that come from its own presuppositions and socially constructed institutional practices. The epistemic authority of scientism is thrown into doubt. This opens the door to a dissenting professionalism and its concern with the communicative context of policy deliberations.

The challenge to the administrative mind does not remain narrowly epistemological, but emerges as also being societal and institutional. The problem of "respecting ignorance and uncertainty," as Gibson titles an essay, indicates that "the self-confidence of large-scale industrial societies is unfounded." While proposing a "distant and difficult goal of establishing societies that respect the boundaries imposed by human ignorance,"[61] he insists that efforts to promote environmentally humble institutional designs must first grapple with established policy processes.[62]

In reference to the toxic waste issue, Bruce Williams and Albert Matheny have particularly advocated "a policy dialogue." They emphasize the need that citizens be able to exercise a "right-to-know" in gaining access to information previously shielded from public view. With such a dialogue, they maintain, serious attention can shift from the mere disposal of toxic wastes to ways of reducing them at their source.[63] Pursued with such a societal and institutional focus, the challenge to the administrative mind raises the possibility of a reorientation within policy professionalism toward practices that, though concerned with immediate issues of reform, are also attuned to a larger agenda animated by the spirit of dissent.

Dissenting Professionalism and the Administrative Sphere

The voices of green dissent have significantly influenced policy professionalism by introducing challenges to agenda setting, problem definition, and epistemology. At the same time, policy professionalism is being contested from within. Some policy professionals have introduced practical innovations that clearly depart from scientistic and technocratic presuppositions. A current of policy theory has also emerged to promote a dissenting professionalism that is emphatically antiscientistic and antitechnocratic. Encouraging the development of counterexpertise, dissenting professionalism draws the politics of expertise into clearer view, questioning the role of expertise itself and highlighting issues in which nonexpert, as well as expert, opinion is clearly relevant.[64]

A key question is how to create an appropriate context for discussing issues in which both nonexpert and expert opinions are significant. Tesh, as we have seen, focuses on the burden of proof as the key concept for promoting an environmentalist epidemiology in response to concerns of the antitoxics movement. Her focus suggests the framework of jurisprudence and the possibility of employing a deliberative forum that is not restricted to experts judging clearly factual questions, but involves citizens as well as experts considering a range of issues that cannot be neatly demarcated in advance by a fixed epistemological position.[65] As important as expert opinions, in this context, are those opinions that draw attention to expert bias.

The problem of expert bias, when recognized and taken seriously within policy professionalism, throws the whole edifice of scientism into question. It is thus that Giandomenico Majone has recommended a "generalized jurisprudence."[66] Focusing particularly on the assessment of technological development, Majone argues that open criticism and public debate are necessary to counteract a central bias of experts: "The initial assumption is that the innovation will achieve what the innovator claims for it and that it will have no negative consequences that could reduce the attractiveness of its practical implementation." Majone concludes that "technological expertise cannot be relied upon to discover the characteristic risks and social implications of new technologies."[67] Lovins similarly maintains that in energy policy "too much expertise tends to obscure rather than illuminate the basic questions at issue."[68]

The point of such observations can be extended to the prevailing pattern of development in advanced industrial society. Environmental impact assessment, along with technology assessment and social impact assessment, were advanced as means of coming to grips with neglected difficulties in this pattern of development, or at least as a kind of "worm in the brain" unsettling to the normal boundaries of administrative rationality. Nonetheless, expert bias often appears in impact assessment both as an unquestioning attitude toward the prevailing pattern and as a tendency to constrain inquiry according to scientistic notions. Thomas Berger, who headed one of the most significant exercises in impact assessment, drew attention to this expert bias as obscuring "the nature of human affairs"[69] and pointed inquiry in a different direction: "If you are going to assess impact properly, you have to weigh a whole series of matters, some tangible, some intangible. But in the end, no matter how many experts there may be, no matter how many pages of computer printouts may have been assembled, there is the ineluctable necessity of bringing human judgement to bear on the main issues.

Indeed, when the main issue cuts across a range of questions, spanning the physical and social sciences, the only way to come to grips with it and to resolve it is by the exercise of human judgement" (2:229). The inquiry Berger headed was significant not so much for the exercise of judgment by an individual, however, as for the process of inquiry itself, which brought citizens and experts together in a forum that tended to equalize their standing.[70]

In such a context, the focus of attention moves decisively beyond the framework of a technocratically oriented policy professionalism: "The supreme analytic achievement," as Majone puts it, "is no longer the computation of optimal strategies, but the design of procedural rules and social mechanisms for the assessment of incomplete and often contradictory evidence."[71] This implies an epistemological shift within policy professionalism from scientism to discursive designs, as John Dryzek has suggested.[72] Similarly, according to Frank Fischer, the shift involves decreased faith in the epistemic authority of technocratic experts together with an enhanced context of communication encouraging citizens to develop "participatory expertise."[73]

Such a communicative shift, or "argumentative turn," has especially been advanced within the professional policy literature,[74] but has not emerged in isolation from dissenting social movements. Dissenting professionalism both reflects the influence of these movements and renders the professional world more receptive to it. Directly contesting the identity and purpose of policy professionalism, the dissident current portrays policy inquiry not as a fixed instrumentality but as a site of contention. Dissenting professionalism promotes participatory expertise and designs for open discourse that would complement a more open and vigorous public sphere.

Despite the prevailing character of policy professionalism, there are thus countertendencies. Not all of these, indeed, take the form of open challenges and declarations of dissent. Some are at work more quietly and inconspicuously from within as a loyal opposition. Frequent efforts to stimulate insight, to promote creative problem solving within the administrative sphere, attest to this. The techniques of management science, though replete with rationalistic imagery conducive to administrative legitimacy, can also become dysfunctional: they provide no help in defining the right problem, so it becomes possible "to solve the wrong problem precisely."[75] On one account, the traps of a narrowly analytic orientation are to be avoided by explicit recourse to dialectics: to an approach that deliberately elicits opposing viewpoints, staging debates to draw out and challenge assumptions that might otherwise remain latent.[76]

Discourse within organizations, as James March and Herbert Simon have observed, typically follows a pattern of categories that deflects attention from uncertainties that could irritate the routine operations of instrumental rationality. This "uncertainty absorption," as they term it,[77] also helps to reinforce the formalized style and imagery of officialdom, to maintain the impression that responsible intellectual activity must be deadly serious.[78]

Disciplined behavior, however, is not always enough. Creative insight also becomes necessary, as March has clearly recognized. Organizational rationality so tends to undermine itself, he argues, that spaces are needed within an administrative apparatus so that a "technology of foolishness" can influence decision making. Of course, this must be a responsible foolishness, in March's view, one that allows for creative insight useful to the organization but does not overstep its bounds by producing dysfunctional consequences.[79]

Implicit in March's proposal for a responsible foolishness is an understanding of the dynamic of power and insight. A technology of foolishness is not readily contained by the functional imperatives of an organizational system, but has a propensity to transgress boundaries, potentially eliciting unwelcome insights into the presuppositions, practices, and patterns of power that sustain the system. If a technology of foolishness becomes irresponsible, it can throw into question the rationality and legitimacy of established power.[80]

March's call for foolishness signals the administrative sphere's recognition of a need for creativity to enliven the administrative mind with new insights. His technology of foolishness implicitly recalls not only the court jester of an earlier era (as reflected, for example, in Shakespeare's *King Lear*) but also the larger tradition of the carnivalesque. Here, as Mikhail Bakhtin has shown, relationships are transposed, hierarchies reversed, fools crowned; the lowly are raised, the marginal takes center stage, the last becomes first.[81] The carnivalesque propensity to reverse key relationships is a common feature of creative problem solving[82]—and is rather typical, as we have seen, of environmental problem redefinition. With a deliberate technology of foolishness, moreover, the insights of the fool are taken seriously and thus become ambivalent in a potential either to help or to threaten the established order of things.

Green dissent testifies that the inclinations of the administrative mind— more precisely, the forms and practices of industry and government constituting the administrative sphere—are not so much part of the solution as part of the problem. In other words, the very constitution of the administrative apparatus in advanced industrial society emerges as an environmental problem, perhaps even the most serious of environmental problems. Incipient changes in policy professionalism and the administrative sphere thus issue a call for attention that cannot be blithely dismissed in the discourse of a green public sphere.

P OLITICS AS WE COMMONLY KNOW it demands that we deny our doubts, that we speak and act with unhesitating conviction, or guile. In the rough-and-tumble of political reality, there appears little opportunity to be tentative, to express honest uncertainties, to play with ideas and possibilities. Politics possesses a tragic seriousness.

Henry Kariel has nonetheless modestly praised a role for the ironic and the inconclusive in a politics where we "decline to end our discourse." He knows that his stance may be outrageous in a world filled with suffering, oppression, horror, and precious few level playing fields. Still, he entertains the idea in the hope of exploring and opening "arenas for political action" in diverse and unexpected places.[1] Kariel is intent not to be single-mindedly fixated on ends alone; he teaches that means are always already ends. A politics of irony and inconclusion thus reveals something of an end in itself, the cultivation of diverse, multidimensional spheres of active public life that redeem the promise of politics.[2]

Quoting Bergson's *Laughter*, Kariel suggests that, if we suspend our gloomy concerns with an air of ironic detachment, "many a drama will turn into a comedy."[3] An ironic and inconclusive politics is, in the end, perhaps an empty politics—one of indirection and indecision, if not moral malfeasance, an inconsequential politics. Entertaining the notion nonetheless suggests at least the possibility of a role for the comic in politics. But is this a possibility for green politics? Immediate appearances are not encouraging.

The Tragic Aspect of Green Politics

A sense of crisis has surrounded green politics since its inception. Its ideas throw the future of humanity into question and raise the prospect of catastrophe—perhaps the very extinction of the human species—unless there is a profound change in the way human beings interact with the rest of nature. No matter what human beings do, their domination over nature is to be remarkably short-lived: progress is coming to an end less than a cosmic blink after it was first hailed as humanity's great mission. The environmental crisis thus heralds a turning point in the confident expectations of the modern age.

Arising in an atmosphere of crisis, green politics seems to fit the story line of a tragedy. The consequences of failure are unthinkable, but the possibility of success often seems remote; a remorseless destiny unfolds despite heroic action. The tragic mood is intensified by the frequent moralism and desperation of some green discourse, in which the undeniably high stakes mix with a crusading sense of high purpose. The human forces threatening nature and the human niche within it are denounced while counterforces are called to heroic resistance.

Anticipating the first burst of environmentalism onto the public stage, Garrett Hardin was moved to quote Alfred North Whitehead on the classical idea of tragedy. The tragic end is inescapable, part of "the remorseless working of things,"[4] and efforts to escape are marked by futility; these actions, in fact, are but further steps toward the tragic end. In the context of environmental problems, Hardin saw tragic consequences arising from the actions of an unrestrained humanity. Yet, he also prescribed actions to escape these consequences, formulating these in a striking and memorable phrase: "mutual coercion mutually agreed upon."[5]

Whether intentionally or not, Hardin's formula summed up with fair precision the basic prescription Hobbes's *Leviathan* long ago advanced during the tumultuous emergence of the early modern state: general acknowledgment of the need for a centralized, authoritarian order of governance.[6] Ignoring the stamp of authoritarian governance on the modern world, Hardin did not see the possibility that his own heroic solution could itself be part of the problem, part of the tragic working of things.

The authoritarian prescription was repeated in the period after Earth Day 1970 by other writers, particularly William Ophuls and Robert Heilbroner.[7] The situation was extreme and called for extreme measures. Humanity was to be saved by a drastic centralization of power capable of taking the measures needed to avoid catastrophe. Following Hardin and explicitly invoking Hobbes, Ophuls thus proclaimed "the tragic necessity of Leviathan."[8]

This authoritarianism arose in sharp contrast to an earlier libertarian, or anarchist, argument to the effect that hierarchical authority is itself the root of ecological crisis. As Murray Bookchin argued in the latter half of the 1960s, a "complete and totalistic" revolution is now both possible and necessary. With the abolition of the authoritarian order, an ecologically harmonious utopia can be created. Guided by ecological principles, the pattern of community life is to be decentralized in the form of "ecologically balanced communes" where "collective abundance and cooperation transform labor into play." It is to be a world of complete, "rounded" human beings, "freed of guilt and the workings of authoritarian modes of training, and given over to desire and the sensuous apprehension of the marvelous." Significantly, there is to be no sharp separation of means and ends, for the libertarian utopia emerges from action that is spontaneous and decentralized, though nonetheless cohesive.[9]

Ecological crisis means that "visionary dreams of liberation" are no longer just desirable possibilities, but have become "compelling necessities" (27). The inevitability of either utopia or catastrophe means that we find ourselves faced with two "drastic alternatives": if not liberation, "the absolute negation of *all* hierarchical forms," then "annihilation" (40). Because the stakes are so high, revolutionary effort turns out to be serious business indeed, aimed at a complete, total solution. Anything less would be catastrophic; indeed, serious errors in analysis and action become "negligence of criminal proportions" (23). "The tension between actuality and potentiality," according to Bookchin, ". . . acquires apocalyptic proportions in the ecological crisis of our times" (16).

That the authoritarian and libertarian solutions share a distinctly tragic aura is not just a reflection of the perceived seriousness of the ecological predicament, but also something that follows from the tragic outlook of the broader tradition. In Plato's *Republic*, the guardians are not inclined to laugh, and the worthy city of the *Laws* is modeled on tragedy in explicit contrast to the unworthiness of comedy.[10] In the Christian Middle Ages, the life of the monastery, devoted to a Christ who did not laugh, foreshadows in its seriousness the worldly missions to follow.[11] Descartes' early modern claim that rationality can render human beings lords of the natural world gains spiritual meaning in the rational, methodical devotions of the puritanical work ethic.[12] As the theological context of the Middle Ages is eclipsed and the metaphysical one of modern philosophy begins to wane, positivism perceives order and progress arising from the stresses of early industrialism.

It is with the passage from theological to metaphysical to positive eras, as positivism told the story, that rationality can finally dispense with irrelevant nonsense and promise a smoothly functioning industrial civilization managed by a secular "priesthood" of experts.[13] Marx, although he glimpsed the comic in history, comes to cast the promise of industrial progress in distinctly tragic terms: to bring the future under rational human control involves inescapable conflict and Promethean struggle to overcome industrial capitalism.[14] Advanced industrial societies, both capitalist and socialist, later come to display awesome technological prowess, even to gain control of nature's ultimate fire, but nature turns out to be more complex and elusive than expected: humanity's very success threatens destruction. To prevent destruction thus becomes another tragically heroic mission.

Against a backdrop of disturbing technological surprises, the naturalist and literary theorist Joseph Wood Krutch came in the middle of the twentieth century to see a "Tragic Fallacy" lingering in the temper of the modern world: "The Tragic Fallacy depends ultimately upon the assumption which man so readily makes that something outside his own being, some 'spirit not himself'—be it God, Nature, or that still vaguer thing called a Moral Order—joins him in the emphasis which he places upon this or that and confirms him in his feelings that his passions and his opinions are important."[15]

What would be the consequences of viewing green politics more as a comedy than as a tragedy? The very suggestion might seem frivolous, but the advantages of thinking in terms of comedy rather than tragedy were strongly suggested by Joseph W. Meeker's *The Comedy of Survival,* which appeared during the early phases of the green movement but has unfortunately not received the attention it deserves.[16]

The problem with an unequivocal endorsement of a comic politics seems obvious. Without clear principles to guide action toward appropriate goals, there is a risk of ineffectiveness, opportunism, and cynicism. As Meeker himself emphasized, the comic protagonist is seldom much of a hero, and is more likely to be a rogue, rascal, scoundrel, knave, fool, picaro, tramp— a survivor, perhaps at any cost. Comic politics, if it takes an ironic stance outside the spectacle of politics, risks a lack of concern about either principles or consequences, a lack of purpose.

Meeker nonetheless followed Krutch's insight to argue that the tragic outlook was the problem, not the solution. What was required, both for human survival and for an ethically respectful relationship to the natural world, was a heavy dose of the comic. Meeker found especially attractive a certain "Chinese fable" that William Faulkner liked to repeat. There was a time, as Meeker recounts the story, "when cats were the dominant creatures on earth," and over the centuries "cat philosophers" attempted in vain "to solve the ethical problems faced by a dominant species."[17] Finally, they gave up, deciding to choose from among the lower creatures a species with sufficient optimism to think the "predicament could be solved," as one of Faulkner's narrators concludes the tale, "and ignorant enough never to learn better": "that is why the cat lives with you, is completely dependent on you for food and shelter, but lifts no paw for you and loves you not; in a word, why your cat looks at you the way it does."[18]

Tragedy treats humanity in heroic, ideal terms, whereas comedy focuses on human frailties, deflating pretences and mocking excesses. The comic mode subverts the tragic hero, cutting humanity down to size and dispelling human delusions of grandeur. In contrast to the tragic portrayal of humanity in terms of godlike aspirations, comedy accentuates human faults and limitations. The focus shifts from the transcendent to the finite; foolish notions, ridiculous situations, the less than exalted functions of the body, the inexhaustible range of human foibles.[19]

Meeker sees ecological wisdom in comedy, a genre not simply frivolous or trivializing that exhibits its own kind of seriousness while attempting to "deflate the overinflated." Like the emperor in his new clothes, the arrogant pretensions of power and moralistic self-righteousness provoke the laughter of comic insight: "The comic point of view is that . . . high moral ideals and glorified heroic poses are themselves largely based upon fantasy and are likely to lead to misery or death for those who hold them."[20] Not comedy, then, but only the pride of a tragic heroism can support the technological quest to dominate nature, along with that quest's terribly ironic consequences. Because tragedy typically involves a struggle to defeat and destroy an opponent, the tragic ending becomes, in Meeker's words, "a funeral or its equivalent": "When faced with polar opposites, the problem of comedy is," instead, "always how to resolve conflict without destroying the participants" (38). The comic art is thus one that involves "accommodation and reconciliation," "flexibility" in response to the "ironies and bewilderments" of life: "When ecological balances are disturbed, comic action seeks their restoration." Comedy wants not victory or progress or perfection, but "joy" (191).

Meeker suggests that the response to environmental crisis is "trapped in a cultural tradition which affirms the supremacy of the tragic point of view" (78). A reconciliation by humans with themselves as natural beings cannot be gained in a tragic mode. While the modern age lacks the cosmic presuppositions necessary to support tragedy in the fully classical sense, the notion of dominating nature echoes a central tragic theme: "Tragic art . . . describes a world in which the processes of nature are relatively unimportant and always subservient. . . . Nobility, honor, human dignity, and spiritual purification depend upon supra-natural forces, not upon conciliation with nature. The tragic view of life is proud to be unnatural" (51–52).

In suggesting an ecological model of "comic integration" (191), Meeker looks back to "medieval cosmology" and invokes the particular example of Dante: "An ecological model of the world will incorporate principles of integration resembling those derived by Dante from his theological model, including a holistic conception of the world's structure . . . and a capacity to think and live in the comic mode" (186). Dante explained the title of his *Comedy*—labeled "divine" by others after he was dead—with reference to the classical idea that comedy moves from misery to happiness.[21] Dante's journey into Hell through Purgatory and up to Paradise thus culminates in the felicity of comic integration. Meeker's comedy of survival, which moves from ecological crisis to a felicitous ecological integration of nature and humanity, is thus modeled on Dante's comedy of salvation.[22]

In his often insightful interpretation, Meeker emphasizes that Dante's apprehension of God culminates in an ambiguous image: "There is no ordering deity in human form controlling the universe from the upper reaches of Paradise, but only pure light, dazzling in its clarity and intensity." Once Dante's vision adjusts, he can discern images with human likeness, but he leaves as an "unanswerable question" the exact design of the universal form and its relationship to humanity (179).

The famous words above the entrance to Hell, however, suggest little ambiguity: "ABANDON ALL HOPE." There is an ultimate order that is rational and everlasting, with one place for ultimate torment and another for ultimate joy. Dante's *Comedy* portrays the invisible cosmos not vaguely, but in vivid images allegorically indicating an awesomely intricate architecture of precise, elegant design: poetic justice.

Throughout the Middle Ages, from Augustine to Aquinas, it was explicitly held that the torments of the damned would be fully revealed to the saints in heaven. With Aquinas, Dante's direct theological predecessor, the purpose of this knowledge also becomes explicit. In *On the Genealogy of Morals*, Nietzsche draws attention to this purpose, directly quoting the words of Aquinas: " 'The blessed in the kingdom of heaven,' he says, meek as a lamb, 'will see the punishments of the damned, *in order that their bliss be more delightful for them.*' " According to Nietzsche, it was thus a "crude blunder" for Dante to place over the portals of Hell the claim that it too was built from "eternal love." The statement discloses a secret, moralistic *ressentiment* in the architecture of the Christian cosmos, for the entrance to paradise does not state another truth that now becomes apparent: heaven was designed from "eternal hate."[23]

In drawing upon Dante as a source to guide the comedy of survival, Meeker does not press far enough to disclose and comically subvert the stark dualism—the fixed opposition without possibility of reconciliation—that defined the terms of spiritual struggle in the medieval cosmos. Dante's poem thus could not evade an unrelentingly tragic aspect, nor could it escape Krutch's tragic fallacy. The entire hierarchical structure of the poem, like the cosmos it represents, rests on the cornerstone of the tragic point of view: that humanity is somehow special, a focus of significant attention in the scheme of things. Tragedy depends on a universe that cares enough about human beings to reward or punish them; it must be, in Meeker's words, "an ordered place where some kind of justice or morality rules."[24] As he points out, there were cosmic certitudes available to Dante that modernity has eclipsed: "Dante's world permitted these basic assumptions as no period since has been able to do, and permitted Dante to construct in his poem the last image of an integrated universe before the fragmentations of the modern world emerged" (181).

Apocalypse Now: The Lost Book of Comedy

A theory and practice of green politics along the lines of Meeker's comedy of survival would confront a perplexing difficulty in finding a coherent orientation for action. Meeker offers an "ecological model" that would include both an integrative, holistic conception of the world, like Dante's, and a capacity for comic engagement. Yet the offer of a comprehensive ecological vision appears very much like an empty, and perhaps dangerous, offer of a new cosmos.

Cosmic aspirations have often been voiced in the green movement, especially by its more spiritually oriented leaders. The difficulty with Meeker's proposal should raise a note of caution for any green cosmological quest. His celebration of Dante's comic integration obscured a moralistic *ressentiment* revealed by Nietzsche's gloss on the *Comedy*. Although Dante presents the most vivid vision of the medieval cosmos ever crafted, the fact nonetheless remains that the comic was largely anathema to those in the medieval world who, living the cloistered life, were most seriously concerned with spiritual salvation.

There is a difficulty in the very notion of comic integration. Taken too seriously, too literally, the ideal of integration has the capacity to stifle comic action. Comedy is irreverent, disintegrative, exposing and disrupting settled patterns of conduct, belief, power, and authority. A comedy might well conclude with a happy ending, a final reconciliation of contradictory elements, but that is precisely where comedy *ends*. Comedy has no final resting place, but seeks always to renew comic tension, to keep the story alive: "the ending of a comedy, like everything else in it, is a joke."[25]

A green politics more comic than tragic would look askance at promises of integration, without altogether rejecting them. In a modernity perplexed by postmodernity, grand narratives of harmony and suggestions of a new cosmos are sure to raise suspicions. Postmodern gestures forestall closure, frustrate any cementing of new and old fragments into an integrated whole, any construction of an order with fixed reference points and stable boundaries. Postmodernity refuses a building permit to any permanent scaffolding for tragedy. By making comic integration the final resting place for his comedy of survival, Meeker implicitly advances the possibility of what might be called comic suicide. Comic integration, that is, ends comedy—kills it—unless further comic gestures are in play to unsettle the integration. A comic green politics could not fail to create parodies of a cherished ecological cosmos, to keep it incomplete if only not to kill it—to include in it, for example, the musings of Faulkner's philosophical cats.

Any order cuts itself off from disorder, but brings disorder into itself by the very act of imposing boundaries on an unfixed, indefinite terrain; the conditions for the order's possibility, as is often said, become the conditions for its impossibility—more practically (and less precisely) speaking, the beginning of its end.[26] By setting a postmodern parody of the popular detective novel in a late medieval monastery, Umberto Eco's *The Name of the Rose* both rehearses the disintegration of the closed medieval cosmos and indicates the permanent impossibility of a new comprehensive order arising out of the ashes. The quiet life of the monastery, home to Christendom's finest library, is disrupted by a series of bizarre and violent deaths. An investigation—methodical, lucky, and (comically) catastrophic—reveals that these and other puzzling events involve a forbidden book. The book in question (which seems to have once actually existed) is Aristotle's treatment of comedy, the lost second book of his *Poetics*.

In his first book Aristotle focused on tragedy, but he also promised a discussion of comedy. Tragedy, according to Aristotle, is marked by seriousness and provokes feelings of fear and pity, yet purifies these feelings through catharsis.[27] Comedy, according to the partial account of the lost book presented in Eco's novel, is regarded by Aristotle as something to praise: it both inspires and purifies the passion to indulge in the ridiculous—it brings comic catharsis. Although comedy indulges in the ridiculous, the human being is not thereby demeaned. As Aristotle taught, the human being is distinguished not by reason and speech alone, but is also set apart from other animals by the *unique ability to laugh*.[28]

Eco suggests that the loss of Aristotle's book on comedy, however it happened (and whether or not it actually happened), constitutes a telling event of Western history. The medieval cosmos was concerned to keep comedy in its place. The monastery was the institution of Christian civilization that, throughout the Middle Ages, dutifully preserved the ancient writings of pagan civilizations. As Christianity in the late Middle Ages came to regard Aristotle as the greatest authority among the ancients, he became known simply as the Philosopher. By indulging in the ridiculous, though, comedy offends not only the seriousness of monastic discipline and order but the sanctity of the divinely ordered cosmos itself. Thus, if the educated were to read an Aristotle praising comedy, the genre could gain a status threatening the very order of Christian civilization. In Eco's novel, the old, blind monk who both hides and protects the book accordingly voices an apocalyptic warning: "On the day when the Philosopher's words would justify the marginal jest of the debauched imagination, or when what has been marginal would leap to the center, every trace of the center would be lost."[29] With premonitions of the apocalypse abounding throughout, the story culminates in a great fire that—consuming the book, the library, the chapel, and the entire monastery—suggests the impending destruction of the medieval cosmos itself. Eco's parody also portrays the disintegration of this cosmos as a fate that may await any modern effort to restore cosmic order.

Much like the apocalyptic fire that consumes the microcosm of the monastery in Eco's novel, modernity has destroyed the old cosmos. Disciplined by orderly governance and freed to become equivalent elements—as both producers and consumers—in an impersonal market mechanism, individuals have been detached from the ties that once bound them to one another in a common world under the "sacred canopy"[30] of Creation. Nonetheless, the modern age does project a central image of cosmic proportions. With mechanism emerging since the seventeenth century as the leading cosmic metaphor in modern science and philosophy, the implicit image of an industrial cosmos was finally fixed as machine technology, the routines of socioeconomic life, and the notion of a big cosmic machine all mirrored and mutually reinforced one another in the modern imagination. This is Weber's "disenchanted" world. It is based on the conviction that there are no "mysterious incalculable forces" and that, thus, "one can, in principle, master all things by calculation."[31]

Although the medieval cosmos disintegrated with the advent of modernity, some fragments were preserved in the mechanistic framework. Especially significant was a continuing provision for the domination of nature.[32] With the dissolution of the medieval cosmos, what changed was humanity's unquestionable subordination to divine authority. Control over nature, especially in the case of the monk, had involved a resistance to temptations— of the body, worldly passions, and one's animal nature—which were feared and despised as threats to the soul and its salvation.[33] With the God of Christendom eclipsed in the modern age as the ordering principle of the civilization, the spiritual quest became mundane.

Progress in the technological mastery of nature became the historical mission of humanity. Eliminating confusion and error in favor of clarity and knowledge, progress aimed for an orderly, efficient industrial civilization guided by an impersonal reason. Progress in mastering nature would also be part of humanity's collective advance to a type of governance that would put an end to brutal oppression and social discord. The industrial cosmos thus invokes the authority of knowledge and power united for a grand purpose—the authority, that is, of the administrative mind.[34]

When Rudolph Bahro likens the "Big Machine" of the industrial system to a train speeding toward "the abyss," he argues that the danger arises out of a destructive form of cosmological faith. Now largely fixed at a psychosomatic level, this faith has unleashed an unchecked drive for acquisition and domination. Salvation thus must involve dramatic changes at a cosmological level, to be brought about through the revival of a monastic form of life: "We need," he declares, "a new Benedictine order."[35] Though perhaps the most prominent, Bahro's is but one voice promoting "ecomonasticism."[36]

Early in the twentieth century, however, Max Weber offered the striking insight that the disciplined, methodical characteristics of modern industry and organization were shaped long ago in the cloistered world. The transformation of monastic discipline into common morality helped produce the bitter fate of all who inhabit the "iron cage" of the industrial cosmos: "For when asceticism was carried out of monastic cells into everyday life, and began to dominate worldly morality, it did its part in building the tremendous cosmos of the modern economic order. This order is now bound to the technical and economic conditions of all the individuals who are born into this mechanism . . . with irresistible force."[37]

Laughter was strictly discouraged, if not banned, in monastic life with the Rule of St. Benedict in the early Middle Ages. Deemed out of place in any life devoted to higher things, laughter remained under suspicion long after the medieval era. One commentator on Eco's novel has indeed pointed to the significance of "forgotten but vital" debates over laughter: "From the early church fathers to the Puritans, the ban on outward displays of frivolity has been an essential part of piety because it points to the tragic aspects of earthly life, the fallen nature of man, and the concentration of the believer on higher matters."[38]

In the formation of the modern world, an ascetic piety became the hallmark not only of religious life but of daily pursuits in the larger world. Frivolity could still abound during the Middle Ages in areas outside the monastic domain and outside ecclesiastical and civil officialdom, but via Puritanism, as Weber noted, the "bitter seriousness" of the religious devotee helped to shape the methodically disciplined productive system of the industrial cosmos.[39] Mikhail Bakhtin has evoked the world that was lost in his description of the carnivalesque: "Carnival festivities and the comic spectacles and ritual connected with them . . . existed in all the countries of medieval Europe; they were sharply distinct from the serious, official, ecclesiastical, feudal and political cult forms and ceremonials. They offered a completely different, non-official, extraecclesiastical and extrapolitical aspect of the world . . . they built a second world and a second life outside officialdom."[40] This is the world that is marginalized, kept in its place by the official cosmos of the Middle Ages, as represented by the monastery in Eco's novel. With the rise of industrialism, the expansive festival of the medieval carnival is reduced to the neatly circumscribed spectacle of the modern circus. The circus became necessary because, as the circus master in Dickens's *Hard Times* lispingly explains to the unsympathetic, fact-filled Mr. Gradgrind, "People mutht be amuthed."

Comedy in Green Politics: The Carnivalesque

The first Earth Day in 1970 was denounced by radicals as an "all day sucker," a cynical attempt by the establishment to deflect oppositional energies away from serious issues, such as the Vietnam War, toward something safe.[41] Even as officials in government and industry became environmentalists-for-a-day, however, Earth Day had the aura of a festival and gave focus to carnivalesque green images exposing and ridiculing the somber specter of the administrative mind.

Despite its tragic aspect, green politics also possesses a significant element of comedy, and this has persisted in the years since Earth Day. It was certainly an image of carnival that gained prominence in the spring of 1983 when twenty-seven members of the German Greens, shown in photographs worldwide, took their newly won seats in the Bundestag, "forming a river of colorful sweaters, shirts, and dresses that flowed down the middle of the chamber between the tiers of black-and-white suited politicians."[42]

Carnivalesque gestures abound in various venues, often deliberately designed to counter the tone of tragic seriousness as well as to mock some of the all-too-human incarnations of the administrative mind. A citizens group stages a funeral for a dead river. Environmentalists at a formal public hearing don humorous hats to underscore their point. Protestors against the clear-cutting of an ancient forest sleep in hammocks that hang from the trees to be logged. The gestures include the actions of such groups as Greenpeace, long a leader in carnivalesque tactics: the unarmed *Rainbow Warrior* sails off to confront a modern navy; inflatable dinghies harass mechanized fishing fleets and whaling vessels; irreverent banners hang high from the towers of a supposedly secure nuclear power plant.

Currently, the leading maxim of one group is *You've got to be funny.* EAAAC?!, a diffuse, loosely affiliated, sometimes clandestine, network of Australian greens, makes humor and absurdity the centerpiece of its actions. (The acronym, pronounced "eek," stands for EcoAnarchoAbsurdist-AdelaideCell.) "They believe," an anonymous source indicates, ". . . that the only way to true environmental change (thus averting the environmental crisis that several of them don't believe exists anyway) is through uncoordinated, diverse, and absurd political actions." Their actions, at times recognizable even to members only in retrospect, are supposed to be more than environmentally sound. A genuine EAAAC?! action must also be spontaneous, unreasonable, and impossible to repeat. Policy proposals, though they must be ecologically rational, also must be patently absurd:

- —Every second tree planted in urban areas must be a fruit tree
- —Bicycles to be provided for people on every third street corner (with baskets)
- —The construction of a museum of "fuzzy logic" and "economic irratio-nality"
- —Thirty-hour week maximum in the workplace, and no overtime
- —Siesta reintroduced (2 P.M. to 6 P.M. in summertime)
- —Subsidies for business folk to purchase and wear clown suits

EAAAC?! may have had its laughs, but it is not without problems. Factional conflicts have begun. Although EAAAC?! members must of course be funny, even this has led to trouble. One element of what has been called the "core" cell is reported to have criticized the rest of EAAAC?! because it is *"not funny enough"*![43]

Green politics possesses a tendency to challenge its own tragic aspect with comic gestures. Taken together, these various gestures are not simply stunts or jokes or mere tactical maneuvers, but express a kind of language. This is the idiom of the carnivalesque, and it is key to the creation of a green public sphere, even if (indeed, *especially* if) communication is to be rational.

Jürgen Habermas has conceived communicative rationality as a way of es-caping problems that early critical theory had encountered when offering its critique of rationality in terms of consciousness. The critique, identifying a dialectic of enlightenment, was meant not only to denounce what usually passes for reason, but also to suggest that any ultimate enshrining of ratio-nality is problematic.[44] By moving rationality out of a monological domain of consciousness to the dialogical domain of communication, Habermas at-tempts to avoid the equivocations of the early critical theorists.[45] He wants a clear affirmation of reason. But his efforts do not resolve everything and, indeed, pose new questions of context and genre.

Even in the best of situations, in a context where we do not think it naïve to believe in a discourse that is open, fair, and meaningful, something trou-bling about Habermas's communicative rationality would remain. For the institutionalization of discourse unavoidably privileges the genre of argu-mentation. It may be argued that this is a justified privilege; there is, in fact, no way to *argue* against this proposition without hoisting yourself on your own petard. But this self-sealing argument on behalf of argumentation, this undeniably rational observation, assumes that a pure genre can exist out-side a simplistic idealization.[46]

As a genre, argument not only seeks coherence, but also has to assume its own self-sufficiency. Argument thus chalks itself in a circle. Strictly speak-ing, it has to be a dialogue, but it constitutes itself as a unitary idiom, aspiring to a single voice that ultimately proclaims *the* conclusion. In this manner, argument takes on the character of a monologue, thereby undermining its dialogical aspect. Bakhtin makes this obvious by invoking the image of a polyphonic carnivalesque in contrast to the authoritarian monotony of officialdom. He especially celebrates a thoroughly dialogical genre, the novel, which conveys "the primordial dialogism of discourse" as an interwoven, open-ended multiplicity of voices: "Language . . . is never unitary."[47]

Unless the green public sphere is implicitly to stamp itself with the monological image of the administrative mind, it must remain sensitive to a diversity of voices, including those of nature. In challenging the bias of industrialist discourse, it must not excommunicate its carnival elements in the name of rationality. And it must not forget to laugh. Confidence in communicative rationality as a dialogical enterprise depends on reason somehow keeping in touch with sources that are not manifestly rational, which do not speak in the language of argument. The prospect of a green public sphere makes comedy vital to green politics.

Comic vs. Tragic?
Story Lines in Green Political Thought

The leading story line in green political thought pictures the industrial cosmos as a tragic doomsday machine, a cosmos in crisis. Despite the carnivalesque features of green politics, their significance is often neglected. Though diversity and democratic openness are celebrated, a principal concern is to delineate sharply the boundaries of the green movement, to give it a name, identity, and purpose that will resist contamination by tendencies that could lead the movement astray, or destroy it. There is an anxious concern to get things right, to be consistent and coherent. The idea of theoretical or practical play hardly enters the picture. As the crisis unfolds, the doomsday machine rushes toward the abyss; there is no time for frivolity.

Crisis, of course, has different meanings.[48] But the sense of the idea seems ultimately to depend on the context of a story, a narrative. In literary terms, indeed, crisis is another word for climax or turning point. So, when we read the script of green politics, what kind of narrative is it? What kind of turning point do we encounter? Are we reading a tragedy or a comedy?

In the standard view of the distinction, tragedy begins with the image of an ideal order but ends in catastrophic disorder. Comedy, by contrast, has a mundane, all-too-human beginning—bizarre, confusing, laughable—but moves toward the harmony of a happy ending.[49] Is the difference between tragedy and comedy basically just the difference between a sad and a happy ending?

In *Tragedy and Comedy*, Walter Kerr argues that this conventional notion is wrong. Happy endings in comedy are "mere pretences," "frauds," "lies": "Comedy is not a form that reaches conclusions." It actually throws the whole idea of a happy ending into question and, as noted earlier, ends in a "joke." "Tragedies," on the other hand, "do not all end in disaster or death; many end most satisfactorily."[50] Contrary to Meeker, in fact, it may be that reconciliation is the final note of tragedy, not of comedy. But what, then, is the relationship between tragedy and comedy?

The classical masks of comedy and tragedy often appear as an either/or duality. Sometimes an intermingling becomes apparent, as in tragicomedies, dark comedies, and the odd mixtures of comedy and tragedy in the theater of the absurd.[51] But is there perhaps a more enduring, less obvious relationship? Consider Kerr's striking description of Marcel Marceau's pantomime *The Mask Maker:* "Here the mask maker is trying on his various masks, quickly substituting one for another. But a particularly gleeful mask, sheer grin from ear to ear, becomes stuck. The mask maker tries to remove it, but cannot. His efforts are confident at first, then increasingly desperate. In due time we know that the real face behind the mask is a thing of maddened frustration, of unadulterated anguish. But all we can see is the perpetual smile. Because M. Marceau is a mime, he is using no real masks; we are looking directly at his face, in which the two expressions, one evident, one intimated, coincide. The fusion is absolute. The comic image dominates . . . yet we see and feel clearly what is behind it, even as it does so."[52] The comic is constantly haunted by a tragic presence. Comedy, Kerr argues, has no independent existence apart from tragedy, though the reverse is not so clearly the case. We do not readily imagine glee behind the tragic mask. There is, he suggests, an "impulse to keep the tragic form pure" (34, 33). In the purity of its form, however, tragedy is also incomplete. It, too, remains haunted by its other.

In stitching together the fragmentary evidence from ancient Greece, Kerr's *Tragedy and Comedy* indicates that the two genres were once actually "one," and he argues that they should again be understood as such (262). When tragedy first gained official standing, Kerr maintains, it took the form of a trilogy followed by a one-play sequel. The tragic trilogy was a narrative of pain and struggle that moved through successive stages. The story did not end in disaster, however, but in reconciliation with the gods. In the follow-up, the same story was retold by the same author, but this time mockingly in the form of a "satyr play," the precursor to satire (22–23): "There is a strong probability, then, that when the comic tone first became recognizable it became recognizable as burlesque of the solemn and sacred. This is what it is there for: to repair an omission. The solemn, the sacred, the tragic, in its upward strain invariably leaves something out."[53] From the perspective of tragedy and comedy as a unified genre, it turns out that

Dante's *Comedy* is not a comedy at all, but—culminating in the reconciliation of heaven—a tragedy without the comedy, without the satirical sequel. Only something like William Blake's little satire *The Marriage of Heaven and Hell* supplies this missing element and completes the form.[54]

Tragedy and comedy might thus be "one," as Kerr indicates, but they also remain *two.* There is no ultimate reconciliation within the form, which remains at odds with itself—split at the center—and hence perpetually open. The two are not contained, as Kerr unfortunately suggests, under a wider umbrella of tragedy.[55] In contemporary terms, the binary opposition tragedy/comedy constitutes a form that openly deconstructs itself: "Comedy derives its very being from the affirmations of tragedy, to which it plays devil's advocate" (309). Perhaps Friedrich Dürrenmatt only presses the matter to its inevitable conclusion when he claims that tragedy and comedy presuppose opposing worlds—one "formed," the other "unformed"—and declares himself a partisan of comedy: "The universal for me is chaos." Only through comedy do we see the "form of the unformed, the face of a world without a face."[56]

Green politics is not tragedy *or* comedy. Tragedy and comedy are narrative genres or, as Dürrenmatt puts it, "formal concepts, dramatic attitudes, figments of the aesthetic imagination" (33). Politics is not simply a narrative genre. Political action and judgment cannot be reduced to the idea of tragedy or comedy, or to some combination of them. Nonetheless narrative ideas, particularly with intimations of emerging order or disorder, do enter into political action, shaping orientations, expectations, judgments, and interactions in ways that may often elude the actors themselves.[57]

Green political thought clearly contains a narrative dimension that calls for recognition. The story of progress—the grand narrative of the industrial cosmos—is typically countered by an ecologically informed story line that anticipates progress ending in catastrophe. What remains constant is the tragic form of the narrative. The pattern remains tragic even when fears of disaster are relieved by hopes for the harmonious order of an ecological utopia. By making this tragic pattern obvious, the comic can help to temper green enthusiasm for a new cosmos.

Cosmic or Comic: The Mirror of Ecology

Ecology makes obvious the inescapable place of human beings in natural cycles and systems, the intricate interdependencies of nature, its complexities and surprises, the unexpected way it often responds to human attempts at control. The industrial cosmos seems far from complete, for its orderly progress is spinning out of control. Is it time for a new cosmos?

The new view of nature suggested by ecology informs a new manner of understanding and caring for nature. The scope of human caring reaches beyond self and humanity to become an ecocentric concern about nature for its own sake. When it expands beyond both egocentrism and homocentrism, however, where does the scope of concern stop? Carolyn Merchant has astutely drawn the apparently irresistible implication. Ecocentrism, as she argues, ultimately involves a concern with the "cosmos."[58] But what cosmos? And what is then left of chaos?

Often implicit in challenges to the industrial cosmos is the idea of restoring cosmic unity in an overall order that will make sense and will have a place (however modest and ultimately temporary) for human beings. The impulse is for a completed whole, perhaps some organic harmony of human/nature. When advanced with cosmic aspirations, however, the ecocentric conception of human/nature has a propensity to erect a new scaffolding for tragedy, leaving out or marginalizing the comic.

Eco's *The Name of the Rose* culminates with William of Baskerville, the monkish stand-in for Sherlock Holmes, contemplating the microcosmic apocalypse of a monastery in flames. At first verging on heresy as a champion of enlightenment, he finally realizes that the whole premise of his methodical investigation—a presupposition of order—was not only flawed, but provided a key element in the eventful chaos that came to spell catastrophe. He had sought a clear pattern behind the crimes in the monastery, but to his consternation found that he had followed a "false pattern" all along.[59] The pattern that emerged in his mind was coherent; it gave him a sensible orientation with which to shape his strategy and direct his moves, but it also entered into an array of contingencies that happened finally to converge in the fire. The mystery's solution brought an end no one wanted or expected.

Having sought a criminal operating with a deliberate plan, William eventually realizes that there was no single criminal and "no plan"—certainly no "plan of a perverse and rational mind"—that could explain the puzzling events: instead, there was "a sequence of causes, and concauses, and of causes contradicting one another, which proceeded on their own, creating relations that did not stem from any plan" (492). The final catastrophe becomes darkly comic. There is no remorseless working of things, no ultimate order, either good or evil.

Chance destroys the seemingly secure order of a monastic world devoted in faith to the larger order of God. Not only is faith in God's order thrown into question, however; so too is faith in any rational order. Having anticipated an enlightened modernity throughout the story, William reaches (not surprisingly for Eco) a strikingly postmodern insight: "The order that our mind imagines is like a net, or like a ladder, built to attain something. But afterward you must throw the ladder away, because you discover that, even if it was useful, it was meaningless" (492).

Any cosmic ordering and mastering of the world to enhance prospects of security and survival betrays a troubling tendency. Yet the quest for contextual orientation is unavoidable. The work of John Rodman is significant in this regard because, though perhaps tempted by cosmic yearnings, he makes no assumption of a firm foundation or ultimate leap to a comprehensive order. Discussing the problem of political orientation in the green movement explicitly in terms of the need for a meaningful cosmic image, Rodman makes this observation: "We lack a suitable myth that comprehends and integrates our feelings and perceptions, articulates our intuitions, allows our actions ritual status, and makes us intelligible to ourselves in terms of an alignment with a larger order of things."[60] His well-known account of the emergence of four forms of ecological consciousness thus also raises the prospect of a new cosmic vision shaped through attention to "ecological models of nature."[61]

Modern political science, he argues, has largely expunged the "overtly symbolic and analogical dimension" of traditional political theory. He particularly invokes Aquinas's medieval cosmology to illustrate a traditional type of "argument by analogy" whereby the forms of "psyche, polis, and cosmos" are shown to reflect one another in a comprehensive structure. He suggests that efforts to model the human world after the image of a larger order may respond to "a perennial human need," and he further insists that the analogical mode of thinking has not been eclipsed by modernity; rather, the interplay of analogy has been driven underground as "mechanism" implicitly mirrors itself throughout the different levels of a tacitly assumed cosmic structure.[62]

Significantly, however, Rodman does not return to a mode of analogical *argument*, but appeals rather to the elaboration of a "metaphoric language which shapes perception and thereby helps constitute the realm being described."[63] Ecology provides but one of numerous cultural sources in an emergence of ecological consciousness that culminates, according to Rodman, in "ecological sensibility."[64] He is well aware that conceptions of nature carry the imprint of human cultures, just as cultural institutions mimic what they project "onto the cosmos." For Rodman, this circle is not something to escape, for it appears inescapable; the thing to do is to pay attention to it: "We should . . . focus on the reciprocal dialectic whereby our images of nature and our images of society shape one another."[65] The point for Rodman, then, is not to make a "forced and futile" effort[66] to create a new cosmos, or to argue for one by analogy, but to evoke a deliberate interplay of images and experiences anticipating "the metaphoric mirroring of psyche, polis, and cosmos" through ecological sensibility. (When he first introduced this concept, indeed, he explicitly called it a "*metaphoric sensibility*."[67]) There can be no grounding on the bedrock of an ecological science for, with an unsettled discipline marked by paradigmatic conflict, one is likely to encounter "shifting sands."[68]

Like other green thinkers, Rodman wishes to celebrate and defend diversity in nature and in human society. Unlike many others, however, he does not stake his position to the tenuous proposition that natural diversity fosters stability, even if it does.[69] He instead maintains that the elimination of diversity means a stifling of natural and human potentialities that call out for protection: "The key to the myth that I see emerging is the principle of metaphoric mirroring in accordance with which certain archetypal patterns —such as the struggle to defend diversity against the juggernaut of monoculture—are seen to be operative in several spheres, e.g. on a biological, a social, and a psychological level."[70] "Diversity and richness of potentiality," he says, "are natural conditions endangered by oppressive monoculture on all levels, and each level is a metaphor of the others."[71] Metaphoric mirroring does not conjure up a new cosmos or supply an order secured by metaphysical principles but exposes the metaphoric foundation of the industrial cosmos and suggests a way to regain a meaningful orientation to context.

Ecology has been called a "subversive science," yet its subversive character comes not from the shifting ground of particular findings, but from orienting metaphors that challenge the presumptions of the administrative mind. As a scientific discipline, ecology often exhibits reductionist features and is perhaps marked more by internal differences and controversies than any grand, unifying ideas. Nonetheless, the scope and nature of ecological concerns also often rule out convincing causal explanations, thereby frustrating the quest for predictability and control.[72]

As the reigning metaphors of the administrative mind become insufficient guides to a complex terrain, attention turns to the advantages of a holism that stresses interdependency.[73] A key question, however, is whether the green orientation will keep alive a play of metaphors, or will end this play by transforming its orienting metaphors into fixed organizational and ethical principles of a cosmic order. When Aldo Leopold drew upon the ecological concepts of his day to proclaim the "land ethic," his point of reference was the whole—the ecological community of which human beings, other animals, plants, minerals, and so on were merely constituent parts. What was right, Leopold maintained, was what was good for the community.[74] Taken seriously, the claim would subordinate the value of diversity to the value of a larger whole, reducing the value of any individual being (human or not) to the value of its service to something larger than itself.

As part of an archetypal pattern, holistic ecological metaphors thus do not resolve issues but serve to bring neglected problems of context clearly into view. Yet is there not perhaps another archetypal pattern that could enhance orientation to context? Is there perhaps a *comic* pattern, much as

Meeker suggests, but without the need to mimic the official, comprehensive order of the Christian Middle Ages?

As the concept of the administrative mind suggests, modern rationality is itself implicitly part of an allegorical narrative that repeats the central myths of Western culture. Charlene Spretnak's *The Spiritual Dimension in Green Politics* is insightful in this regard, as she quotes the poet Gary Snyder: "Our troubles began with the invention of male deities located off the planet."[75] An earth-based spirituality with "reverence for the mysteries of the life force," Spretnak maintains, was displaced by adoration of "a remote judgmental sky god—first Zeus, then Yahweh."[76]

"Tragedy," according to Kerr, "makes a great curved arc into the heavens. . . . Comedy never leaves the ground."[77] The comic, Bakhtin has similarly suggested, brings us "down to earth," into "contact with the earth as an element that swallows up and gives birth at the same time." As related to the body, coming down to earth means focusing away from the upward, heavenly regions—the face and the head—and toward the "lower stratum"— "the genital organs, the belly, and the buttocks."[78] The world's "comic aspect," he shows, was preserved and celebrated throughout the Middle Ages in the expansive, "festive laughter" of a popular culture that stood outside and against the reigning piety and asceticism of Christian officialdom. The unbounded laughter of the earth, its "regenerating and renewing" capacity, became constricted, even forgotten, with the decline of the carnivalesque and the rise of modernity's worldly seriousness.[79]

The connection Bakhtin draws between festival and comedy in the Middle Ages recalls the age in ancient Greece preceding the differentiation and polarization of tragedy and comedy, an archaic time of pretheatrical ritual and festival, even predating the ascendancy of Zeus in a well-ordered, hierarchical cosmos. Comedy, observes a careful student of the origins of Greek theater, "takes us back to the masked dances of prehistory, beyond . . . the dawning distinctions of times, domains, and places." As the etymology of "comedy" suggests, its origins are in festival, in the *komos*, "a joyous and festive procession," enacting myths in celebration of the earth.[80]

A version of one such story reflects the rise of the Olympian Zeus in a comprehensive order of things—the patriarchal cosmos—yet also records the resistance of Demeter, the Earth Mother. Persephone, Demeter's beautiful young daughter, has gone missing. As yet unknown to Demeter, the girl has been abducted into the underworld by Hades, at the behest of his brother Zeus. Searching vainly for her child, Demeter issues a curse and the world withers: nothing can thrive, nothing can be born. Haggard and dejected, the grieving Earth Mother stops and rests. Then, along comes Baubo, the clowning belly goddess, a bizarre figure of a woman, who dances and wiggles her body suggestively: "The dancing female . . . had no head whatsoever, and her nipples were her eyes and her vulva was her mouth. It was through this lovely mouth that she began to regale Demeter with some nice juicy jokes. Demeter began to smile, and then chuckled, and then gave a full belly laugh. And together the two women laughed, the little belly Goddess Baubo and the powerful Mother Earth Goddess, Demeter."[81] Provoked to laughter by Baubo, Demeter eats and gains strength to resume her quest for Persephone. The Earth Mother, discovering the truth of her daughter's abduction, mounts a challenge to Zeus that is partly successful. She regains Persephone, except for the winter, and the springtime fertility of the earth is thus restored, thanks to laughter.

Persephone can, of course, be regarded as an aspect of Demeter, just as the Earth Mother can be regarded as an aspect of Gaia, the Great Mother, whose form was the first to emerge from the primal chaos and from whose body all differences were born. In a contemporary context, the tendency toward holism in ecology can be suggestive of a new cosmos, and the image of Gaia has accordingly been pressed into service, but not the image of Baubo, even though her ludicrous form also reveals an aspect of the Great Goddess.[82]

Far from founding a new cosmos, ecology in a key sense comically subverts efforts to fashion one. Ecology suggests human limits, particularly the limits of the human capacity to comprehend and model the world. A recognition of these limits does not await the confirmation of a scientific hypothesis, but informs the (often forgotten) nature of scientific knowledge itself as limited and tentative, as a kind of knowledge that in principle can neither assume nor finally demonstrate a comprehensive order.

The mirror of ecology, in Rodman's sense, thus does not necessarily suggest some ultimate order or harmony; disorder is also present, a touch of chaos in the cosmos, an element of the comic.[83] No doubt, there can be a place for ecocentric concern within the cosmos, but the cosmos is not closed (therefore, is not fully cosmic) and provides no permanent scaffolding for tragedy. A metaphoric mirroring in these terms can offer a place for comedy as well as tragedy in green political thought. Both are aspects, neither complete, of orientation to an uncertain, ultimately unfathomable, context. There is thus a place for Faulkner's philosophical cats, even if these cats implicitly argue against ecocentrism, or at least suggest that there is something a bit absurd about it.

Uncertainty looms over the industrial cosmos, despite the often energetic efforts of its apostles. Perhaps even more important is the enormous scope of *ignorance* that both ecology and environmental problems reveal. As Robert Gibson has emphasized, it is not just a matter of "gaps" in knowledge that further research might fill, but of a "general darkness with scattered pinpoints of light."[84] Ignorance and uncertainty provoke the question of what constitutes an appropriate "green approach to knowledge." A certain modesty is clearly called for, and it has been aptly suggested that green political thought has to question its own convictions, "to embrace uncertainty and therefore the need for constant self-interrogation on what people are being asked to believe."[85]

If ecology indicates the interconnection, complexity, and significant unpredictability of nature, we can also hold up the mirror of ecology to reveal the corresponding character of human affairs. The intricate, continually surprising maze of politics and history compels us to think always with a question mark. We must act with conviction, but with the understanding that we might be (somehow must be) wrong. That paradox provides at least one principle for orientation in a world beset by stark conceptual oppositions: certitude and uncertainty, conclusion and inconclusion, the serious and the ironic, the heroic and the ridiculous, the tragic and the comic. Viewed abstractly, such principles often seem to be either/or possibilities, fixed alternatives between which one must choose. With any pair, there appears to be an irreconcilable contradiction; one possibility excludes the other. What is left is a tragic choice.

Yet this misses the comic insight that practical life is filled with paradoxes that cannot be logically reconciled but that can sometimes be resolved through inventive action that bypasses, transcends, or unexpectedly reconfigures the abstract terms of the opposition. This possibility arises if one acknowledges that conceptual structures are not to be enshrined as ideals but regarded as inevitable exaggerations whose convenience varies with the situation. Categories, one literary theorist has said in stressing the limits of his own conception of the comic, "are only a compromise with chaos."[86] In life, if not in logic, concepts are always imperfect because they either take too much in or leave too much out.

Only when not taken too seriously do concepts help provide the kind of orientation adequate to actual contexts of judgment and action. Politics, in this sense, is a comic juggling act that defies fixed concepts. Though obscured by the polarized (often perilous) oppositions typical of political life, this play tacitly affirms a type of public life that goes beyond narrow conflicts and maneuvers. The virtuosity of the adroit political actor[87] thus helps to suggest the kind of playfulness that would be necessary (though not sufficient) for a responsible, reasonable, and civil form of public life in which we would decline to end our discourse. By invoking comedy as well as tragedy, green politics is able to anticipate this playfulness as part of the discourse of a green public sphere.

WHEN GREEN DISCOURSE TURNS TO normative issues, the focus is typically on ethics rather than politics. Criticizing this tendency, Bob Pepperman Taylor has observed that even the ethical focus tends too much toward "issues of personal consciousness" and makes adherence to ecocentrism something of a "litmus test" for being truly green.[1] Although Taylor recognizes that it is not the only position in environmental ethics, he rightly sees ecocentrism as having staked a largely successful claim to the moral high ground in green ethical discourse.

Taylor further notes a tendency toward moralistic impatience with debate and "a significant hostility toward democracy."[2] The ecocentric position in environmental ethics, he argues, presses toward a definitive conclusion: a philosophical reconceptualization of the human/nature relationship that can provide a final moral standard not to be questioned, but obeyed. The worrisome political consequence of an ecocentric litmus test, he suggests, is that ecocentrism comes to find itself "increasingly marginalized or threatened" and then "assumes the self-righteous posture of an ideological minority" (100).

Andrew Dobson's conception of green political thought, while pressing beyond a narrow ethical framework, also makes ecocentrism the distinguishing feature of genuinely green politics.[3] To link green politics with ecocentric ethics in this way is to erect a moral posture not subject to compromise with—or contamination by—positions conceived merely in terms of human interests. In making this link, however, Dobson also helps to reestablish the ancient connection, increasingly attenuated in the modern era, between politics and ethics. To recognize this connection in a green context underscores the importance, as we shall see, of reconsidering the meaning and value of politics.

Aristotle provides a common point of departure for various contemporary efforts to overcome the modern gulf between ethics and politics. Often, these efforts aspire to the shared identity of community.[4] Aristotle could take for granted a continuity between ethics and politics because he began with the polis and its ethos as a common world for deliberation and action. He could assume the shared understandings, values, and norms of a *we*, a common collective identity. For Aristotle, participation in ethical and political life was oriented by norms of human excellence, by virtues that human beings could exercise in their capacity as rational beings. Key among these virtues was *phronēsis*, a prudence displayed in practice through deliberation, judgment, and action undertaken in accord with the values and norms of the polis.[5] In modern and postmodern contexts, however, a common identity cannot simply be taken for granted.

For all their aspirations to ecocentrism, green practices obviously remain profoundly human and risk becoming exercises in bad faith if they neglect or deny their human character. This does not mean that ecocentrism, in some significant sense of the word, is necessarily incoherent or impossible, but it does mean that ecocentrism cannot stand apart either from an inescapably human center or from the cultural presupposition of a *we*. Ecocentric notions could help in constituting a *we* for ethical debate and deliberation, but these efforts remain human, indeed all-too-human.

A neglect, even an implicit denial, of human identity becomes obvious at moments of moralism in the green movement. Rather than a forthright acknowledgment of the need to nurture a common humanity of mutual respect and compassion, there is frequently a repetition of moralistic clichés in a manner that fails to recognize their parochial character. The charge of human arrogance, for example, is an especially prominent gesture,[6] but the force of this charge springs neither from nature nor humanity at large. The charge gains full significance only within a particular cultural context: the Christian portrayal of pride as a vice (the sin of the chief rebel angel no less) and humility as a virtue.[7] Competence in ethical and political practice requires more, however, than humility. Also needed is the confidence that is inseparable from responsible action.

The highly personalistic notion of ethics in green moralism tends to reinforce the modern gulf between ethics and politics.[8] An individualistic posture denies the *we*—the shared context of understanding and value—that makes for meaningful discourse in ethics and politics. The creation of this shared space and identity emerges as a principal task of green politics. It is necessary if green politics is ever to be anything other than part of a movement for social change, if there is to be a context, that is, in which green politics can be fully practiced in all its functional, constitutive, and performative aspects.

These considerations raise the question of communicative ethics, as debated in a green context by John Dryzek, Robyn Eckersley, Andrew Dobson, and others.[9] Whatever the limitations of communicative ethics, as advanced by Jürgen Habermas and others,[10] the idea draws attention to the nontrivial conditions needed simply to conduct a reasonable discussion, if not to achieve some ideal rational discourse. To reject communicative ethics would still leave the question of how there can be an appropriate context for any ethical discussion, environmental or otherwise.

For those who follow Habermas (to one extent or another), concepts of communicative ethics gain political significance in reference to the public sphere or, perhaps, diverse networks of public spheres.[11] An environmental ethics focusing on the need for an appropriate context for communicative practice would thus point, in political terms, to the need for a green public sphere. Green politics would need to focus not only on gaining immediate results, but also on developing the conditions necessary to promote its own practice.

John Rodman's concept of four forms of ecological consciousness, which we encountered in prior chapters, is particularly significant here. The concept suggests a broadening of homocentric toward ecocentric concern, culminating in ecological sensibility as an appropriate basis for environmental ethics.[12] From a communicative perspective, nonetheless, what becomes striking about Rodman's orientation is its very focus on consciousness. Shifting from the paradigm of consciousness to the paradigm of communication reveals Rodman's "ecological sensibility" to be conceptualized primarily in subject-centered terms that neglect communicative context. Inimical to environmental ethics, this neglect is clearly fatal to any prospect for a green public sphere.

What is needed, in a conceptual sense, is a break with the subject-centered notion of ecological sensibility in favor of a culturally oriented ecological ethos. The significance of the distinction is that, while the notion of sensibility focuses attention on the individual human's encounter with non-human nature, the cultural and communicative idea of an ethos emphatically draws attention to human-centered relationships as well as to human/nature relationships. With the idea of an ecological ethos, an ambivalence arises between homocentric and ecocentric orientations; indeed, it becomes difficult to specify a center.

Environmental Ethics and Responsible Judgment

In his seminal contribution to environmental ethics, Aldo Leopold bluntly states the conclusion that comes from an ecological perspective: "Man is . . . only a member of a biotic team."[13] This amounts to a dramatic reduction of humanity's place in the scheme of things as seen from the homocentric viewpoint. Human beings no longer have any privileged position; they stand on an equal footing with the other constituents of an intricately balanced whole, an ecological community, which now takes its rightful place at the center of things.

The human species is thus nothing but an element of a natural system. This fact is the lesson of ecology. The arrogant homocentric vision of nature as a hierarchy with humankind at the top is exposed as a delusion, replaced by an egalitarian vision that levels the natural order and rules out the pretensions of human reason. Once we take this ecocentric conception seriously, however, we immediately confront a remarkably ironic paradoxic. For it is a conception that decenters the human and, at the same time, places humanity at the center of things. As soon as humanity is expelled from its privileged position, it is readmitted, so to speak, by the back door. Human reason is divested of its pretensions, but placed in judgment of all being.

If human beings are to be governed by reflective judgment rather than immediate impulse, exercising restraint in their interchange with nature, then the human species would appear not to be just an element in a natural system, but something unique in nature. Alone among natural beings, human beings are deemed ethically responsible for their actions.

To see something paradoxical in ecocentrism does not mean that it is necessarily incoherent or that ecocentric ideas may not influence reflection and discussion. Awareness of the paradox simply helps avoid the notion that we humans are capable of somehow leaping out of our own skins and judging from a point of view that transcends our humanity. Full acknowledgment of the paradox is necessary to achieve a balance of confidence and humility and to foster judgments that are humanly responsible.[14]

Forms of Ecological Consciousness

Ecocentrism nonetheless remains of key significance in reconsidering the human/nature relationship and reinterpreting what it means to be human. Rodman portrays ecocentrism as a form of ecological consciousness developing both historically and conceptually from earlier forms. By his account, an ecocentric "ecological sensibility" emerges from (and remains rooted in) the more homocentric orientations of resource conservation, wilderness preservation, and moral extensionism.[15] Rodman's account is not without its difficulties, but it is helpful in considering the prospect of an ecocentric human *we* for both environmental ethics and green politics.

Resource conservation.[16] Early in the twentieth century, the movement for resource conservation arose in opposition to the waste of natural resources. This protest posed no challenge to the rise of industrialism; on the contrary, resource conservation was inspired by the same "gospel of efficiency" that inspired the movement for scientific management in government and industry. The focus of resource conservation was on promoting an enlightened use of nature for human purposes—taking into account not only immediate gains, but also the broader interests of both present and future society. Moral concern focused exclusively on the interests of human beings.

Wilderness preservation.[17] The promotion of wilderness preservation arose along with the cause of resource conservation, and the two have often been found in an uneasy alliance. At times, the case for preserving wilderness is made in terms of providing a recreational resource. However, aesthetic and quasi-religious themes pervade the wilderness preservation literature, which is suffused with images of the beauty and sanctity of nature. Experiencing wilderness becomes part of a process of self-reflection. The processes of nature without are seen also to be within. One emerges with a profound understanding that the natural order is no longer something other, but is integral to one's self: the individual becomes a human being who has sensed the meaning of being nonhuman.

Moral extensionism.[18] If resource conservation promotes prudent action toward nature, and if wilderness preservation sometimes evokes a reverential attitude, then moral extensionism demands that obligations be accepted. Moral extensionism, dedicated to the cause of legal and ethical rights for natural entities, is rooted historically in eighteenth- and nineteenth-century movements against cruelty to animals. The emphasis on rights today generally attempts to balance the human need for natural resources against a moral concern for the interests of other creatures. A central issue that emerges is where to draw the line of moral concern. Should concern extend beyond the bounds of sentient life, beyond the bounds of animal life, beyond the bounds of life? What sorts of entities, in short, deserve moral consideration? Strict homocentrism is abandoned, yet the hierarchical scale of humans, nonhuman animals, plants, and minerals remains visible. As we descend the ladder, we find decreasing levels of moral concern for *sub*human beings. With no fundamental change in perceiving nature or interpreting the human identity, the homocentric ground of ethics is preserved.

Ecological sensibility.[19] Elements of previous forms are preserved, but radically reconstituted, in ecological sensibility. We find concern about the ecological foundation of human society, a sense of continuity between humanity and nature, and moral concern for natural entities. Ecological sensibility goes beyond all of this, however, shifting its focus to natural systems—not to manage them, but to appreciate the diversity, interconnection, complexity, and dynamic integrity of their forms. Influenced though not limited by contemporary scientific ecology, ecological sensibility recognizes "that thistles, oak trees, and wombats, as well as rainforests and chaparral communities, have their own characteristic structures and potentialities to unfold, and that it is as easy to see this in them as it is in humans, if we will but look" (89).

Ecological sensibility would, if developed fully, involve a transformation in the human perception of nature together with a "revolution in ethics." The human/nature interchange would center on "a style of cohabitation that involves the knowledgeable, respectful, and restrained use of nature." There would be a "pattern of perceptions, attitudes, and judgments" that would normally render unnecessary the discussion of rights and obligations. For ecological sensibility would incorporate a moral sensibility—adhering to a principle of "noninterference with natural processes"—that would dispose human beings toward "appropriate conduct" (88).

What remains unclear, however, is how the other forms of ecological consciousness relate to ecological sensibility. Human beings become attuned to the intrinsic qualities of natural systems, their structures and potentialities, and come to discern something valuable about them—that is, to respect their "intrinsic value" and to accept as a matter of obligation "that one ought not treat with disrespect or use as a mere means anything that has a *telos* or end of its own—anything that is autonomous in the basic sense of having a capacity for internal self-direction and self-regulation" (88–89). We are told that because ecological sensibility will guide humans toward appropriate conduct, there will not normally be a need for the explicit discussions of rights and responsibilities characteristic of moral extensionism. Ecological sensibility indeed allows us to see that, with its implicit hierarchies, moral extensionism is itself morally suspect, degrading to the structures and potentialities of nonhuman, natural being.

How are we to decide or deliberate upon hard cases, though, or even identify hard cases? Will there indeed still be hard cases when the promise of ecological consciousness is fulfilled? Proceeding on the basis of a teleological conception that he hopes escapes homocentrism, Rodman proposes characteristics such as "diversity, complexity, integrity, harmony, stability, scarcity" as indicating value in natural entities and systems. Reference to such a "cluster of ecological values," he maintains, can provide practical criteria for judging among alternative courses of action and even for appraising the "relative value of different ecosystems" when priorities have to be established (90–91). To the end of the list, however, he notably adds an "etc.," as if to suggest that the range of criteria is perhaps simultaneously inexhaustible, indeterminate, and obvious.

When Rodman directly poses the question of what could justify such a cluster of ecological values, he offers a reply that is not only strikingly weak but rather peculiar in an argument that seeks to escape homocentrism: "It is," he says, "possible for human beings to hold such values." He suggests a thought experiment for people who do not: Imagine a world without such qualities. Rather than coming to a clear conclusion, however, his argument here simply takes a twist as he acknowledges that how one appraises the various values in the ecological cluster involves a "balance" that "fluctuates" in a changing context (91). Rodman is thus vague as to what justifies or even constitutes the value cluster that is to guide decision making.

Rodman acknowledges the teleological—indeed, Aristotelian—character of his conception and faces up to the question of whether the attribution of *tele*, or ends, to natural systems does not merely impose a human quality on nature at large. He denies this, but in doing so curiously has recourse to what he terms "observable fact," as if factuality were an entirely unproblematic notion and facts merely registered an objective nature in itself. More convincing and potentially significant is his ensuing claim that we can discern characteristic structures and potentialities in the natural world "if we will but look." To help us look, he suggests as a guidebook the whole of Leopold's *A Sand County Almanac* (not just the chapter on "The Land Ethic"). Here the field naturalist's wonder is expressed through an imaginative effort to portray the differing significance of things from the standpoint of other natural beings: "What melts away as we become intrigued by this plurality of perspectives is the assumption that any one of them (for example, ours) is privileged" (89).

By encouraging us to look for structures and potentialities in the natural world, Rodman invokes his central category of an ecologically informed *sensibility*. What we do not arrive at is some observable fact, but a wondrous sense of simultaneous similarity and difference: "While we can never get inside a muskrat's head and know exactly what the world looks like from that angle, we can be pretty certain that the view is different from ours" (89). Here a particular phrase of Rodman bears repeating: this is what we can see "if we will but look." Discerning structures and potentialities in nature becomes inconceivable apart from human interests and perspectives, giving rise to a creative and imaginative sensibility.

What stands forth in Rodman is the implicit idea of a human *telos*, an idea of human excellence that is profoundly human centered. If they are to achieve this excellence, human beings cannot escape being concerned with themselves and their potential, even if they are paradoxically able to fulfil this potential only by relinquishing and overcoming arrogant notions of human superiority.

The amazing human capacity to reconfigure the human/nature relationship through ecological sensibility both puts humanity in its place and reveals to human beings something about themselves that only a false humility can stop from evoking a sense of admiring wonder.[20] Indeed, one could argue that ecological sensibility, which requires a profound recognition by humans of themselves as a natural species—thus, in a sense, as nothing special—cannot develop fully without a profound recognition, minus the arrogance, of just how special (or peculiar) human beings are.

What is missed in not pressing ecological sensibility this further step is clearer understanding of what it means to be human, of how humans cannot step out of their own skins—out of the domain, that is, of human perspectives and interests. Even the bizarre effort by some humans to do so betrays their inescapable humanity. Beyond arrogance and false humility, there is the possibility of a balance between humility and confidence that fully recognizes human beings as natural beings but does not lose touch with the peculiarities and mysteries of being human. Only with such a balance can responsible human judgment be exercised individually and collectively in a way that takes human potential seriously, though not too seriously.

Rationality and Environmental Ethics

Rationality has acquired something of a bad name in green circles, and perhaps for good reason. Certainly, there is good reason if rationality remains identified with narrow-minded instrumentalism or formal analysis. Rodman may have a valid point when he suggests that the cultivation of sensibility is more important than a lot of explicit talk about what is right and wrong, good and bad. Yet it is difficult to see how one can altogether avoid rationality—and Rodman does not pretend to—when understanding, assessing, and enriching the sensibility of oneself and others. Making claims supported by reasons is not everything that is involved here, but it is certainly a part.

The positivist conception of rationality as a value-free, neutral instrument becomes untenable as soon as one grasps the Kantian insight that the very idea of rationality presupposes the autonomy of a rational being: thus inextricably linked, reason and freedom exhibit intrinsic value that demands the respect of any rational being. Of course, this idea not only founds a form of deontological ethics, but is also vulnerable to deconstructive moves that have thrown into question the modern idea of the essentially rational and autonomous subject.[21]

The problem of the rational subject was dramatically posed by Max Horkheimer and Theodor Adorno, key figures of early critical theory, in their book *Dialectic of Enlightment*. The virtues of rationality become at best ambivalent as Horkheimer and Adorno relentlessly turn reason against itself, revealing enlightenment's empty sensibility, its heart of darkness. Unrelenting rationality, trying to be pure, closes itself off from contamination, but ends up narrowing itself to the point of being irrational. Interestingly, Rodman's portrayal of ecological consciousness also addresses the problem of a sensibility twisted by the arrogance of homocentrism and inattention to the natural world. What Rodman shares with Horkheimer and Adorno—betraying common Hegelian roots—is a focus on consciousness, the sensibility of the subject, ultimately the problem of the *I*.[22]

The most prominent current effort to resurrect an unambivalent commitment to rationality follows in the tradition of critical theory, but significantly shifts attention from consciousness to communication, from *I* to *we*. In Habermas's conception, rationality is understood in communicative terms as presupposing an ethics.[23] Drawing on Habermas, Dryzek has attempted to work out a concept of communicative rationality as "green reason" while suggesting communicative ethics as a viable basis for environmental ethics. Shifting attention from consciousness to communication may, indeed, serve to overcome some of the perplexities arising from Rodman's account of ecological sensibility and allow us to conceptualize the possibility of an ecocentric *we*.

If Rodman draws our attention to ecological sensibility, what is ecological *insensibility* and how does it relate to the problem of rationality? Horkheimer offers the story of an early antivivisectionist society whose members wished to inspect a research laboratory. They received this chilling response from a researcher: "He told them that, although the animals were by no means asleep, the visitors would not hear a single sound. A simple transection of their vocal cords had deprived the animals of the ability to give voice to their suffering!"[24] The horror evoked as we imagine the silent shrieks of the tormented animals might obscure another horror. For the simple transection of the vocal cords has cut the researcher off not only from the natural being under study, but also from himself as a natural being. Simultaneously, the researcher denies the pain of the victim and deadens his own sensibility. Undertaken with apparent peace of mind, the conduct of inquiry turns into a cruel parody of reason.

The instrumental rationality of planned, systematic action in pursuit of predetermined ends[25] cannot be the whole of rationality. The very capacity to develop models of the world involves the possibility of deliberate, self-conscious reflection on one's identity, character, and commitment. Rationality also means turning the focus of attention to the very models one has constructed and recognizing that all such objectification has an intrinsic limitation: it cannot grasp one's full experience; something always is left out. A human being enthralled by instrumental rationality risks being cut off from the world of sensuous experience and reified, turned into an abstract thing. Left to its own devices, instrumental rationality lacks the critical capacity to recognize this.[26]

In a well-known passage from *Dialectic of Enlightenment,* Horkheimer and Adorno have precisely stated the price paid for instrumental rationality: "Men pay for the increase of their power with alienation from that over which they exercise power."[27] As dictatorial manipulation becomes the signature of rationality, the scar from a terrible wound marks the rational, masculine individual: "Men had to do fearful things to themselves before the self, the identical, purposive, and virile nature of man, was formed, and something of that recurs in every childhood. The strain of holding the I together adheres to the I in all stages; and the temptation to lose it has always been there with the blind determination to maintain it" (33). Horkheimer and Adorno's mythic archetype is the cunning Odysseus, who willingly exposes himself to the irresistible song of the sirens while bound upright to the mast of his ship. We witness here the terrible scene of the determined *I* maintaining itself while fully conscious of its sacrifice, tormented by "a promise of happiness" that today's narrow self can no longer hear.[28]

In their critique of enlightenment, Horkheimer and Adorno are thus concerned not only with a narrow, instrumental rationality, but also with the sacrifice of sensibility required by the formation and maintenance of the rational individual. Yet their critique remains ambivalent, for they themselves base their own discussion on a rationality aware of its limits (xiii–xv). What becomes unmistakable is that rationality is never a mere instrument, but involves commitment. In focusing on rationality in the subjective terms of consciousness and the *I,* however, Horkheimer and Adorno do not probe the issue of rationality in a context of communication dependent on the formation and maintenance of a *we.*

Consciousness and Communication

The problem of a *we* is central to the efforts of Habermas and others to develop a communicative ethics. The main point is that a rational discourse requires a "communication-community" founded upon a collective commitment to a process of inquiry and discussion that is free and open. A necessary condition for rational inquiry, in other words, is collective adherence to norms that are intrinsic to genuine communication. Force and manipulation, for example, are ruled out because their intrusion signals the point where communicative rationality ends and domination begins. Rational discourse demands, quite to the contrary, a commitment by all participants to the mutual recognition of the autonomy and responsibility of one another. Communicative rationality cannot be divorced from freedom, equality, sincerity, and understanding—the norms that underpin communicative ethics.[29]

Communicative rationality is conceptualized as an ideal, which may be more or less approximated, or flagrantly violated, in practice, but is necessarily assumed by the participants in any serious discussion. In communicative ethics, no definitive conclusion can be taken for granted on any substantive issue. What are prescribed are the principles guiding the interaction of participants in ethical discourse, primarily a principle of symmetry establishing a level playing field for all affected parties. Habermas's version of communicative ethics particularly stresses regulative principles and seeks through ethical discourse to gain agreement among the parties on questions of justice.

Yet the formalism of Habermas's approach has led to a suspicion that he has simply replicated for communication what Kant did for consciousness in founding a deontological ethics upon the presupposition of rational subjectivity. The rational *we* of Habermasian discourse thus falls under suspicion of harboring problems similar to the *I* of Kantian rationality. Each, true to a rigorous fixation on a self-contained ideal of pure rationality, appears to exclude or neglect too much. Can communicative ethics exclude deliberate inquiry into what is valuable and good? Can it neglect a cultivation of moral sensibility? Is there, in other words, not a risk that the circle around the rational *we* might be drawn too tightly, choking ethical inquiry off at its source?[30]

Similarly, does the bifurcation of consciousness and communication, of the subjective *I* and the collective *we*, not represent a false choice? Does communicative ethics not need both, in some practically significant sense of these terms? At one point, Habermas refers to "the constituents of a rational form of life."[31] But what, in fact, is needed for a rational form of life? What needs to be included or excluded?

In his book *Reason and Compassion*, R. S. Peters also invokes the idea of "a rational form of life,"[32] like Habermas apparently drawing upon the late linguistic philosophy of Wittgenstein. Peters, however, deals with rational commitment in both individual *and* collective terms, distinguishing yet relating the problems of consciousness and communication, the *I* and the *we*. The will to think and speak with accuracy and consistency is, he argues, not something to be taken for granted. To exercise rationality—even in a narrow sense of the term—thus depends not upon the absence of passion, but upon the vitality of certain "rational passions" (74). Anyone "committed to the use of reason" (75), Peters maintains, necessarily acts on the basis of some profound concerns: "the determination to get to the bottom of things, to find out what really is the case, what the correct interpretation is or what the right thing to do or think is." "Linked with this," he adds, "is the feeling of humility which is necessary to the whole-hearted acceptance of the possibility that one may be in error" (79). To call someone rational, Peters argues, is to imply that the individual is so moved by the rational passions that they largely give shape to the person's identity and character.

Peters portrays an irrational individual, in contrast, as one who reaches conclusions "on the basis of inadequate evidence" and "is a victim of prejudice and ego-centricity." The individual, being "biased and short-sighted," is insensitive to what others say; such a person is, in sum, "obtuse, wilful, arbitrary and pigheaded" (79). The kind of commitment required by rationality becomes strikingly obvious, Peters suggests, once we recognize what a rational agent simply cannot be.

The very concept of rationality harbors a notion of human excellence and implicitly advances norms that bind individuals, inasmuch as they are rational, to a mode of conduct appropriate to a rational form of life (103). Although it may be difficult, if not impossible, to imagine any human being as fully rational in this sense, this difficulty does not erase the significant practical difference between one who takes seriously the requirements of reason and one who simply does not care.

A rational form of life, more significantly, cannot be restricted to the private existence of the insular individual. Here Peters attributes to rationality an "essentially public character" such that the rational *I* presupposes the communicative context of a *we*, even when the *I* is apparently lost in thought (77–78). Rationality is, he maintains, public in a dual sense: "It is public not just in the sense that its vehicle is language whose concepts and rules of syntax are pubic possession, but in the further sense that, even when it takes place in the individual's head, it is an internalization of public procedures—those of criticism, the production of counter-examples and the suggestion of different points of view" (78). To engage in genuine discourse is to adopt an orientation to others that excludes disregard, manipulation, or force; it means treating others with care and respect. As the title of Peters's book suggests, reason becomes practically linked with compassion. This means that the ethics of a rational form of life involves not only collective adherence to procedural norms, but also a common sense of what is morally appropriate. Moral education becomes necessary for the cultivation of both individual moral sensibility and a shared ethos.

A Discursive Ethos

The norms intrinsic to the *we* of a communication-community may be questioned in the course of discussion, but they may not be violated: to violate them is to end the discussion. In other words, the norms of the communication-community can be directly criticized only by one who tacitly accepts them.[33] A collective recognition of the norms already presupposed in a rational discussion thus provides an orientation for moral education.

Practice in rational discourse is surely necessary for cultivating and maintaining a discursive ethos. In the process of openly engaging one another in discourse, people cannot remain narrowly self-centered. Mere caprice and whim are displaced by moral concern toward oneself and others. Moral education involves the individual gaze turning inward, so to speak, as people consider their own identities, but this gaze also turns outward to others, both to the members of the communication-community and to a larger context.

In a discursive ethos, we can glimpse a basis for a measure of agreement on ethical matters. Although we cannot say that a communication-community is necessarily devoted to any particular norms besides those intrinsic to its own existence, we can say that a rational form of life would require individual sensibilities and a shared ethos conducive to free inquiry and the open exchange of ideas.[34] Hence, the scope of disagreement would, in practical terms, likely be confined to a range of judgments consistent with a common moral sense. This does not mean that all moral sensibilities would have to converge to a point of common identity, constituting some undifferentiated *we*. A shared ethos, while providing the potential for agreements in ethical discourse, could well allow for significant differences among particular sensibilities and could encourage diversity as something desirable.

Although a communication-community would have to maintain relations of mutual respect among its members sufficient to allow for rational discourse, such a commitment to reason does not give any clear guidance concerning relations with the world outside the community's boundaries.[35] There are no necessary norms to guide the communication-community in this regard, none that are necessary, that is, in the strong sense that their violation would ipso facto put an end to discussion within the rational community. Strictly speaking, an ethical orientation for dealing with the external world thus cannot simply be assumed but must be considered in the course of discussion.

Yet, can no measure of agreement on this ethical orientation be expected? We are not dealing with the whims of irresponsible people, but with members of a community devoted to a rational form of life that requires commitment not only to particular norms of discourse, but more generally to an ethos. Such an ethos would practically involve not only adherence to certain abstract norms of rationality, but also a common acceptance of what is reasonable.

To speak of a communication-community is not to speak of any concrete institution, but of conditions we necessarily *suppose* to be adequately in place whenever we seek to communicate in the mode of rational argument. Abstractly conceived, the idealized *we* of the communication-community appears very much like the idealized *I* of the Kantian rational subject. The community seems cut off, utopian—out of place in an imperfect world. Yet, as soon as the idealization is viewed in a practical context, considerations of reasonableness obviously become necessary for any such community to exist. The idealized image can thus inform and guide practice through judgments that, though concerned to promote the norms intrinsic to rationality, reflect an awareness of how idealized concepts are themselves both necessary and necessarily flawed.

How are the abstract norms to be interpreted and applied in practice? Any answer to this question would have to appeal to an at least implicit notion of reasonableness. In practical terms, a rational form of life would require a context of economic, social, cultural, political, and (nota bene) ecological conditions[36] allowing for its existence. An assessment of issues arising from these requirements would depend on notions of reasonableness constitutive of the ethos. Already, then, the attention of the communication-community is drawn to a larger context. Issues arising from that larger context are part of its agenda, and members of the community would have to discuss them in the context of the shared ethos that makes their discussion possible in the first place.

Conceived as an arena in which relations of domination are in principle excluded, the communication-community offers an image against which domination can be contrasted, rendered clearly visible, and criticized. An obvious practical problem arises from the possibility that relations of domination outside the community might penetrate and distort it, that pervasive irrationality might render the community's own existence untenable. The communication-community thus anticipates a supportive economic, social, political, and cultural context, providing continuity—rather than stark antagonism—between the reasonableness of the community's own ethos and the qualities of the larger domain in which it is located. Any reasonable conceptualization of the community as a domain of rationality would have to recognize certain bounds, but not necessarily fixed barriers.

An Ecological Ethos

Rodman draws attention to different forms of ecological consciousness, but the differences seem to be recognized only to be absorbed in the form of ecological sensibility. The point is to reach a stage at which the earlier differences become reconciled and irrelevant. His entire conception indeed downplays the significance of ethical discourse, and he clearly states that the discussion of appropriate conduct tends to become unnecessary as ecological sensibility dialectically emerges.

What if we were to imagine the different positions not as forms of consciousness, however, but as *voices*? Does the rise of ecological sensibility effectively silence the voices of resource conservation, wilderness preservation, and moral extensionism? Are they left with nothing to say? By transcending the homocentrism of these earlier positions, ecological sensibility seems to be the telos, the self-sufficient fulfillment of ecocentrism. But then ecocentrism, secure in its truth, would also put itself beyond discussion.

The culturally oriented idea of ecological ethos directs attention away from individual experience toward a context of communication. It is certainly possible to imagine an ecological ethos existing outside the context of a communicatively rational form of life—maintained, for example, by tradition, myth, or dogma. But an ecological ethos could also exist together with a discursive ethos. An ecological ethos here would not be a kind of doctrine, the end of discussion, but the beginning of discussion. There would not simply be four forms of ecological consciousness, but four ecological *voices* with the possibility that even more voices might speak up. An ecological ethos could live with these differences, and the discursive ethos of a rational form of life would depend on them.

Communicative ethics might seem unavoidably homocentric and hostile to the very possibility of an ecological ethos.[37] In addressing this concern, Dryzek has drawn attention to the ecological basis that is necessary for any community and thus for the practice of communicative ethics itself. Portraying nature as "a silent partner in every conversation," he suggests it is at least reasonable that the human participants afford nature "a measure of respect."[38] It must nonetheless be admitted that nature, on this account, could in principle still be reduced to the status of merely serving a community of rational human beings.

Communicative ethics, however, is not necessarily homocentric, but simply human—as is the content of all ethical views, whether ecocentric or homocentric. As a particular human community, a rational form of life clearly has a human center and is not ruled by necessary norms in its dealings with nonhuman nature. But this does not mean that the community may not discuss ecocentric ideas and possibly adopt them. Given the community's commitment to reason, indeed, how could such a discussion be avoided?

Normative discourse in a human communication-community can clearly be concerned with nonhuman beings. This point can be made even more strongly: Human beings participating in a rational form of life could not reasonably avoid considering the moral dimension of their relationship with nonhuman nature. To do so would be to focus on the difference between the human and the nonhuman, ignoring the significance of the continuity.

A community combining an ecological ethos with a discursive ethos would need to listen to ecological voices, including those that speak on behalf of resource conservation, wilderness preservation, moral extensionism, and ecological sensibility. Other ecological voices might demand attention as well. To persist unquestioningly in the domination of nature would simply help sustain a mystification of human/nature relationships.

The very rationality of an ethical discussion hinges on overcoming such mystification. Reflection on the homocentric bias in the traditional view of human/nature relationships reveals a decided irrationality: intense resistance to fully recognizing the continuity of humanity and nature and, especially, to fully admitting the animality of human beings. Freud saw in this resistance a "repugnance."[39] Yet if rationality involves critical reflection on one's identity and character,[40] then no rational animal can avoid coming to terms with itself as an animal. Adequate consideration of the human/nature relationship would call for an ecological ethos, shaped among human beings as they collectively deliberate on their interchange with nonhuman nature.

Voices of Nature

How could a consideration of human/nature relationships be adequate? A necessary step would be identifying the relevant voices, listening to them and responding to them. The voices of nature demand a hearing. Christopher Manes, far from simply accepting the silence of nature in every conversation, in fact draws attention to the "buzzing, howling, gurgling" of a nature that has been silenced: "Nature *is* silent in our culture . . . in the sense that the status of being a speaking subject is jealously guarded as an exclusively human prerogative."[41]

Listening to the voices of nature obviously assumes an understanding of what nature is. While Manes objects to Georg Lukács's famous statement that "nature is a societal category,"[42] Manes's own view relies not just on the lessons of ecology but also on insights into culture. Indeed, his very idea of listening to nature draws upon shamanistic traditions that hold that the key to nature's secrets lies in a language of the animals, especially to be heard in the voices of birds. Without entering the complexities of constructivism and objectivism,[43] we can recognize that Manes becomes inconsistent whenever his account of the voices of nature assumes a nature in itself, observable apart from a cultural context.

Similarly, in Rodman's account of ecological sensibility, the structures and potentialities of natural systems are, he suggests, clearly observable. But to demonstrate his point—and to help promote a sensibility capable of discerning natural structures and potentialities—he makes reference to Leopold's *A Sand County Almanac*. What is strikingly obvious about Leopold's portrayal of ecological communities is its carefully crafted metaphorical character. As Rodman's account makes clear, Leopold presents no merely objective fact but a way of focusing attention, of looking and listening; and Leopold plays on the notion of objectivity when he invites people into the mysteries and insights of "thinking like a mountain": "Only the mountain has lived long enough to listen objectively to the howl of a wolf."[44] Rodman's ecological sensibility—a mixture of scientific and aesthetic categories—thus exists in a tension between the apparently literal and the obviously metaphorical.

That tension is reflected in Dryzek's explicit discussion of how communicative ethics could become green. Rejecting a "regressive emphasis" on spirituality in much green literature devoted to the resurrection of nature,[45] he directs attention to insights arising from ecological science. Not wishing to keep nature silent, he indicates how nature is easily ignored in a contemporary world exhibiting "gross failings in human perception [that] can be called into account by standards of communicative reason": "Communicative ethics," he argues, "suggests improved perception" (209). Like Rodman, he also draws attention to structures and potentialities in natural systems, taking as his primary point of reference James Lovelock's "Gaia hypothesis," a suggestion of structure and potentiality on a planetary scale. Yet Dryzek also identifies in Lovelock's account of Gaia an equivocation between "two extremes": a reductive model explaining stability in the earth's climate paired with a "surprising" appeal to spiritual imagery. Attempting to steer between these two extremes, Dryzek concludes that the Gaia hypothesis (along with testimony from a postmodern biology) "indicates that there is agency (but not divinity) in the natural world" (205).

Dryzek's aversion to spirituality in the green apprehension of nature is linked to his reasonable concern that cultural tendencies in a spiritual vein, as they become fixed in dogmatic faith, have proven to be at odds with a rational form of life. Dryzek's recourse to "agency" in nature, however, seems to assume that it could be apprehended and interpreted in a literal fashion as something objectively given. It may well be that the participants in a rational form of life would come to regard the principle of agency as a more convincing interpretation of nature than one based on images of an ancient earth goddess. However, both a model of climatic change and a concept of agency—no less than goddess imagery—remain cultural constructs that retain distinctly metaphorical features that cannot be neatly reduced to a strict, literal correspondence with an objectified nature in itself. Depending on how they are interpreted, these constructs all serve both to reveal and conceal. All remain elements within a linguistically constituted form of life; the trick in communication is knowing how to understand and assess them within the terms of that form of life.

The eclectic green search for spiritual alternatives has critically explored the major world religions, has resurrected an ancient goddess heritage, and has been attracted to the animistic beliefs of aboriginal cultures. The spiritual sources inspiring much of the green movement will surely appear dubious from the standpoint of the disenchanted modern world. What is noteworthy, however, is the very eclecticism of the green search. This spiritual eclecticism often appears shallow and artificial, but it also suggests a tendency to view traditional myths and images in an "as if," metaphorical way: to appreciate them, to be inspired by them, but not to believe in them literally with an unwavering, dogmatic faith. At least in this way, green spirituality is not necessarily at odds with the development of a rational form of life.

Dryzek stresses that communication is a natural human capacity: "We can communicate not only because we are human, but also because we are natural" (207). But the search for green spiritual alternatives can be viewed as a quest for a kind of communication, an idiom, appropriate to an understanding of human beings as natural beings. Spiritual myths and images can carry a metaphorical significance, communicating indirectly meanings that cannot be flatly and directly stated, but only suggested and evoked—meanings that can be constructed and conveyed only in a manner that is, in a word, poetic. This mode of communication is not rational argument, but it may well be needed in a form of life conducive to argumentative practices.

Leopold's call to think like a mountain pointed explicitly to his ecologically grounded argument that an extermination of wolves strips a mountainside of vegetation because of an unchecked population of deer. But his image is suggestive beyond that and can call forth human efforts to imagine what it means not to be human, to listen to nature, and to reinterpret human/nature. The "council of all beings"[46] is a device people have sometimes used to do this deliberately in a collective way, drawing both upon the kind of ecological insights offered in work such as Leopold's and upon spiritual traditions, especially aboriginal animism. A council of all beings gathers people together in a ritualistic setting, in which each person assumes the identity of a natural creature, object, or complex (e.g., a snake, a stone, a forest). Each member concentrates attention on a particular being, wearing perhaps a costume or mask, and gives human voice to the nature and meaning of that being, presuming to speak on its behalf. Such practices, combining aspects of the argumentative and the ritualistic, might appear silly and contrived, but there is no reason simply to assume that they—or something like them—cannot play a valuable role in developing an ecological ethos within a rational form of life.

The very fact that such practices are so easily ridiculed indicates that they are unable to stand without argument on their behalf. Only true believers are likely to take them on faith. If they are to be discussed seriously in a larger context, such practices would probably best be conducted not too seriously—their ridiculous character being openly acknowledged, even celebrated. More precisely, they should perhaps be conducted with an altogether different kind of seriousness, the seriousness that Bakhtin notes in the "ambivalent and universal laughter" of the carnivalesque.[47] The comic Baubo can be regarded as key to the creative aspect of Gaia, and a council of all beings may indeed be seen as implicitly recalling the archaic roots of comedy.[48]

Although spirituality often animates ecofeminism, this does not mean that a spiritually oriented ecofeminism is necessarily at odds with rational discourse. Ynestra King has identified the potential for "a rational reenchantment" as indeed defining "the project of ecofeminism": "We thoughtful human beings must use the fullness of our sensibility and intelligence to push ourselves intentionally to another stage of evolution. One where we will fuse a new way of being human on this planet with a sense of the sacred, informed by all ways of knowing—intuitive and scientific, mystical and rational."[49] Of course, this is to state more an agenda than a conclusion. What is rational reenchantment? How might all these things fit together? Questions such as these require discussion in the process of forming an ethos that is both discursive and ecological.

Argument—the explicit statement of claims and criticisms, with reasons given for each—is by itself insufficient to a rational form of life, but it remains an important test. More important than the outcomes argument, though, is the commitment that underlies it. An ecological ethos within a rational form of life remains open to question and cannot become an unquestioned ecological faith without also becoming irrational.

Communicative reason requires an understanding of the irrationality upon which the human domination of nature has been founded: a delusion of grandeur and a denial of the animal nature of the species. When the ethos supporting the domination of nature is exposed as fostering a distorted self-image of human/nature, environmental ethics and communicative ethics come to share the common task of reexploring and critically reinterpreting the human/nature relationship, of fostering an ecological ethos as part of a rational form of life.

Environmental Ethics and Green Politics

Even within a shared communicative context, an ecological ethos would harbor internal tensions and differing perspectives about what is reasonable in regard to substantive issues. For example, how could Rodman's noninterference principle be applied in practice? This principle is clearly at odds with what ecology most clearly teaches us: We are connected. What human beings do or do not do is part of a complex pattern of interdependence. Neutrality is not an option. The very existence of humanity as a natural species requires selectivity with regard to nature: what to eat, where to live, what to change, what to let be. This dictates that, for human life to continue, the integrity of certain natural forms must be violated.[50]

All sorts of compromises would be necessary, along with the need for deliberate discussion about what is reasonable and appropriate. But for the sake of this discussion, there would have to be continuing agreement on the principle of maintaining a conducive communicative context. A communicative environmental ethics cannot be exclusively concerned with substantive ethical issues of the human/nature relationship, but needs to include concerns about how discourse is to proceed in an obviously imperfect world. Because the very conditions of rational and reasonable discussion are often blatantly violated on the uneven field of human conflict, in other words, there must be concern about means as well as ends, about how to establish and maintain something approximating a rational form of life. Not only an ecological ethos is needed; so too are economic, social, and institutional conditions necessary to make the communication-community something more than a vague hope.

The ethically concerned communication-community thus reveals a clear political connection. Green politics, viewed in communicative terms, anticipates the prospect of a green public sphere, a realm of public discourse informed by an ecological ethos. For the sake of this public sphere, discussion needs to focus on the cultivation and protection of a *we* that, whatever its plurality and diversity, still provides a common world of meaningful discourse. Public debate, as an exchange of differing opinions that exposes and illuminates the multifarious dimensions of a problem, not only promotes reasonable deliberation and responsible judgment on specific issues: the practices of a public sphere themselves help constitute a common world.[51]

But what is the membership of this public? What is the principle of inclusion or exclusion? We might wish to stress the importance of permeable and indefinite boundaries, but what clearly remains is an inescapably human center—however perhaps ecocentric in its outlook—created and constantly maintained by the centripetal force of debate itself. If this human center is forgotten, neglected, or wished away, the green public sphere would tend toward irresponsibility.

The modern quest to dominate nature was guided from the outset by political metaphors, principally by images of authoritarian governance.[52] Some of the key figures in the promotion of ecocentric ideas have responded with political metaphors of their own. Aldo Leopold thus speaks of the human being as a "plain member and citizen" of an ecological community,[53] and Lovelock calls Gaia "a very democratic entity."[54] Such metaphors could well prove helpful in promoting an ecological ethos and a green public, so long as they do not lose their "as if" quality. There is a tendency in ecocentric discourse, however, to take a further step and find a way of somehow construing nature as literally a "democratic subject."

Peter Hay poses this issue explicitly in the case of a controversy arising from the designation of one-fifth of the Australian island state of Tasmania as World Heritage Area (WHA).[55] Long home to a politically vital and significant green movement, Tasmania has a larger proportion of its area so designated under the 1972 United Nations convention than any other comparable jurisdiction in the world. According to Hay, differing views on the proper relationship between human beings and wilderness underlay the emergence in the 1980s of sharply conflicting positions on the issue and a larger "anti-green backlash" (7). He focuses attention not on such obvious antigreen forces as mining and timber interests, however, but on people who have traditionally used the wild areas for recreation—fishing, hunting, horse riding, off-road vehicle excursions—and who fear this use will be limited or halted by WHA status.

The traditional recreationists particularly complained that an extensive public participation process was stacked against them, and the greens countered that the recreationists' claim to be protecting a valued cultural tradition was disingenuous, especially when it came to their off-road vehicle enthusiasm. What implicitly becomes clear from Hay's account is that there has not only been a disagreement on wilderness policy issues, but also an underlying agreement—at least in principle—on the conduct of public debate. The claims of the opposing parties implicitly appeal to intrinsic norms of a communication-community, particularly those of sincerity and a level playing field.

Hay's main concern, in the light of an antigreen backlash, is that homocentric democracy is insufficient for the achievement of the ecocentric goals of the green movement. In thus posing the question of the democratic subject, Hay distinguishes between "two democratic communities—a more restricted one, confined to humans, of democratic participants, and another far broader one of democratic subjects, embracing all of life, whose interests must be taken into strict account in human decision-making" (16).

Of course, Hay veers away from the idea—so far, limited to Orwellian allegory—that other creatures of the earth could become active in democratic politics. There seems no escaping the obviousness of the point Albert Weale makes in response to ecocentrism: Democratic decisions will "necessarily be made solely by humans." "Democracy is a discursive practice and other species, let alone other types of non-living entities, are not (yet?) able to participate in that practice."[56] Hay's political point, in this regard, turns out to parallel the common distinction in ethics between an ethical agent and a being worthy of ethical consideration: A nonhuman being cannot be conceived as a political agent but can be afforded due consideration by those who are political agents.

The question of what consideration ought to be given nonhuman beings thus becomes a focus for political discussion. But such a discussion remains emphatically human and, even if strongly influenced by an ecological ethos, clearly dependent on human interpretations of nonhuman interests. Any attempt to avoid a frank recognition of this principle would not promise to expand democracy to the nonhuman world, but would expose a latent authoritarian tendency, an impulse to secure a principle by putting it beyond dispute: "If the conception is genuinely democratic," as Weale puts it, "one cannot impose a priori constraints on the outcome of discussion and debate" (342). What Weale invokes here is not just a democratic principle but a principle of rational discourse. Although an ecological ethos is arguably also needed for a context conducive to rational discourse, the underlying point that emerges here is that an ecocentric authoritarianism would be at odds with the ethos of a rational form of life.

Green activists of course do not normally enjoy anything like a context conducive to rational discourse, and it is thus hardly unreasonable for them to adopt a strategic posture in the midst of political conflict, to employ tactical moves for the direct achievement of green goals. Concern with promoting a green public sphere, however, turns attention to opportunities that might be missed in simply seeking tactical advantages. What opportunities might be missed for an exchange of opinions that actually clarifies issues, allowing participants to acknowledge room for agreement, even to gain entirely new and unexpected perspectives?

In the Tasmanian dispute over WHA status, for example, did the recreationists have any concerns about their traditional practices that could be considered reasonable within an ecological ethos? Was the green position beyond all reasonable criticism? These questions readily arise because, as we have noted, the opposing sides both appealed to common standards of public debate. Hay's account at least suggests the opportunity for a further exchange of opinions, of claims and counterclaims supported by reasons.

Pursuing such a discussion would serve to enact, even if most imperfectly and incompletely, a green public sphere open to an exchange of differing opinions. The ethos of a rational form of life would connect the divided realms of ethics and politics. Green politics, informed by an ecological ethos, would no longer have to be defined in terms of what it opposes but could come into its own.

People are obviously capable of recognizing and respecting nonhuman interests as well as human interests. The task is not to get beyond human interests but to consider which human interests guide appropriate, or even admirable, conduct. To imagine leaping beyond human interests for the sake of nonhuman nature is a move that threatens to undermine itself—either explicitly or implicitly—through a denial of human/nature. The human being is cast again as the tragic hero who possesses a special responsibility and importance in the scheme of things. It is possible, however, to entertain a more complex, less exalted understanding of human beings and their ethical responsibilities. This interpretation would grasp the comic as well as the tragic aspects of the human condition, soliciting compassion for the frailties and fallibilities of those all-too-human beings who—all of us included—are the only potential participants in a green public sphere.

AN UNUSUALLY FRANK PUBLIC CONFESSION can be found in Mark Sagoff's book *The Economy of the Earth:* "I speed on the highway; yet I want the police to enforce laws against speeding. . . . I love my car; I hate the bus. Yet I vote for candidates who promise to tax gasoline to pay for public transportation. . . . I have an 'Ecology Now' sticker on a car that drips oil everywhere it's parked."[1] Sagoff intends his confession to underscore a crucial distinction between consumer and citizen: "The political causes I support," Sagoff explains, "seem to have little or no basis in my interests as a consumer, because I take different points of view when I vote and when I shop" (53).

Sagoff presses the point home with his example of a Disney venture to build a ski resort in the Mineral King area of the Sierra Nevada mountains in California. Surveying the preferences of his students, he found that, though many expressed an interest in visiting a Mineral King resort, almost none favored its construction (51). The consumer in them differed from the citizen in them.

The distinction between consumer behavior and citizen action is vital for efforts to enhance democratic practice through discourse and deliberation in a public sphere. To assume the role of the citizen is to enact an identity in which narrow interests and perspectives—the centerpiece of liberal politics—become marginalized. In this context, debate—the essence of politics, according to Hannah Arendt—is not merely a means by which individuals seek to achieve ends in accord with a clear and fixed ordering of their preferences. As an interchange of considered opinions, debate can foster an imaginative interplay of identities, interests, and perspectives that encourages evaluations and judgments from an enlarged viewpoint. More than political outcomes are important, for the very process takes on value for those who participate in it.[2]

The idea of a green public sphere contradicts an image of human beings as essentially consumers, sharing this standpoint with proposals for a discursive form of democracy.[3] Yet the green public sphere arises in opposition not only to the citizen quiescence of liberal democracy or to market models of politics that reduce the actions of a citizen to an expression of consumer preference.[4] What is distinctive about the green public sphere is its questioning of industrialist presuppositions, a challenge at a cultural level that serves to reconstitute what we take as reasonable.

Both by its form—a realm for democratic discourse—and by its distinctive cultural content, the green public sphere promises a way of life that reconfigures human creativity and imagination together with human/nature relationships. The promise gains credibility as a historical possibility for the simple reason that a green discourse has emerged, making it possible to formulate and discuss ideas that industrialist discourse formerly excluded or marginalized. Now that the terms of industrialist discourse have been seriously thrown into question, even put on the defensive at times, industrialism can no longer stand forth steadfastly on its own terms, but must incorporate green imagery and attempt to speak the "language of environment."[5] Slick efforts at "greenwashing" invidious corporate and governmental practices may well testify to green weakness and a potential for co-optation.[6] At the same time, though, these very efforts also proclaim the potency of a green discourse, well inscribed at the level of cultural practices, that can no longer safely be ignored.

Some of Sagoff's personal practices may be "disgusting," as John Dryzek has suggested with tongue in cheek,[7] but they can also be viewed as episodes in a green comedy lampooning the desperately insecure, possessive individual[8] that furnishes the industrial cosmos with its human fodder. Looming large in the modern world, this image of the human being is widely portrayed as representing the human essence. Sagoff's confession does not counter with an alternative image of the human essence, but does enormously complicate the situation. He simply shows that any enshrining of possessive individualism as a unitary human essence arises from a simplistic abstraction that refuses to acknowledge the obvious.

There is no doubt that the image of the possessive individual captures important possibilities of human identity and inclination. Modern civilization, indeed, was largely made possible by a cultural reconstitution and restriction of human identity to accord with the possibilities circumscribed by this image. As economic activity came to be construed on the model of a self-regulating market, the rational economic individual was no longer despised, but prized as the centerpiece of human order and progress. From Hobbes to Locke to Adam Smith and onward into the ensuing tradition, there was a curious reversal as narrowly acquisitive behavior came to be viewed as reflecting more the virtue of industriousness than the sin of greed. Indeed, the proper role of the state became that of maintaining a framework in which greed could do its good work. Mastery of nature was externalized; it no longer meant self-control of bodily passions, of internal nature—as it had with monastic discipline—but a redirection of the passions for the sake of achieving collective human control over external nature.[9] The irony in all this, as Smith seemed to appreciate,[10] was that the pursuit of happiness offered little that was intrinsically rewarding; the great human project was, in effect, reduced to a "joyless quest for joy."[11]

Despite the much-heralded freedom to choose enjoyed by the individual in modern capitalist democracies, this individual has been shaped by socioeconomic structures and disciplinary practices making for collective order and predictability. This feature of modern civilization has been achieved in no small measure by a systematic maintenance of individual insecurity that, in its turn, makes anxious and relentless striving the common denominator of those driving the motor of human progress.

The comic dimension of Sagoff's confession can also illuminate the antipolitical character of a green ethical discourse that focuses on individual sensibility and decision. Such a focus simply mirrors and inverts the celebration of possessive individualism as a domain of free choice. Drawing strength from a religious heritage that held the acquisitive impulse—indeed, all worldly passions—to be morally suspect, green ethical discourse often tends to celebrate individual restraint and sacrifice while proclaiming hope for the person's transcendence of a narrow and wayward self. This focus obviously follows a tradition that, concerned with the condition of the individual soul, taught that confession was good for it.

What is admirable about Sagoff's confession is that it becomes an anticonfession, comically deflating the impulses of green moralism. This anticonfession reveals a human comedy that might well have amused Faulkner's philosophical cats. By poking fun at himself as part of that all-too-human common run of humanity, Sagoff shows that green change on a collective level depends far less than is often supposed on the individual's propensity to do good deeds. What seems really crucial is the context of individual action, including opportunities to engage in the debates of a green public sphere.[12]

Political Debate and the Three Faces of Politics

When Arendt speaks of debate as the essence of politics, she is thinking of debate as action.[13] She does not prize the conclusions reached in debate so much as the activity of debating, its performative and theatrical features. By portraying politics as an intrinsically valuable activity, a site of illuminating and inventive virtuosity, Arendt advances a concept sharply at odds with conventional instrumental notions. She thus speaks out against the modern chorus that, in various ideological tones, demands that politics prove its value through results.

To think of politics being intrinsically valuable is so rankling to received opinion that the idea may be difficult not only to accept but even to comprehend. It is prone to be rejected as unreasonable or, indeed, preposterous— a mere aesthetic indulgence. At the very least, however, Arendt's concept has the revelatory power of an exaggeration that allows us to recognize, and perhaps enact, an aspect of politics that the prevailing instrumentalism of modern times tends to obscure and diminish. As was suggested in the introductory chapter, her concept does not necessarily compel us to exclude other reasonable senses of politics, and her general conceptualization of the active life provides a scheme that can be used in distinguishing three distinct, though of course related, faces of politics. Along with Arendt's radically noninstrumental, performative aspect of politics, we can recall two clearly instrumental aspects: the functional and the constitutive.[14]

All three aspects of politics are involved in the prospect of a green public sphere, and each calls for independent attention. To discuss the functional, constitutive, and performative aspects of green politics, however, it is important first to understand something more of the complexity of Arendt's position, beginning with her point that politics thrives only in a valued context.

Political action—valued for its own sake as artful performance, virtuosity—flourishes only in a public space defined and created for it: an arena in which individuals may as equals stand forth distinctively among one another. Arendt identifies a solicitous, persuasive form of speech as the prevailing manner of interchange among the participants in political debate. Not only is "physical violence" excluded from these relationships, so too is a "non-violent form of coercion, coercion by truth."[15] Opinion implies plurality, as distinct from the singularity of truth, and political debate involves an exchange of opinions that illuminates a common situation rather than imposing a conclusion. "In matters of opinion . . . our thinking is truly discursive," Arendt argues, "running as it were, from place to place, from one part of the world to another, through all kinds of conflicting views" (242).

The ancient Greek polis provides Arendt with her inspiration in asserting the intrinsic value of political action. Public space in modern civilization, however, lacks centrality and significance. Arendt finds the modern promise of politics only on the margins of modernity—at moments of dislocation in the status quo, particularly in revolutionary times.[16] But such times are also dangerous times. Especially with the emergence of mass society and the devaluation of politics to a mere means, there is a danger of the collapse of public space, the abolition of politics in favor of authoritarian governance or, in that uniquely twentieth-century experience, totalitarianism.[17]

Nonetheless, there is commonly a moment in revolutionary situations when the value of politics is glimpsed, typically with the temporary emergence of a form of council politics. The American Revolution provides, for Arendt, one clear example in which the value of politics was at least partially recognized and institutionalized. But this was because the American Revolution, unlike most revolutions and revolutionary movements of the modern era, did not raise "the social question," did not bring into its debates the pressing necessities of human beings in extreme deprivation. However laudable the goal of social justice that arises from the recognition of such deprivation, the historical experience, as in the French and Russian Revolutions, has been that an overriding concern with the social question presses the open space of political debate toward collapse.[18]

What is the intrinsic value of political debate? Arendt provides different answers. In *The Human Condition*, she draws attention to the "glory" of citizens in the agonistic Greek polis.[19] However, in *On Revolution*, she shifts focus to a promise of "public happiness," which was especially advanced in the founding of the American republic.[20] Elsewhere, she speaks in a similar vein of "the actual content of political life": "the joy and gratification that arise out of being in company with our peers, out of acting together and appearing in public, out of inserting ourselves into the world by word and deed."[21]

Public happiness rather than glory becomes her principal accent, in fact, as she assesses the promise of politics in a modern context. Her point of reference ultimately turns to the generational politics of the 1960s, taking the Berkeley Free Speech Movement as a key point of departure: "This generation discovered what the eighteenth century had called 'public happiness.'" Participating in public life, in other words, serves to open "a dimension of human experience that otherwise remains closed," a dimension that "in some way constitutes a part of complete 'happiness.'" It was thus, according to Arendt, that an "experience new for our time entered the game of politics: It turned out that acting is fun."[22]

Functional politics, for Arendt, would not be fun. It would not be politics at all, but management—at best, economic and governmental administration providing for the satisfaction of human needs. Curiously, Arendt takes a rather ambivalent position in regard to administration in the modern world, at times stressing its connections to deceptive and self-deceptive distortions of politics—even to the totalitarian abolition of politics—but at other times indicating the capacity of an administrative apparatus to meet human needs and thereby help to provide all with the "opportunity" to engage in a life of political action.[23] The substance, if not the name, of a functional politics is presupposed as part of the context securing a world of performative politics.

At the same time, a politics of performance cannot dispense with constitutive politics, but is literally founded and maintained through it. The establishment of a public space provides a stable framework for action with all its "frailty," "futility," "boundlessness," and "uncertainty."[24] Although violence is excluded from political debates, it inescapably enters into political foundations. In Arendt's view, order can be created and maintained only by exclusion as well as inclusion: in celebrating action in a public space, she is acutely aware that such space does not arise from the nature of things but must be constructed, humanly constituted. A space for politics—indeed, the whole artifice of human civilization—is something made; and all making, including the conceptual framework underpinning the design of institutions, includes an element of violence.[25]

The problem of foundation thus becomes pressing for Arendt, especially so as she suggests that the promise of political action in modern times characteristically comes to the fore in revolutionary situations. Indeed, a crucial ambivalence in Arendt becomes evident when, following her unique interpretation of Machiavelli's *virtù*, she proclaims virtuosity of performance to be the characteristic political virtue.[26] For, just like Arendt, Machiavelli was singularly concerned, as she in fact stresses, with the problem of foundation;[27] *virtù* for him clearly pertained not only to an art of performance, but also to an art of making: the construction, maintenance, and renewal of civil order.

A purely performative politics, valued for its own sake, would ultimately be self-referential: it would be about itself, a domain of virtuoso performances. This is what is most frustrating for many about Arendt's celebration of politics: it ultimately seems empty, form without substance, a politics without political content. It was thus left to a close friend of Arendt to pose publicly a simple but probing question about the actors engaged in the debates of an Arendtian public realm: What do they talk about?[28] Arendt seems to rule out much of the commonplace content of politics. She is not only averse to posing the social question, for example, but would also seem to rule out the issues of social policy.

Whatever content Arendt might propose for public debate, however, it is important to stress that the particular content does not really matter for a performative politics. What matters, most importantly, is that the content not undermine the potential for a meaningful exchange of opinions in a shared public space. Posing the social question carries this danger, Arendt argues, because its imperatives are so pressing that they threaten to disrupt the space of public discussion. However, her point would hold not only for the social question, as posed in the French Revolution, but for any demands that would overshadow the public shaping and sharing of opinions.

Issues of social policy, in Arendt's view, even if they threaten no disruption, still do not count as topics of political debate. The reason she gives may be surprising: it is that issues of social policy (e.g., the provision of adequate housing) are not typically legitimate matters of opinion. Arendt strikingly takes it as given that modern society ought to provide adequate housing, but even more strikingly indicates that housing needs are a matter to be determined by experts—not as a matter of opinion.[29] However naïve and startling such a trust in technocrats—and the administrative mind—may be, her position implicitly provides an opening for a rethinking of politics that includes functional and constitutive, as well as performative, aspects.

It turns out that a self-referential politics may not be so hollow after all. Arendt's very attempt to illuminate the nature of active political life by conceptually narrowing the scope of politics obviously involves a controversial matter of opinion. Even by Arendt's standards, one topic surely appropriate for political debate would be the nature of politics itself, the scope and limits of the political. Because she does not attempt to anchor her judgments metaphysically and advances them under no other guise than that of considered opinions in a world of appearances, the expression of her political thought constitutes a mode of political action—an intervention into politics about the very meaning of politics.

In response to Arendt's intervention, it seems evident that the illumination she offers by narrowing the scope of the political comes with considerable sacrifice. The problem is not simply that the focus of her concept clashes with other reasonable notions of politics, but also that her conceptual scheme deflects attention from the place of political debate in the functional and constitutive domains.

Functional Green Politics

The comforting allure of the administrative mind, its promise of rationality, looms large in the domain of functional politics. Here the traditional managerial concept of visible authority, of hierarchical command and obedience, tends to combine with notions of technocratic management, in which the rationality of an authority figure is displaced by a more anonymous systems rationality.[30] With some variant on the image of the administrative mind taking center stage, attention is in any case diverted from the inconvenient contingencies of an uncertain context.

When ecological rationality becomes a problem for industrialism, however, uncertainty unsettles the industrialist project of order and progress. The idea of a rational industrial civilization, a progressive socioeconomic system under knowledgeable guidance, is thrown into question. As the human/nature relationship comes onto the public policy agenda, a door opens for functional green politics.

Functional green politics presents a face of reform, of working within existing systems to enhance their potential for ecological rationality. This approach is of course soundly rejected by those radical greens who insist that reform measures are bound merely to reinforce an environmentally destructive industrialism. This fear, acutely focused on obvious dangers of advanced industrial society, tends to conjure up a monolithic structure and grants it too much coherence and stability, thereby neglecting the dysfunctional features of industrialism that the green movement has helped expose to public view. A fuller focus on the irrationalities of industrialism recasts the stark opposition between radical and reform orientations by suggesting that functional reforms carry, at least, an ambivalent potential: either to reinforce or to redirect established dynamics.

DYSFUNCTIONS OF INDUSTRIALISM: THE PROBLEM
OF COMPLEXITY

By drawing attention to obvious dysfunctions of industrialism, environmentalism dramatically exposes a complexity that the administrative mind would prefer to ignore.[31] There is no better witness to the inclinations of the administrative mind than Herbert Simon, who, recognizing omniscience in decision making to be a hopeless fantasy, sought to reaffirm the potential of rationality in administrative organizations by proclaiming its necessarily bounded character. For all practical purposes, Simon insisted, the "devious consequences" of complexity "must of necessity be ignored." One must assume instead the possibility of isolating "from the rest of the world a closed system containing only a limited number of variables and a limited range of consequences."[32] Administrative practice follows "a drastically simplified model" that assumes that "the real world is mostly empty," "that most significant chains of causes and consequences are short and simple" (xxix). Simon here bears witness to a key belief that has guided the administrative sphere throughout the course of industrialization: Complexity is no real problem.

Complexity, however, has become an increasingly obvious challenge to the administrative sphere of advanced industrial society, a problem duly noted even from a technocratic perspective.[33] The typical technocratic response has attempted to capture a broader range of elements and interactions through large-scale systems modeling. Yet, this kind of effort cannot escape a problem Dryzek has stressed: "Any system model, no matter how large and complicated, embodies but a single perspective on reality." Systems modeling is pulled as well between (1) the need to capture all relevant elements and interactions and (2) the need for a model simple enough to be useful. Yet the biggest problem with the technocratic response is that it proceeds with an objectivism that cannot take account of the complexities arising from human action and social interaction, especially those stemming from technocratic intervention itself: "Wholescale commitment to the approach would demand abdication of . . . control to a computer model in the hands of an administrative agency."[34]

COMPLEXITY AND COMMUNICATION:
THE PLACE OF DEBATE

Technocratic commitment to the orderly functioning and development of advanced industrial society has long dominated policy professionalism. Despite its unmistakable technocratic accent, however, policy professionalism has also long harbored countertendencies and notable democratic inclinations inspired by Deweyan pragmatism. Both Charles Lindblom's incrementalist muddling through and Harold Lasswell's contextually oriented preference for creativity count as currents that have run, at least in significant part, against the mainstream.[35] More recently, John March's promotion of a "technology of foolishness" has questioned the prevailing rationalism of the administrative sphere.[36] Now a clear tension in policy professionalism has emerged between those committed to the conventional technocratic approach and those wanting an approach that is more discursive, open to wider participation by nonexperts. The keynote of this dissenting professionalism, in a word, is debate: a dialogical challenge to the monological administrative mind.[37]

Although dissenting professionalism remains primarily attuned to functional politics—and thus a framework of reform—the discursive accent of the approach points to a constitutive prospect, more precisely a discursive redesign of policy processes and the administrative sphere. Similarly, green interventions into the functional domain, while addressing particular policy issues, also work a larger influence in both agenda setting and problem definition and through an epistemological challenge to the administrative mind. This larger influence suggests a constitutive element to functional green politics, especially where it intersects with dissenting professionalism to promote discursive redesign.

Dryzek's well-known promotion of discursive democracy principally pertains to the level of constitutive politics but also involves a dissenting policy professionalism engaged at the level of functional politics. He envisages an approach to public policy with an accent on participatory democracy rather than technocracy. It is an approach capable of grappling with problems of complexity by going beyond both narrowly analytic instrumentalism and systematic rationalism to enhance communicative rationality: "Coordinated problem-solving," he says, "will occur to the extent of communicative rationalization in the decision process."[38] Dryzek particularly presses this point home in an environmental context, suggesting that communicative rationalization offers a path to ecological rationality.

The problem-solving potential of communicative rationality, according to Dryzek, escapes the limits of an analytic instrumentalism or a systemic rationalism primarily through the discursive interaction of diverse perspectives on a problematic situation. There is a kind of debate, in a word, that enhances policy learning. Yet Dryzek's concept of communicative rationality, largely following Habermas, proposes criteria not only to guide practice but also to criticize it.

Objections to the proposals of dissenting professionalism often stress their supposed lack of practicality or, what is more to the point, political feasibility. Such an objection is relevant if one focuses only at the level of functional politics, but the issue takes on a different aspect if viewed in terms of the constitutive dimension. The concept of communicative rationality poses a challenge to prevailing practices by anticipating the institutionalization of discursive designs for decision arenas, particularly a provision for dramatically greater openness to public participation than is typically found in the administrative sphere of liberal democracy.

The very notion of constrained or distorted communication at least implicitly depends on a contrasting concept of genuine communication. Whatever problems might ultimately be found with such a concept, it at least focuses attention clearly on the difference between narrowly self-interested maneuvering and cooperation in a process that is oriented to a shared goal of understanding. Dryzek's concept of discursive designs, indeed, anticipates such cooperation as, at least in significant part, displacing the strategic interaction typical of liberal democratic politics. The examples of discursive design that can be brought to bear are no doubt sparse and imperfect, but they nonetheless indicate that communicative contexts can be designed and developed to supply incentives for a significantly better approximation to communicative rationality than is usual in policy deliberations.

With its open interplay of perspectives, communicative rationalization would, as Dryzek argues, appear well suited to coping with problems of complexity, particularly in an environmental context. But are problems of uncertainty and ignorance thus necessarily overcome, even if some ideal of communication is significantly approximated? A claim that communicative rationalization necessarily leads to ecological rationality could of course not acknowledge the frailty and fallibility of the human condition. If these are acknowledged, the most that can be claimed is that better communication is the best bet, and this in fact seems to be Dryzek's point.

ECOLOGICAL COMMUNICATION

What is better communication? In Dryzek's view, it is, first of all, communication that excludes, or at least decenters, practices of manipulation and domination in favor of an equalized, respectful interchange among participants. Such an interchange characterizes Habermasian discourse, an explicit and deliberate discussion of issues that excludes all force except the "force of the better argument."[39] Noting the clear homocentric focus of a communicative ethics restricted to human dialogue, however, Dryzek has made an attempt "to rescue communicative rationality from Habermas" with a concept of "ecological communication."[40]

Moving cautiously toward an ecocentric position, Dryzek maintains that communicative rationality requires enhanced sensitivity to the "signals emanating from the natural world." These signals call for the "same respect" we give to the signals of human beings and require "equally careful interpretation" (21). At the very least, he would argue, human beings cannot engage in ecological communication while intent on the domination of an alien nature. What is needed is an appreciation of human/nature relationships: "Of course, human *verbal* communication cannot be extended into the natural world. But greater continuity is evident in non-verbal communication—body language, facial displays, pheromones, and so forth. And a lot goes on in human communication beyond the words, which is why a telephone discussion is not the same as a face-to-face meeting" (21). Recognition of the continuity of embodied human communication with the signals of nature provides a pathway to ecological communication, which Dryzek links to scientific practices emphasizing "not manipulation and control, but rather understanding and communication." Human "communicative interaction with the natural world," he maintains, "can and should be an eminently rational affair" (21–22).

In his effort to rescue communicative rationality from Habermas, Dryzek is guided both by ecocentric ethical concern and a wish to enhance ecological rationality. Yet, by expanding the sphere of human communication to include ecological communication, Dryzek does not simply press from a homocentric toward an ecocentric orientation, but also serves to change the focus on humanity by emphasizing those embodied forms of human communication that clearly demonstrate a pervasive human/nature interchange. In doing so, moreover, Dryzek relies, quite strikingly, neither upon scientific findings nor upon formal considerations (à la Habermas) regarding the nature of communication. Dryzek clearly relies instead upon a mode of political judgment—considered opinion appropriate to a democratic debate—that is not above giving reasons but can never offer final, uncontestable proof. In this way, his position both anticipates and partly constitutes a green public sphere.

Dryzek's account of communicative rationality serves to throw into question the centrality that Habermas gives to explicit and deliberate argumentation as the ultimate test and guarantee of rationality. To restore the communicative link between humanity and nature, in other words, Dryzek

draws in genres of communication able to evoke those subtle understandings that typically prove elusive to the forceful, yet often clumsy, grasp of
direct, literal-minded argument. These understandings are not necessarily
ethereal. They are a matter of culture. Clearly, they can be shared by a
human community, and in an environmental policy context, such understandings may well prove vital to a technology of foolishness able to escape
conventional constraints and thereby frame problems for effective action in
the cause of ecological rationality.

PUBLIC SPHERE AND ADMINISTRATIVE SPHERE:
THE POLICY CONNECTION

Habermas locates the public sphere, as we have seen, apart from the state
in the realm of civil society. Discourse in the public sphere does not directly govern but influences government in an indirect fashion through the
communicative power of opinion.[41] Dryzek largely reaffirms this distance
between the state and the public sphere, though he highlights a plurality of
public spheres arising from a heterogeneous array of social movements. In
stressing their potential opposition to the state, his primary thrust is strategic. It is through oppositional public spheres that the imperatives of the
state "in the shadow of capitalist political economy" can most effectively
be challenged, or somehow circumvented, in the promotion of discursive
democracy.[42]

Habermas conceptualizes the state in systemic terms, indicating that
the discourses of the public sphere provide no substitute for the "systematic inner logic" of public administration.[43] Dryzek makes a similar move
in referring to the "structural necessities" or "imperatives" of the state in
a global capitalist context, particularly those of maintaining conditions of
economic profitability and social order.[44] By speaking of necessities, Dryzek
suggests a fixed and stable system operating according to inescapable constraints. Even though he thus highlights systemic resistance to change—
particularly change promoting discursive democracy—the whole point of
his analysis is to identify possibilities for democratization.

To find these, Dryzek shifts metaphors to speak of "pressures" rather than
necessities.[45] It turns out, indeed, that these pressures are not oriented in
any single, consistent direction, but also operate at cross purposes in the
manner of systemic contradictions. Pressures for enhancing profitability
through private accumulation, for example, are at odds with maintaining
order through social welfare. He is aware that cross-cutting purposes can
provide opportunities for apparently unrealistic change.

Dryzek recognizes that the discursive designs he celebrates are not necessarily located only in the domain of civil society: they enter into the state
as well. He indeed explicitly acknowledges "*incipient* discursive designs"
within the state.[46] However, he emphasizes that the pressures facing the

state render it a highly constrained communicative context, in contrast to the open public spheres of civil society. In the state, manipulation regularly masquerades as genuine communication, routinely undermining communicative rationality. Dryzek understands the state, nonetheless, as a sphere of communication as well as a site of systemic imperatives. This understanding allows conceptually for a point of connection between the state and public spheres, even for overlapping discursive practices.[47]

Implicitly at least, Dryzek does not conceive the state simply in formal terms as a separate seat of public decision-making authority. He evidently also understands the relationship between the state and the public spheres of civil society in more fluid, complex, and dynamic terms as part of a public policy process that extends well beyond the state. By not fixating on the state as a formal institution, one can conceptualize two discursive spheres set off against one another, as noted in the first chapter: an administrative sphere and a public sphere. Each contains its own unity and diversity, its own internal plurality of spheres, and its own communicative constraints.

The green public sphere has a complicated relationship with the administrative sphere. Often employing their own experts, for example, reform-oriented environmental organizations typically seek direct entry to the administrative sphere, to the central arenas of the policy process. If these organizations themselves begin to operate as part of the administrative sphere, they also come under the criticism of more radical, grassroots groups that picture themselves in a relentless oppositional posture. Neither light nor dark green influences, however, stand altogether apart from the policy process.

Particularly at the levels of agenda setting, problem definition, and epistemology, a complex of green influences intervenes in the policy process at a functional level, establishing particular points of interplay between the administrative sphere and the domain of the public sphere. This functional intervention carries with it a constitutive prospect. If the discourse of the administrative sphere reflects awareness of the dysfunctions of industrialism exposed by complexity, the administrative sphere will be more open to the technology of foolishness as a means of enhancing adaptability. Under such circumstances, the voices of the green public sphere will be more clearly heard in the administrative sphere. An adaptable administrative sphere, of course, may well avoid both functional and constitutive change toward substantial greening, but such change at least becomes a more imaginable possibility.

AMBIVALENT POTENTIALS OF SYSTEM ADAPTATION

The systems metaphor looms large in the domain of functional politics, often part of a technocratic idiom employed to contain dissent while reaffirming the established order and dynamics of power. The apolitical, managerialist discourse of policy professionalism constructs its context as a stable system that merely requires reliable maintenance through a regulated cycle of inputs, throughputs, and outputs. However, the systems metaphor contains an idea of dynamism that suggests no system imperatives are altogether fixed: systemic relationships are continuously produced and reproduced through a process that cannot rule out change.

Employing a systems-theoretic model to disclose surreptitious, even unconscious, alignments of power, Peter Bachrach and Morton S. Baratz have helped recast the meaning of inputs, throughputs, and outputs in a political system. Their model also suggests a way of understanding more precisely the relationship between functional and constitutive politics. They portray actors, employing different sources of power, who attempt either to maintain or to change existing patterns of policy outputs. The actors seek entry to a "channel of policy choices," but access to the actual decision-making arena requires overcoming both ideological and organizational barriers. The actors try, in other words, to make "inputs" into decision making, but entry can be routinely, even automatically, denied by prevailing "values, myths, and beliefs" or by "procedures, customs, and institutions."[48]

Those who seek change usually confront a "mobilization of bias" that tends to exclude interventions threatening the established order of things.[49] Typically excluded are radical departures in agenda setting and problem definition, as well as epistemological challenges that could upset prevailing criteria of policy knowledge and procedure. The stronger and more pervasive the exclusions, the more they appear to follow systemic imperatives of the established order. Under changing circumstances, however, such imperatives can become incompatible with one another and thus self-defeating to the system. This not only is the chief insight of the Marxian notion of contradiction, but also is a commonplace of systems theory concerned with the adaptability of dynamic, open systems. By advocating a technology of foolishness to counter the rigid rationalism of the administrative sphere, March offers a remarkable example of a deliberate effort to enhance the adaptability of systems whose very orderliness threatens to become dysfunctional.[50]

Without some explicit or implicit criteria of meaning establishing the identity of a system, systems theory lacks the ability to say when functional adaptation becomes a transformation of the system at a constitutive level. Efforts to enhance the adaptability of a system may also initiate or reinforce patterns of activity with consequences that go beyond what is intended. In Bachrach and Baratz's model, the pattern of inputs and throughputs produce effective policy outcomes that loop back to increase or decrease the sources of power that can be brought to bear by actors engaging the policy process.

Apparently minor adjustments can thus enter into a larger pattern of unexpected and unintended results. An effort to add adaptability to a system particularly carries an ambivalent potential: the outcome depends on a context—of politics, culture, and history—that mocks any effort at comprehension and control. Of course, a challenge to system imperatives will provoke a panoply of defense mechanisms. But no one can say in advance that the defenses will be effective. More to the point, no one can say that the defenses will play out in a way that necessarily protects a coherent and cohesive system from undergoing a transformation. The problem is not simply one of indeterminate identity or of human ignorance, but also is a matter of possible incompatibilities—contradictions—within the system that, in effect, set it against itself.

Even within the conventional policy literature, incrementalism heralds an ironic "science" of muddling through that provides a reminder of disjointed, contextual contingencies that demand adaptability rather than synoptic rationalism. Although characteristically understood and practiced as a cautious, step-by-step approach that rules out major change, incrementalism in principle simply rejects the idea that major policy departures—or, indeed, historical transformation—can be comprehensively planned and executed: change inescapably exhibits adaptive patterns, however much these might be obscured by rationalistic expectations and imagery.[51]

POLICY DISCOURSE: THE QUESTION OF
ECOLOGICAL RATIONALITY

By drawing attention to ecological irrationalities of industrialism, green politics promotes ideas for a wide array of policy responses at a functional level. The ideas involve a well-known assortment of policy tools—market-based, command-penalty, persuasive—as well as anticipatory mechanisms such as environmental impact assessment and new institutional arrangements to focus attention on environmental problems.[52] The big question for policy discourse, however, is whether any combination of such responses will, in the long run, add up to ecological rationality. The notion of sustainable development, focusing attention directly on this larger question of ecological rationality, has elicited both rationalistic and incremental strategy proposals, as well as competing visions. Ecological modernization is a slogan that even more explicitly addresses the question of ecological rationality in a context of functional politics.

The meaning of ecological modernization is contested, but the basic idea involves both a critique and endorsement of modernity. The critique lies in an acknowledgment that the process of modernization has, to date, issued in obvious ecological irrationalities, that even early efforts to grapple with environmental problems have been marked by a neglect of ecological interdependencies and complexities. The endorsement lies in the notion that a process emerging from modernization itself could ensure ecological rationality. Central to this idea is confidence in the capacity of advancing technology to achieve ecologically appropriate technological systems, designed to avoid waste and pollution by dramatically reducing the total use of energy and material, particularly in the form of hazardous substances. But is there any basis to this confidence other than renewed faith in the irresistible momentum of progress?

Ecological modernization can be portrayed simply as an outcome of market dynamics, a result that comes automatically so long as the market operates according to undistorted price signals. Although certainly simplistic, this position underscores the important point that technological development under capitalism is tied, to a significant extent, to calculations of benefits and costs in a competitive context.

The potential for environmentally friendly technology is enhanced to the extent that technological innovators and developers take environmental costs into account in their designs. Celebrating the magic of the market, however, typically fails to recognize that the externalization of costs is not something separate from market dynamics, but is a direct (and often deliberate) consequence of market behavior.[53] Industrial capitalism has not resulted from some innocent market dynamic, but from a historical complex of power relationships, centered in the administrative sphere, that has given shape to the actually existing market (in contrast to textbook fantasies) and has promoted a particular pattern of technological development.

Recognizing the actual potential of ecological modernization requires clear attention to the context of power. Indeed, the very ability to imagine ecological modernization as a possibility arises from the influence of green politics on the routine operations of advanced industrial society and on the normal functioning of the policy process. Ecological modernization obviously requires the extraordinary ingenuity of human technological design. Clearly, as well, this ingenuity can be mobilized on behalf of environmentally friendly technology in a context of market competition, provided that price signals transmit the appropriate incentives *and* that the design process is guided by a recognition of ecological interdependencies and complexities. For these conditions to be met, the market would not suffice and industrialist fantasies could not go unchecked. The impact of green politics on the discourse and outcomes of public policy becomes crucial—as can be seen in places, such as Germany, where ecological modernization has been most clearly advanced.[54]

In the promotion of ecological modernization, there is a marked tendency to move immediately beyond the critique to reaffirm modernity. The overriding idea is that ecological modernization serves to get progress back on track, only in a more intelligent, ecologically rational way. The critique of modernity contained in the idea of ecological modernization nonetheless serves to promote a questioning of the meaning and desirability of progress. The recognition of ecological irrationality tends to throw into question not only the means but also the ends of progress: modernity appears flawed and incomplete by its own standard of rationality because the irresistible momentum of progress rules out rational deliberation over its purpose and direction. It is thus that Maarten Hajer, under the influence of Habermas, has raised the prospect of discursive ecological modernization, a process of development shaped by public deliberation on both ends and means.[55]

A discursive process of ecological modernization would have to involve both functional and constitutive aspects of green politics. Clearly, the administrative sphere would have to change, extensively employing discursive designs and opening its policy deliberations decisively to green influence. No spontaneous opening can reasonably be anticipated, however, even though there have been significant green achievements to enhance public involvement in environmental policy. Any opening, not to mention transformative greening, of the administrative sphere would require persistent struggle by an array of green political actors. Direct green intervention in established policy arenas would not be enough. The discourse of an expansive green public sphere would also be needed in the broader context of the policy process.

Constitutive Green Politics

Constitutive green politics vacillates between systematic affirmation and systematic negation of the established order[56]—between, in other words, two basic strategies: either making adaptive changes or seeking total social transformation. Constitutive green politics thus varies in relation to functional politics, tending either to reproduce or transform prevailing patterns. Within these two general tendencies of reformism and radicalism, however, are some complex and significant variations.

VARIETIES OF REFORMISM AND RADICALISM

Despite their differences, reformism and radicalism can both proceed from a standpoint of synoptic rationalism. Even though it seeks to reform rather than transform things, technocratic reason bases its legitimacy on a systematic survey of policy options and a supposed ability to master all things by calculation. Comprehensive radical strategies for social transformation are similarly rationalistic, offering something of a mirror image of technocratic reason.

By adopting an uncompromising posture, green radicalism serves to highlight the danger that green reforms might well be absorbed and rendered ineffective by the established order. Against reformism, green radicals emphasize the need to thoroughly transform prevailing institutions and ways of viewing the human/nature relationship. In the absence of coherent and plausible programs for radical transformation, however, desperate scenarios of crisis and catastrophe become inviting: "The very best thing for the planet," one radical green has thus declared, "might be a massive worldwide economic depression": "Amid the terrible hardships this would create for countless people, at least the machinery would stop for a while, and the Earth could take a breather."[57] Needless to say, this repugnant hope ignores the obvious range of potential consequences arising from such a scenario. Social insecurity and human misery could intensify human conflicts and promote neglect of environmental concerns as people desperately sought to protect themselves; there could also be increased terrorism, even warfare of a type and on a scale that would prove enormously destructive to life on Earth.

To the extent that reform and radical postures remain steadfast in their commitments either to affirm or negate the basic order of things, these positions are inclined toward exaggerated totalizations. Occupying a space between the poles of systematic affirmation and systematic negation, *radical reformism* undermines these totalizations. It is attuned neither to narrow political feasibility, as normally conceived in policy professionalism, nor to some sweeping program of comprehensive change, but to subtle points of vulnerability in the established order, to possible changes that, though not directly challenging the established order, could gradually lead to radical change.

Radical reformism thus seeks to fill the gap left by the perplexing lack of a coherent and plausible strategy for comprehensive transformation. The approach, nonetheless, typically aspires to a comprehensiveness of its own, to a strategic posture able to survey the whole sufficiently to identify false paths and to provide reliable direction either to a cohesive green party or a unified green movement. Radical reformism, in other words, continues to have recourse to a stable strategic center, to an image of the administrative mind.

Quite in contrast, incremental reformism—long posing a challenge to technocratic policy professionalism—gives thought neither to radical change nor to comprehensive plans determined by a strategic center. Incremental reformism instead places confidence in adaptive processes involving a plurality of actors. This approach to policy professionalism bears a remarkable resemblance, in this regard, to an emerging approach to radical change.

Disillusionment with prior theory and practice of radical change has given rise to a decentered approach to social transformation. This approach to transformative politics has particularly been developed to avoid problematic features of the Marxian legacy. Abandoning dependence on a strategic center, as we have seen, such transformative politics is oriented by a counterhegemonic posture toward established institutions and by the goal of radical democracy.[58] Neither the source nor the character of this opposition is homogeneous; it involves diverse social forces that resist efforts at comprehensive coordination and direction. The approach dispenses altogether with a centralizing move and strategically relies on the emergence of a decentered hegemony through the complementary interplay of heterogeneous social movements.

INCREMENTAL RADICALISM: A DECENTERED "STRATEGY"?

Green ambivalence between incremental change and radical opposition does not necessarily require a definitive resolution through some either/or decision. The always shifting ground of public discourse suggests another approach. The prospect emerges of an environmentalist strategy, decentered in its orientation, breaking decisively with the epistemological presuppositions of the administrative mind. The ambivalence and tension of a diverse green movement might thus be retained within the general orientation of an *incremental radicalism.*

The possibility of a conceptual linkage between reformist incrementalism and transformative radicalism arises because both possess a decentered character. Still, as contrasting orientations, the two appear to be worlds apart. The one stresses accommodation and compromise within existing institutions; the other, confrontation and refusal. One is a world suited to the reform-oriented environmental professional; the other, to the radical green activist. Each position, nonetheless, is attuned to differences and to an interplay of divergence and adaptation within a context of plurality and diversity. From a certain perspective, then, incrementalism and radicalism can be imagined as complementary aspects of a decentered approach, even though determined opposition between them typically remains the rule.

Current departures in policy professionalism, as noted in chapter 4, promise to make dissenting voices more significant in policy discourse. One radical response to this possibility would be to reaffirm a rigorously oppositional stance, rejecting any incrementalist tendencies. Yet another possibility, however, would be to avoid the temptation—against which theorists of transformative politics often warn—to think in exclusionary terms and to imagine that social change can be directed from some untainted posture of theoretical purity. This possibility suggests the need for a flexible orientation, for a greater appreciation of irony and paradox. The potential for even a partial convergence of dissenting policy professionalism with a decentered transformative politics at least throws into question a stance of pure and simple resistance, even though the rationale for a strong oppositional accent is certainly not eliminated.

Contemporary environmental policy, though shaped through its institutionalization in the administrative world, at least partly remains the achievement of an environmentalism critical of this world and its industrialist orientation. The radical critique is right to emphasize that established institutions have an enormous capacity to absorb and reshape divergent initiatives. However, it is a mistake to think that any such initiative is somehow intrinsically destined to suffer this fate, for the outcome depends on the dynamics of a broader context of forces, of which green radicalism is itself a part. Within this context, the contention between incremental and radical approaches may be expected to have results that no single party could predict or control.

Even to speak of a decentered strategy, to introduce a term like incremental radicalism, appears of course to anticipate a comprehensive point of view and thus to betray confidence in rational strategy. Yet this is no unbounded confidence, for the approach offers question marks rather than guarantees. And the opposition between incremental reform and transformative radicalism is not going to disappear simply because it becomes possible to conceptualize a mediating ground between them.

A decentered strategy is really not a *strategy* at all in the conventional sense of the word, for it cannot—with any specificity—tell what is to be done, what is to be undone, or even what the ultimate goal is. Thinking in terms of a decentered strategy, however, can expose the limits of fixed positions and conventional strategic thinking while enhancing contextual orientation and warning against the overconfidence of true believers. This warning also readies the ground for an enhancement of the green public sphere.

A NET THAT WORKS: BETWEEN MOVEMENT
AND PUBLIC SPHERE

A decentered green strategy has emerged with the practices of the environmental justice movement, which is characterized neither by centralized organization nor by common adherence to doctrinal beliefs, but by a "networking across issues and groups" that binds together an "eclectic pluralism."[59] Focused on the grassroots, the networking of environmental justice links locality to locality in both national and international contexts. Networking, as David Schlosberg has argued, mobilizes diversity as a "countermeasure" to mobile arrangements of power, particularly to the capacity of capital to shift rapidly from one locale to another within increasingly globalized relationships of political economy.[60]

Because of this kind of networking, the environmental justice movement can celebrate itself as a "net that works."[61] The image of Jonathan Swift's Lilliputians using a multitude of threads to tie down the giant Gulliver has been invoked to characterize the orientation of the movement as a whole:

"At the core of the Lilliput Strategy is [a] process of linking together a net out of a variety of otherwise isolated groups, communities and issues, and putting that net to work."[62] The idea of a net that works highlights the potential of the environmental justice movement to be instrumentally effective. The effectiveness of environmental justice as a movement arises because of interactions in different contexts and levels of political action, interactions serving "to generate real forward motion."[63]

The practices of the environmental justice movement thus tend to substitute the image of a decentralized network for a centralized organization. The attention of the discourse, however, remains fixated on the metaphor of movement, particularly movement that presses forward to achieve a goal on the horizon. The fixation is metaphorically peculiar because, though networks may well grow and expand, they do not move forward. The image of moving forward subordinates a network to ends beyond itself, but these are ends that could not be served by the network unless it had first been spun as a fabric of communicative exchanges—relationships valued, that is, at least in part for their own sake.

The First National People of Color Environmental Leadership Summit was held in Washington, D.C., in 1991. Although culminating in a collective commitment to "a new movement" for environmental justice,[64] the summit dramatically featured the emergence of respectful communication across differences of race, gender, region, and culture that had previously led to division. Participants remarked on "the openness to difference, the listening to others, the mutual respect, solidarity, and trust that were both expressed and affirmed at the conference." "Difference was forged into unity," Schlosberg concluded: "Participants entered diverse; they left both diverse and united."[65] The summit, in Dryzek's terms, was clearly an instance of discursive design in civil society, part of a larger, emerging public sphere. Networking in the environmental justice movement both depends on the communicative relationships of such a public sphere and has the capacity to strengthen them.

The environmental justice movement has often been defined in opposition to other elements of the green movement, particularly to environmentalism conceived as a white, middle-class movement concerned with protecting environmental amenities, conserving natural resources, and preserving wilderness. This kind of environmentalism is readily portrayed as having conspicuously ignored environmental injustice. Especially in an America that has yet to live down the slavery of its past, the charge of environmental racism has been potently effective in promoting the cause of environmental justice. But it is notable that environmental justice is typically promoted by exposing blatant injustice, particularly injustices visited by human upon human. The very phrase environmental justice achieves an irresistible discursive impact by asserting a demand that no decent person could oppose.

An unquestionable phrase can be remarkably helpful in promoting the instrumental effectiveness of a movement. But such a potent phrase can also become a slogan closing off discussion and undermining the potential for open discourse in a public sphere. The phrase environmental justice exhibits an ambivalence in this respect. As a unifying symbol, these words set the concerns of environmental justice off from the green movement as a whole. The words indeed have often resounded as an accusation against environmentalism, protesting its insensitivity to human injustice while tending to denigrate key green concerns about ecological rationality and ecocentric values. Environmental justice as a movement, however, has a decentered and diverse character that is significant for its discursive practices.

Drawing attention to manifest injustice rather than proclaiming an ideal of ultimate justice to be righteously pursued, the movement has allowed for an exchange of diverse perspectives. This was especially evident at the First National People of Color Environmental Leadership Summit. The summit significantly brought urban-based African American activists together with American aboriginal activists. By Paul Ruffin's account, the effect of the encounter was dramatic. After he had long felt bitter about the typical focus of white environmentalist concern, his exchanges with aboriginal participants allowed him for the first time to feel "the moral imperative of protecting animals and trees and land."[66] In the end, the summit's "Principles of Environmental Justice" not only supported "ecological unity and the interdependence of all species," but also proclaimed "spiritual interdependence on the sacredness of Mother Earth."[67] The open-ended notion of environmental justice, in other words, allowed for mutual questioning, a discourse in which participants could perceive and transcend the narrowness of their positions without abandoning their key insights and commitments. Such a discursive enhancement of standpoints within environmental justice also suggests a broader potential for enriching discourse in a green public sphere.

Although perhaps bitter, the accusation in the phrase environmental justice was not simply a condemnation but also a challenge throwing into question the meaning and commitment of environmentalism. The accusation, that is, was also a provocation, at least implicitly the initiation of a debate. There are signs the debate has been joined. As a consequence, the green movement has broadened and become more diverse, though not necessarily more cohesive as an instrument. There has been no final agreement, but there has been enhanced potential for meaningful disagreement. The effect of environmental justice as a decentered movement, in other words, has not only been to broaden and further decenter the green movement, but has also been to expand and reinforce the emergence of a green public sphere.

A constitutive green politics of incremental radicalism cannot escape ambivalence, but the ambivalence can at least be conceptualized and acknowledged. In this context, there can be neither an instrumentalist application of knowledge nor a dialectical unity of theory and practice. The possibility of conceptualizing incremental radicalism as a strategy is not, though, without practical potential.

Theorizations enter into practice, but there remains a disjunction between theory and practice. The very ambivalence acknowledged by incremental radicalism presupposes diversity rather than unity—a plurality of interests, perspectives, purposes, and approaches that contend and conflict as well as coalesce. Conceptualizing incremental radicalism means understanding the practical limits of the position. The position can be advanced as *one* needed in the present historical context without assuming that the theoretical validity of the position entails a need to eliminate other positions.

As a paradoxical antistrategy, incremental radicalism depends in practice on quite the opposite—on no one position, *even itself,* becoming fully dominant in the discourses of theory and practice. The approach thus embraces diversity, but cannot celebrate to the extent of guaranteeing some ultimate harmony or happy ending. The ambivalence within incremental radicalism spells theoretical self-limitation, a lack of closure, loose ends, which rule out practical guarantees—which, in fact, indicate that such guarantees are not worth the paper they are printed on.

The approach does not demand a focus in green politics that is either fully constitutive or fully functional, but recognizes that the two aspects of politics are interrelated. Significantly, the constitutive dimension of incremental radicalism is consistent with the needed inclusiveness and diversity of a green public sphere but does not signal a lack of critical judgment.

The propensity for advanced industrial society to co-opt and absorb oppositional elements is clear enough. This does not argue for the insignificance of incremental changes in that form, however, but for the importance of a radical opposition to counter co-optive tendencies and to maintain a tension, without which the administrative mind would be prone to close in further upon itself. Emerging tendencies toward new forms of environmental policy are not inherently destined to be stillborn, but have ambivalent potentials that depend on largely unmanageable contexts.

Clues for intervention are indeed evident in the apparent dysfunctions of industrialism. Slogans like sustainable development and ecological modernization cut both ways. They suggest that development is sustainable and that modernization can be ecological; they thus promise solutions that do not necessarily disturb the fundamental dynamics of industrialism. Yet, in promising solutions, they also acknowledge a problem, a deficit in the rationality of advanced industrial society. They acknowledge that this social form is not, at least yet, ecologically rational. The slogans thus serve both to reinforce prevailing assumptions and to open a space where disputes are possible over the viability, desirability, and meaning of development and modernization.

Ecological modernization, as we have seen, partly suggests that deficits in ecological rationality arise from a lack of sufficient modernization. The likely remedy would thus seem to be little but a prosaic functionalism: more of the same. Indeed, the notion of ecological modernization typically involves intensified reliance on capitalist market relationships in a global context. The discourse of ecological modernization appeals, at least in significant part, to the impetus that competitive economic relationships give to technological innovation. With appropriate incentives, technology assumes the lead role in achieving ecological rationality.

The inconvenient question that thereby arises from this appeal to the market, however, is why incentives have not—yet, at any rate—proven ecologically appropriate. No one seriously suggests that consumer enlightenment, by itself, will secure the path of ecological modernization. Typically, there is instead a reliance on state—or, in an international context, quasi-state—institutions of governance to steer the market in an appropriate direction, either directly or indirectly.

The only conceivable alternative to such state involvement would be the creation of a more perfect market.[68] At first glance, a celebration of the free market seems simply to reinforce the status quo, particularly to fit nicely with corporate demands to "free enterprise" from the costs and inconveniences of regulation and social welfare. However, the celebration of an idealized market, though undoubtedly naïve about actual relations of power, implicitly points to the patterns of public and private power that have shaped the project of industrialization.

Perfecting the market would require the abolition of both public *and* private power in the market, and this would mean a radical transformation of power relationships on a scale that free market advocates do not fully contemplate.[69] The necessary challenge to power is but mildly suggested when green activists vociferously oppose such things as the state promotion of nuclear power, the state-sponsored clear-cutting of rain forests by giant corporations, the construction of new airports and superhighways, diplomatic and military interventions to secure the oligopolistic control of oil, the monocultural practices of agribusiness oligopolies, and the development policies of quasi-state international agencies. A serious effort to perfect the market would, in the end, tend to undermine itself by throwing into question *what the market really is*. What is left of the market, indeed, if it is considered detached from the ensemble of vast public and private power that has historically promoted, shaped, and defended actually existing capitalism and its spectacular wealth?

There has perhaps never been a more ironic statement on capitalism than *The Communist Manifesto*, an irony that Gramsci grasped when he interpreted Marx as once having said "that no society breaks down and can be replaced until it has first developed all the forms of life which are implicit in its internal relations."[70] Inasmuch as it relies on the dynamics of capitalism, ecological modernization in this light can appear as being something more than business as usual, as being potentially part of an incremental process of radical change. At least, ecological modernization is not merely an adaptive response to the dysfunctions of industrialism, but also an opportunity to contest the meaning and desirability of modernity.

The possessive individual—motivated by some combination of insatiability, insecurity, and the work ethic—remains the centerpiece of contemporary political economy. Policy discourse typically presupposes this action type, this model of the actor, to the extent even of supposing this one peculiar construct of history and culture to be a full portrait of humanity.[71] Yet, if technological change exacerbates unemployment to the point that prevailing approaches to social policy lose their credibility, the stage will be set for a serious consideration of significant policy departures. Proposals to guarantee a basic income for all citizens, as discussed in chapter 4, provide one example of a policy initiative with the potential to alleviate dysfunctions of industrialism while at least partially attenuating the practical importance of possessive individualism.

No automatic radical transformation, of course, can be expected to come from such a policy initiative. However, deliberations on its design and implementation would set the stage for forms of political action promoting a cultural reconstitution of the human identities and motives that now prevail in advanced industrial society. A social policy that served to alleviate the threat of unemployment by partially decoupling income and work performance would also tend to diminish the kind of social insecurity and moralistic stigmatization long maintained by the welfare state (and simply reinforced by recent neoconservative policies). Such a change in social policy would place the meaning and purpose of work squarely on the agenda of public discourse.

The idea that "we work too much" for our environmental good also sets the stage for a green discourse on social policy and the work ethic.[72] Beyond that, policy change to alleviate the anxieties of the possessive individual could help in constituting the green public sphere as a domain for free, equal, and open discussion.[73] With greater free time and a reduced need for constant employment, there would indeed be greater opportunity for enhanced discussion in a green public sphere.

The image of the administrative mind suggests a unity, a guiding intelligence, that conceives and directs the path of historical development. Yet, despite the advent of a world of administration revolving about concentrated economic and state power, this world was not constructed simply according to the plans of centralized powers but also through an apparently complementary ensemble of particular practices, involving painstakingly detailed work, initiated to resolve specific problems of order arising from power relations in diverse arenas of economy, state, and society.[74] If the present order has risen from a pattern composed of such contingent elements, then it also makes sense to conceive any possible transformation of this order as proceeding according to a similar pattern of planned, unplanned, and fortuitous events ultimately beyond anyone's full comprehension or control. Does anything more orderly not defy the limits of credibility?

Performative Green Politics

What is the purpose of green politics? It makes sense to think of a functional green politics promoting reforms to alleviate the ecologically irrational dysfunctions of industrialism. It also makes sense to think of a constitutive green politics devoted to transforming the existing order after the model of some kind of ecological utopia. All sorts of combinations of functional and constitutive green politics would also at least make sense, whether or not one agreed with them. But the very idea of a performative green politics valued for its own sake, with no purpose outside itself, seems bizarre — virtually a contradiction in terms, a denial of all that makes green politics important. What becomes of any concern with ecological rationality? What, moreover, becomes of ecocentric concerns? Would valuing green politics for its own sake not merely render it ineffective for green purposes while reinstating a human institution at the center of things?

WHY POLITICS?

To recall the homespun remark of an American president (made in quite a different context), a lot depends on whether you can imagine being able to walk and chew gum at the same time.[75] Arendt accentuates the intrinsic value of politics as performative artistry, but this value can be acknowledged, even celebrated, without denying the extrinsic value of what can be achieved through functional and constitutive politics.

One rationale for Arendt's emphasis on the intrinsic value of politics is that this value has been so neglected by modernity that politics itself is threatened. Without a celebration of the intrinsic value of politics, neither functional nor constitutive political activity has any apparent rationale for continuing once its ends have been achieved. Functional politics might well be replaced by a technocratic management of advanced industrial society. A constitutive politics intent on social transformation might well be eclipsed by the coordinated direction of a cohesive social movement. In neither case would any need be left for what Arendt takes to be the essence of politics: there would be no need for debate.

Green authoritarianism, following in the footsteps of Hobbes, has been all too ready to reduce politics to governance. Similarly, proponents of deep ecology, usually vague about politics, at least have been able to recognize totalitarian dangers in a position that disparages public opinion in favor of objective management.[76] Any attempt to plot a comprehensive strategy for a cohesive green movement, moreover, ultimately has to adopt a no-nonsense posture while erecting clear standards by which to identify and excommunicate the enemy that is within.

Green politics from its inception, however, has challenged the official-dom of advanced industrial society by invoking the cultural idiom of the carnivalesque. Although tempted by visions of tragic heroism, as we saw in chapter 5, green politics has also celebrated the irreverence of the comic, of a world turned upside down to crown the fool. In a context of political theater, instrumentalism is often attenuated, at least momentarily displaced by a joy of performance. The comic dimension of political action can also be more than episodic. The image of the Lilliputians tying up the giant suggests well the strength and flexibility of a decentered constitutive politics. In a functional context, green politics offers its own technology of foolishness in response to the dysfunctions of industrialism, even to the point of exceeding the comfortable limits of a so-called responsible foolishness.

Highlighting the comic, these tendencies within green politics begin to suggest an intrinsic value to politics. To the extent that this value is recognized, politics is inimical to authoritarianism and offers a poison pill to the totalitarian propensities of an industrialized mass society.[77] To value political action for its own sake, in other words, at least has the significant extrinsic value of defending against the antipolitical inclinations of modernity. But what is the intrinsic value of politics? Arendt would locate this value in the virtuosity of political action, particularly as displayed in debate. Although political debate surely has extrinsic value,[78] this does not exhaust its value. Debate is a language game that, to be played well, cannot simply be instrumentalized for the services it can render but must also be played for its own sake. Any game pressed into the service of external goals tends to lose its playful quality; it ceases to be fun.

It was in reflecting on the social movements of the 1960s that Arendt proclaimed the discovery that political action was *fun*. It was fun even though it sprang from moral purposes and even though political debate also enhanced the rationality of opinion formation. Arendt's affirmation of the apparently frivolous value of fun sharply contrasts with her earlier celebration of glory, even of public happiness. The affirmation nonetheless suggests a particular promise of politics, a promise especially contained in the comic dimension of green politics.

THE DEBATING GAME

Some quarter of a century after he first wrote *The Comedy of Survival*, Joseph W. Meeker has issued a revision with a new emphasis. The point, Meeker now maintains, is not simply to promote an environmental ethic, as he had previously suggested, but to challenge the work ethic with a "play ethic."[79] Meeker's idea of a play ethic depends on a distinction between "finite" and "infinite" games. Finite games have "clear goals" and are familiar from a variety of contexts, including "politics as usual." But play has only one purpose: "to please its participants and keep them playing." "When goals or objectives appear," he says, ". . . play disappears." The goal of an infinite game is "infinite play," which Meeker calls "a manifestation of the comic way." In play done for its own sake, the point is to maintain the game and keep it interesting.[80]

The language game of political debate, however, is typically played for keeps. Debate is oriented toward a conclusion. Arguments are crafted with a purpose in mind: to persuade, to reach agreement, to come to the truth of the matter, or simply to win. In this perspective, debate is a finite game focused on an extrinsic purpose. Conversation, Henry Kariel has suggested, typically provides a sharp contrast; it wanders more or less aimlessly, and it is precisely this meandering quality of conversation that suggests its implicit purpose: to keep the conversation going and to maintain the relationships that constitute it.[81]

It is along similar lines that Kariel urges his point that the promise of politics is to be realized in declining to end our discourse.[82] What Kariel thus suggests is that the intrinsic value of politics comes through a form of communication that cannot be restricted merely to debate, to argument as it is normally practiced. To flourish, an intrinsically valuable politics must enact its own genre, must be guided by its own metaphors. With a striking contrast between two metaphors for argument, George Lakoff and Mark Johnson may help to suggest the character of a thoroughly noninstrumental politics: "Imagine a culture where an argument is viewed as a dance, the participants are seen as performers, and the goal is to perform in a balanced and aesthetically pleasing way. In such a culture, people would view arguments differently, carry them out differently, and talk about them differently. But *we* would probably not view them as arguing at all: they would simply be doing something different. . . . Perhaps the most neutral way of describing this difference . . . would be to say that we have a discourse form in terms of battle and they have one structured in terms of dance."[83] Only through such a wrench of imagination can we perhaps fully grasp what Arendt means when she characterizes politics as one of the performing arts. We witness a display of inventive and illuminative communicative skill, an exchange of opinions valued for its own sake. In this sense, political debate assumes the aspect of an infinite game, in which the players are committed to playing the game and keeping it going.

POLITICAL SPACE

To be understood and promoted, the performative aspect of politics needs to be clearly distinguished, made a focus of attention. But this is not to make the performative aspect of politics into some pure, independent form entirely detached from instrumental aspects. Action as performance cannot stand alone, as Arendt herself indicates in her portrayal of Greek political life: "a definite space had to be secured and a structure built where all subsequent actions could take place, that space being the public realm of the *polis*."[84] Constituting a "space of appearance"[85] is a necessary condition for action; in our terms, performative politics depends on constitutive politics.

What gets included and what gets excluded, what gets recognized and what gets neglected—these are key questions in creating a public space of appearance. If there is no neutral or ultimately impartial organizational principle by which to answer these questions, there is, as Arendt seems to suggest, an arbitrary and (in a broad sense) even violent element that enters into any foundation.[86] Even the most open, flexible, and inclusive public sphere must have some kind of boundaries to define it and make it recognizable.

Constituting a space for politics means far less the construction of any physical location than it does the creation of a *we* for public discourse. For Arendt, the chief political act needed in the constitution of political space is the act of promising. "Promises," she says, "are the uniquely human way of ordering the future, making it predictable and reliable to the extent that is humanly possible."[87]

Constituting a space for politics is also a fragile prospect at best if politics is valued only in instrumental terms. Despite the lack of an impartial founding principle, a partiality for politics thus remains a key constitutive element for a public sphere. Arendt particularly fears the potential for social movements to cut off debate violently, in effect eliminating the possibility of politics. The arbitrariness of creating a sphere for public debate is attenuated, she suggests, to the extent that the constitutive acts themselves incorporate an organizational principle affirming the intrinsic value of politics.[88]

It is thus significant that the *we* of a public sphere presupposes implicit or explicit mutual promising among the actors who comprise it. Clearly, such promising cannot be reduced to a formal contract among possessive individuals, for the substance of the promise, what is being constituted through it, depends on the enactment of a different kind of identity: that of the citizen rather than the consumer. The promises immanent to a green public sphere provide for a meaningful context of debate. This context sets the terms of what is arguable, of what can be debated and how. The context thus sets off an "arguable world," a place "where things are discovered, conflicts are fought, people agree and differ afresh."[89] What the context cannot do, however, is to exclude the openness that debate demands.

The green movement often seems to confront strategic imperatives that pose anxious questions of closure. Who is in and who is out? Who is and who is not genuinely green? The project of constituting a green public sphere cannot of course avoid questions of closure. Boundaries cannot be entirely eliminated if there is to be meaningful disagreement. The metaphor of the green public sphere nonetheless suggests a new orientation to problems of identity and boundary. The openness needed for debate could in principle be driven out of a green movement—or even out of a green community[90]— but not out of a green public sphere.

IMAGINE THE WORLD TURNED upside down.[1] What if, instead of propagating the industrialist inclinations of a consumer society, the prevailing media of communication instead promoted the green cause of a conserver society?[2] What if the same resources now devoted to product promotion were instead devoted to product investigation and exposure? What if the full range of environmental impacts of every product were minutely scrutinized, continuously monitored and updated, placed on warning labels, and given the same amount of public exposure as their selling points? What if this exposure included exhaustive attention to how these impacts were visited upon the human population as well as upon nonhuman nature—the distribution of environmental costs and benefits according to race, gender, class, and country?

What if the alignments of power behind each initiative for economic development received similar attention? What if uncertainties were emphasized rather than glossed over? What if, in public debate, precaution not only became the watchword, but the burden of proof was shifted so that environmental damage was assumed in the absence of compelling evidence to the contrary?

Such an extraordinary inversion of discourse would mean that public life had undergone a fundamental change, a dramatic greening. A privileged industrialist discourse would have been displaced by a privileged green discourse. For now, however, such a discursive focus remains the province of a nascent green public sphere emerging in opposition to the prevailing framework of industrialism.

Constituting the Green Public Sphere

To speak of a green public sphere is not to impose something altogether alien on green politics, but is to suggest a metaphor able to help refocus and enhance emerging activities. A deliberate project of constituting and enhancing the green public sphere is possible as a focus of green politics, but this focus is deflected by the metaphor of movement, particularly when it alludes to a comprehensive strategy of radical social transformation.

Such a comprehensive radical strategy would neglect incremental changes —centered in functional politics—with the ability to enhance the scope and vitality of the green public sphere. Somewhat paradoxically perhaps, as much of our discussion in earlier chapters has suggested, the relevant incremental changes may not even involve environmental policy, as conventionally understood, as much as a broader range of policy domains. Social and economic policy, for example, could at least conceivably be designed to reduce the insecurities and anxieties that tend to diminish the capacity of citizens to focus their concerns on problems of the environment. Similarly, communications policy could direct attention to ecological matters in various ways, particularly by requiring product advertisements to include environmental impact warnings, just as health and safety warnings are sometimes now required. Because functional politics is prone to a technocratic rationalism inimical to vital discursive contexts, a further step in communications policy would be to promote regular media access for environmental counteradvertising, including "adbuster" satires.[3]

The perspective of dissenting policy professionalism could help to encourage the incorporation of discursive features into policy design and implementation generally, with the policy process understood broadly to include not just state institutions but also the full complex of administrative spheres and public spheres. Key here would be the promotion of citizen participation and deliberation as related to matters ranging, for example, from policies for public funding in election campaigns (as at least a partial check on the power of concentrated wealth) to provisions for supporting citizen interventions into environmental impact assessments.

Green politics serves to enhance and expand the green public sphere by promoting debate conducted on the terms of green discourse. Though these terms themselves often remain vigorously contested, the emergence of a language of environment offers enough commonality for meaningful disagreement. Yet, it should be stressed that the creation of the common language remains due, in no small part, to green political activities guided by the instrumentalist metaphor of a progressive social movement.

The idea of a green public sphere raises in a particularly pointed fashion the problem of the relationship between means and ends. The prevailing historical context of power renders the nascent green public sphere vulnerable; there is no guarantee that it will not be stillborn. It emerges in a context where its very survival, much less promotion, depends on strategic actions to fend off attacks. This problem gives rise both to internal strife in the green movement and to a temptation to establish coherence by excommunicating those elements that threaten to lead the movement astray, to deflect it from a clear path.

The problem becomes especially pressing when industrialism begins to speak the language of environment through deliberate efforts of greenwashing. These efforts dramatically throw into question the boundaries of the green public sphere, and the problem has no miracle solution. The green public sphere cannot escape a need for boundaries and rules in its language game, however contestable and flexible they might remain. Unlike the green movement, though, the green public sphere is inherently committed to debate—not just to tolerate but to cultivate and provoke disagreements. The contested boundaries of the green public sphere are thus prone to remain indeterminate, fuzzy, highly permeable, and in flux. Unlike the green movement, the green public sphere remains especially conducive to a performative politics valuing debate for its own sake. The green movement could survive without much debate, but the end of debate would spell the end of the green public sphere.

As a forum for debate, the green public sphere is inconceivable apart from an idiom, a relatively stable pattern of linguistic usages, providing for the practice of green discourse. It is the language of environment, George Myerson and Yvonne Rydin maintain, that allows for "arguability." This green language, they suggest, is a linguistic "net" that "holds in place the practices of communication and arguing, but is itself continually pushed into new shapes—stretched and torn in places, made slack and compressed in others." As a net, the language of environment is thus "a dynamic system of changing connections spread across society . . . busy with environmental arguing, competitive and collaborative, controlled and spontaneous."[4]

The green public sphere, then, is not a clear-cut institution, but involves a changing pattern of interconnections among sites where green discourse is practiced. Conceptualizing the green public sphere in this way makes it possible to resist taking the spatial metaphor in the sense of some literally determinate location. Green discourse may be centered in civil society, but it is practiced in diverse places, from the grassroots to the corridors of power. Of course, the language of environment is spoken with different accents and at times—all too often—as a foreign tongue. It is spoken more or less fluently in such settings as grassroots groups, environmental organizations, green political parties, and certain academic settings. Newsletters, conferences, journals, public television and radio, films, telephones, fax machines, and the Internet—all these media are frequently conducive to the green idiom. It is spoken rather awkwardly, when allowed, in the administrative sphere, whether of state institutions or of business corporations. Still, it plays a role in influencing agenda setting, problem definition, and epistemological criteria in the policy process, especially if that process is understood to go beyond formal institutions. Certainly, the green public sphere is not limited to any particular country, but generally matches the increasingly globalized pattern of economic and governmental relations.[5]

In arguing that democratic deliberation on environmental problems markedly tends to enhance environmental rationality and commitment, Adolf G. Gundersen maintains that deliberation must be public[6] but does not entirely depend on formal public institutions or gatherings: "deliberation need not be restricted to a town meeting or even to a strictly public place." "Nor," he goes on to say, ". . . does deliberation depend on a direct confrontation with one's neighbors or fellow citizens. As Socrates demonstrated long ago, deliberation requires only an interlocutor. And it's a good thing; is there anything more incongruous than a global public meeting?" (150–51). The green public sphere certainly includes public meetings, but much more as well. In this sense, it is like the polis as conceived by Arendt, not a "physical location" but "the organization of people as it arises out of acting and speaking together": "its true space," she says, "lies between people living together for this purpose, no matter where they happen to be."[7] This is a space that can be enacted in many venues, for example, as Arendt indicates, by "only ten of us . . . sitting around a table" for an open "exchange of opinions."[8]

Communication is obviously a necessary feature of any social movement, but communication does not necessarily take the form of debate. Indeed, the strategic imperatives of a social movement often tend to inhibit an open exchange of differing opinions. To the extent that such an exchange is considered valuable, whether for intrinsic or extrinsic reasons, the movement will be inclined, however, to constitute itself as a public sphere.

The Ethos of the Green Public Sphere

Enhancing the green public sphere could become a clear and pressing priority for green political action. This would mean promoting the green public sphere as a context of arguability in which industrialist presuppositions do not prevail. In some significant sense, it would mean promoting an ecological ethos.

Would this require a clear commitment to ecocentrism? Robyn Eckersley has claimed that, aside from all arguments favoring ecocentrism in principle, "the cultivation of an ecocentric culture is crucial to achieving a lasting solution to the ecological crisis."[9] Crucial to a green public sphere, however, would be the maintenance of arguability about ecocentrism rather than any general commitment to it. There could well be serious disagreements, but the green public sphere would need an ecological ethos disposed at least to take the question of ecocentrism seriously, to treat it as meaningful, reasonable, and worth discussing. "Do rocks have rights?"[10] In a green public sphere, even such an apparently absurd question would deserve attention to explore seriously from multiple vantage points its possible relevance and significance.

Besides an ecological ethos, there would need to be a discursive ethos, sealed perhaps by what Hannah Arendt indicates as the power of "mutual promise."[11] This need raises questions, though, of rationality and genre. With its epistemological challenges to industrialism, green discourse certainly throws technocratic rationalism into question. Is this questioning simply for the sake of a more comprehensive rationality, though, or does it portend a thorough break with rationality, a displacement of the genre of rational argumentation by some qualitatively different genre?

In its diversity, green discourse includes both the form of rational argumentation and forms of communication that appear to be sharply at variance with all rationality. These other genres, however, are not necessarily irrelevant to argument. A big question is whether these other genres actually threaten rationality or somehow enrich it. Norbert Kostede is especially alert to the threat of green anti-intellectualism: "Even where the limits of human knowledge are themselves concerned . . . we still have to remain on the territory of rational discourse, and must resist the temptation to enter the realm of meditation or spiritual insight. In their private individual or collective lives, people are of course free to do as they wish; if approaches which are valid here were to be applied in the public sphere of politics and were to become the basis of political strategies, this would be a recipe for disaster."[12] For Kostede, the territory of rational discourse offers a safe haven from anti-intellectual intrusions into the public sphere. Argument is thus privileged as a public genre, displacing all others. From this rather Habermasian perspective, personal adventures in meditation and spiritual insight can have no public standing. Strictly speaking, however, even in terms of rational argumentation as conceived by Habermas, neither meditation nor spiritual insight could be ruled out as an experiential basis for arguable propositions.

The question would be whether good reasons could be explicitly and coherently stated in the course of debate. Similarly, whether such things as meditation and spiritual insight have any appropriate relationship to the green public sphere would be an issue for public debate—a debate that would require explorations and understandings going beyond mere rationalistic prejudice. The genre of serious, rational argument cannot stand as an a priori roadblock to unsettling possibilities, but can serve simply as a crucible.

Even in this limited capacity, however, the genre of rational argumentation would enclose the green public sphere with a singular homogeneity. The rational argument would have the final word, beyond which there would be no appeal. Objecting to Habermasian homogeneity in public life, Iris Marion Young suggests the possibility of "heterogeneous publics of passion, play and aesthetic interest" promoting issues for public discussion. In this context, even "the practice of such discussion" serves to affirm "the proper place of passion and play in public." Young thus suggests the possibility of a form of open discourse not restricted to the genre of argumentation, but admitting other gestures, for example, "guerilla theatre and costumes," "chants, music, song, dancing." Such forms of communication also serve, she says, "to make political points."[13]

If followed in the shaping of a green public sphere, Young's suggestions would encourage a diversity of expression. She insists that playfulness, passion, and a multiplicity of genres have a "proper place" in public life. Notably, though, she does not make this claim by chanting, singing, or dancing, but by rationally arguing: giving and defending reasons in an explicit and coherent manner. She thus assumes, at least implicitly, that rational argumentation does have some justified privilege in this connection, though it may not be the privilege of an ultimate trump card. In effect, she affirms an intellectual seriousness that does not rule out playfulness.

Although indispensable to serious debate, straightforward argumentation cannot avoid incredible assumptions, dubious faith both in its concepts and in the rules of its language game. The rationalistic inclinations of the Western spiritual tradition, with its deification of reason and truth, helped inspire and sustain this faith in secular contexts, especially—and ironically—with the Enlightenment critique of religious dogmatism. The Enlightenment heritage, however, has been shown to be prone to its own dogmatism, so that the presuppositions of any straightforward rational argument are now burdened with a question mark.

Hegel's ingenious dialectical effort to avoid the question mark has met with the response of Horkheimer and Adorno's *Dialectic of Enlightenment*. Within the Western philosophical tradition, Theodor Adorno's subsequent exercises in negative dialectics and Jacques Derrida's deconstruction of logocentrism have, among many such efforts, further served to underscore the limits of rational argumentation.[14] So too have insights drawn from some non-Western sources, such as, to cite what is possibly the most extravagant example, Zen Buddhism. Often, there is understandable concern that the heretical questioning of rationality leaves itself open to sheer arbitrariness and irrationalism. What is noteworthy, however, is the profound intellectual seriousness that obviously guides this questioning.

It is for the sake of such seriousness that Mikhail Bakhtin celebrates the "textual carnivals" of dialogic genres such as the novel, opposing the monologue of straightforward, literal argumentation; in the novel, indeed, "the direct and unmediated intention of a word presents itself as something impermissibly naive."[15] A rational argument permits conflicting arguments, but not the fullness of diverse voices. Privileging argument to the exclusion of other genres ushers in a uniformity of voice and rules out as irrelevant a heterogeneous context of voices—including the voice of laughter—that could expose this uniformity and its naïveté.

The monologue of rational argument may seem to ensure against irrationalism, but argumentative seriousness also affirms a self-righteous certainty, a dogmatism merely masked by the claim of openness. Bakhtin thus identifies in modern culture "a specific form of seriousness, strict and scientific," that in principle must exclude "all intolerant dogmatism."[16] This seriousness, however, is incomplete and prone to dogmatic intolerance, according to Bakhtin, as can be seen in the experience of Western officialdom, from the Middle Ages to modernity. Against rationalistic seriousness, Bakhtin celebrates a "true ambivalent and universal laughter [that] does not deny seriousness but purifies and completes it" (121–22): "Laughter purifies from dogmatism, from the intolerant and the petrified; it liberates from fanaticism and pedantry, from fear and intimidation, from didacticism, naiveté and illusion, from the single meaning, the single level, from sentimentality. Laughter does not permit seriousness to atrophy and to be . . . forever incomplete. It restores . . . ambivalent wholeness" (123). "True open seriousness," Bakhtin further maintains, is fearless in the face of laughter. Such seriousness "fears neither parody nor irony . . . for it is aware of being part of an uncompleted whole" (123).

Bakhtin shows that the crucible of serious argument is incomplete, for seriousness itself needs to be "tested in the crucible of laughter" (121). It is thus that he refers explicitly to the wholeness of tragedy and comedy: "The antique culture of tragedy did not exclude the laughing aspect of life but coexisted with it. The tragic trilogy was followed by the satyr drama which complemented it on the comic level. Antique tragedy did not fear laughter and parody and even demanded it as a corrective and a complement" (121). In speaking of a restoration of true wholeness, Bakhtin may create suspicions that he harbors his own naïveté in the form of a utopian idealism. However, it is notable that the completed whole can never be sealed shut, in his view, for what paradoxically completes the whole is ambivalence, a question mark unsettling to the naïve self-confidence of authoritarianism.

In speaking of the net of environmental language, Myerson and Rydin suggest, à la Bakhtin, that it might well "be imagined as a 'textual carnival'": "A carnival is . . . dynamic, full of connections made and broken in the melée. And a carnival . . . mixes people and voices: the prestigious and peripheral, authoritative and popular, would-be weighty and knowingly transient." As a contemporary textual carnival, the net of environmental language offers a place "where high and low can exchange views and change places."[17] In this regard, the language of environment contains the comic dimension that, despite the prevailing tragic narrative, at times comes out in green politics.

Timothy Doyle has implicitly invoked the carnivalesque in proposing a green politics of "resilience," in contrast to a simple politics of resistance. Doyle draws metaphorically on the ecological notion of resilience as typically involving such characteristics as "inter-connectedness, complexity, flexibility, adaptability, amorphousness, ambiguity and diversity." He particularly singles out the importance of ambiguity, conceived as "a tolerance of different political approaches," and affirms the need for many green positions on the same issue, suggesting that different, even conflicting, positions are a sign of health.[18]

Doyle draws attention, as we saw in chapter 5, to the environmental absurdism of the Australian group EAAAC?! He underscores the importance of humor for political resilience and quotes an EAAAC?! member's astute, absurdist insight into the sources of ecological crisis: "The constipated are at the root of much that is evil in the world today. Bureaucracy operates on a symbiotic relationship with constipation; economic rationalism is a euphemism for constipation. . . . I speak as one who knows; yes, I confess, I was once a member of the constipated cabal myself. I know the intense frustration, discomfort and irritation which governs their lives, and makes them hate the world and wish to obstruct the development of the good, the right and the true."[19] Doyle thus affirms a comic resilience at odds with the tragic aura of much green political thought: "Self-righteousness burns people up. . . . To run against more powerful tides takes an enormous amount of courage and creativity; but, without humour and life balance, this can only lead to self-destruction. Martyrs need not apply!"[20] Implicitly, Doyle promotes a form of green politics that—including clearly functional, constitutive, and performative aspects—is supportive of a green public sphere.

Earth First! provides another example of the comic in green politics, but offers a cautionary tale. The group first gained attention with its "Cracking of Glen Canyon Damn." In 1981, five people—four men and one woman—marched out onto the Glen Canyon Dam on the Colorado River in Arizona with a plan to "crack" the dam. They tossed something over the edge, and then "a tiny black gash" appeared in the concrete. The crack, however, was actually a large roll of plastic that the Earth First! activists had unfurled. "The crack," as it appeared from a distance, "was a wisecrack, a daring bit of humor in an environmental movement that had become glum and solemn. . . ."[28]

The event deliberately alluded to a "comedic, rag-tag" bunch of ecoactivists portrayed in Edward Abbey's novel *The Monkey Wrench Gang*. Abbey was even on hand to watch and to comment that he "would advocate sabotage, subversion as a last resort when political means fail."[22] It is telling that Abbey counsels abandoning politics if "political means" appear instrumentally ineffective, for Earth First! lacks the absurdist, more fully comic, orientation of EAAAC?! Rik Scarce, indeed, sums up the Earth First! position in these succinct terms: "No more muddling through. No more compromise."[23]

A celebration of resistance is clear, but what is missing is the kind of resilience that Doyle advocates. Humor alone offers no guarantee in constituting a green public sphere. Humor, indeed, can obviously be both cruel and oppressive. To see this, one need look no further than the misanthropic —indeed, racist—tenor of some of the notorious jokes (one hopes they were jokes!) promulgated in Earth First! literature by "Miss Ann Throphy."[24] By giving comfort to the uncompromising defenders of the earth, to true believers, Earth First! humor here lacks the ambivalent seriousness that, in Bakhtin's terms, serves to provoke "universal laughter."

Bakhtin refers to an unbounded laughter that demeans nothing, has no particular target, but recognizes and expresses an ambivalent wholeness in human/nature. What Bakhtin has in mind may best be suggested by a story a Western philosopher relates of a dialogue with a Zen Buddhist scholar concerning the Zen view of "ultimate reality." Although both knew better, the two engaged in a serious, convivial argument and went so far as to draw and exchange diagrams. As they talked, seeking "concepts to carry the weight of [their] mental probings," they continued to draw "until there were nearly a dozen diagrams strewn about on the table." At that point, they recognized again what each had already known: the utter insufficiency of concepts and arguments to grasp or convey what they were trying to comprehend: "He finished the last diagram and then began to laugh, and his laughter increased steadily in intensity. I sensed what had happened, and laughter overcame me as well. The laughter continued until tears rolled down our cheeks in shared delight at our presumption. . . . He shook his head in merriment, and then blurted out, 'Forgive me. I am sorry, but somehow this always happens to me when I try to talk about ultimate reality.'"[25]

The enhancement of the green public sphere depends on mutual promises that extend beyond explicit commitments. Whatever its differences, the *we* constitutive of this sphere depends on a shared discursive as well as ecological ethos. Yet, the green public sphere also needs an understanding of its own limitations and an ability to get the joke.

Not everything, of course, is a joking matter. The horrors of human history cannot be erased, even if they could be ended.[26] To celebrate the debates and disagreements of the green public sphere is not to forget that greens occupy an often hostile world, in which opposing forces take not only such common forms as well-financed propaganda campaigns and law suits, but also various forms of violence that extend to state-sponsored terrorism (France) and judicial murder (Nigeria).[27] Still, the green public sphere offers at least the frail prospect of a forum in which Bakhtin's ambivalent seriousness could come to hold sway.

Anyone who battles a monster had better take care, Nietzsche once said, not to turn into a monster.[28] An uncompromising green politics intent on ecological resistance threatens to succumb to a kind of resentment that, in the end, could undermine not only the intrinsic value of political action but anything further one might hope to gain from politics. A resilient green politics, though it offers neither a grand scheme nor much in the way of tragic heroism, is nonetheless consistent with the character of a green public sphere.

Those intent upon changing the world, including greens, are all too often inclined to stake an implicit or explicit claim to the privilege of their standpoint. In some respects, this may often be a justifiable privilege, but any claim to privilege courts an irresponsibility inconsistent with a discursive ethos. The claim tends to erect a wall around the privileged *we*, such that recognition and respect for others at times come grudgingly if at all; confidence displaces humility as well as much awareness of how the *we* is itself limited, even damaged, by the historical forces that have shaped it.[29]

Green politics arises in a context of public life where industrialist discourse has long prevailed. The emergence, expansion, and enhancement of a green public sphere denies industrialism its unquestioned supremacy. If one wishes to assess the potential of the green public sphere to contribute to historical change, that potential is no doubt modest and cannot develop on its own. But it is still clearly indispensable to the constitution of a human civilization able to incorporate an ecological ethos together with a discursive ethos. By encouraging the emergence of a green public sphere, green politics also offers the at least fragile promise of a place in which citizens might enjoy what is now seldom imagined, the intrinsic value of politics.

1 · WHAT IS GREEN POLITICS?

1 See Gallon, "The Green Product Endorsement Controversy."

2 Dobson, *Green Political Thought*, 1.

3 Ibid., 2–3, 7–8. Dobson makes a rather formal conceptual point, arguing that unlike ecologism, environmentalism does not constitute a properly conceived "ideology." However, his conception leaves out the significant sense of ideology as false consciousness or as a support for dominant powers. Cf., e.g., Marcuse, *One-Dimensional Man*. Dobson's conception of ideology, in fact, closely resembles the idea of utopian thought as contrasted with ideology in Mannheim, *Ideology and Utopia*. Also see Eckersley, "Green Political Thought."

4 Marcuse, *One-Dimensional Man*, chap. 10.

5 Cf. Dobson, *Green Political Thought*, 14.

6 Die Grünen, *Programme of the German Green Party*, 6.

7 See, e.g., Paehlke, *Environmentalism and the Future of Progressive Politics*.

8 Reich, *The Greening of America*.

9 See Dalton, *The Green Rainbow*, chap. 1.

10 Hjelmar, *The Political Practice of Environmental Organizations*, 88–98.

11 Shaiko, "Greenpeace U.S.A."; Wapner, *Environmental Activism and World Civic Politics*, chap. 3.

12 See, e.g., Diamond and Orenstein, *Reweaving the World*.

13 See Schlosberg, *Environmental Justice and the New Pluralism*. For a concise history in an American context, see Hartley, "Environmental Justice"; on the international scene, see Sachs, "Upholding Human Rights and Environmental Justice."

14 Bateson, "Conscious Purpose versus Nature." Also see Leiss, *The Domination of Nature*, chap. 1.

15 Dryzek, "Ecological Rationality," 5, 8.

16 Dryzek, *Rational Ecology*, 245.

17 Goodin, *Green Political Theory*, 168.

18 See Dobson, *Green Political Thought*, 7–11; cf. Eckersley, *Environmentalism and Political Theory*, chap. 3. This issue is addressed in chap. 6 below.

19 See Cohen, "Strategy or Identity"; cf. Goodin, 13–17, 54.

20 Goodin, 15.

21 Eckersley, "Greening Liberal Democracy," 222. Also see Dobson, "Democratising Green Theory."

22 See Rodman, "Four Forms of Ecological Consciousness Reconsidered."

23 Eckersley, "Greening Liberal Democracy," 223.

24 See, e.g., Paehlke and Torgerson, eds., *Managing Leviathan*; Press, *Democratic Dilemmas in the Age of Ecology*; Jänicke, "Democracy as a Condition for Environmental Policy Success."

25 Goodin's position supports liberal democracy, but on instrumental grounds, in principle leaving the door open for authoritarianism on such grounds.

26 See Torgerson, "Domination and Liberatory Politics."

27 See Lindblom, "Another State of Mind."

28 See Dryzek, *Democracy in Capitalist Times*.

29 See the treatment of liberal democracy in the work of Macpherson, particularly *The Real World of Democracy* and *The Life and Times of Liberal Democracy*.

30 See Habermas, *The Structural Transformation of the Public Sphere*; Calhoun, *Habermas and the Public Sphere*.

31 See Habermas, *Structural Transformation of the Public Sphere*, chaps. 5–6. Cf. Foucault, "The Eye of Power" and *Discipline and Punish*. For an early treatment of propaganda as a "concession to the rationality of the modern world," see Lasswell, *Propaganda Technique in World War I*, 221.

32 See Crozier, Huntington, and Watanuki, *The Crisis of Democracy*, esp. the contribution by Samuel Huntington.

33 The divisions of authority that have emerged under liberal democratic constitutions tend to attenuate administrative power to the extent that the institutions of parliament and the courts sometimes provide official points of entry through which citizens can exert influence on a largely closed process. However, these potentials are ambivalent because parliament and the courts can also operate to support administrative closure. How these potentials play themselves out remains part of ongoing struggles with considerable history. These struggles are reflected in Mill's *Considerations on Representative Government*. Although Mill is often portrayed as something of a participatory democrat (e.g., see Carole Pateman, *Participation and Democratic Theory*, chap. 1), his book indicates significant concern to shield the affairs of governance and administration not only from the influence of public opinion, but also from parliament.

34 Habermas, "Further Reflections on the Public Sphere," 452.

35 Fraser, "Rethinking the Public Sphere," 132–36.

36 Habermas, *Between Facts and Norms*, 367. Cf. Dryzek, *Discursive Democracy*.

37 Dryzek, *Democracy in Capitalist Times*, 151–54; Dryzek, "Strategies of Ecological Democratization," 115–21.

38 Ibid., 118, 119. The flexibilty of liberal democracy is an achievement of democratic struggles that has been inscribed in constitutional provisions for civil rights and the division of powers. I take it for granted here that such constitutional provisions would be needed both in a discursive democracy and in a green state. Cf. Eckersley, "Green Justice, the State and Democracy"; Christoff, "Ecological Citizens and Ecologically Guided Democracy."

39 Dryzek, "Strategies of Ecological Democratization," 120.

40 See Alford and Friedland, *Powers of Theory*, esp. chap. 17.

41 See Torgerson, "Limits to the Administrative Mind," esp. 160 n. 95.

42 Offe, "The Separation of Form and Content in Liberal Democratic Politics," 8.

43 The separation of state and public sphere in Habermas corresponds conceptually with a deeper opposition between the two key categories "system" and "lifeworld." See *The Theory of Communicative Action*, vol. 2. This division, as he conceives it, is between the invasive, monological functioning of market mechanisms and state administration (i.e., the system) and a resistant cultural domain of dialogical communication (i.e., the lifeworld). Because the two are constituted on radically different principles, Habermas creates an anomaly in his conceptual scheme when he speaks tentatively of a "democratization" of administration, even of "participatory administrative practices" (Habermas, *Between Facts and Norms*, 440–41).

44 See Torgerson, "Limits of the Administrative Mind."

45 Lindblom, *The Policy-Making Process*, 4.

46 See Schrecker, *Political Economy of Environmental Hazards*.

47 Leiss, *The Domination of Nature*, 22.

48 Zamyatin's *We*, although written in Russian, was first published in English translation (1925) and influenced Orwell's *1984*.

Political theory is, of course, often exercised through interpretations of artistic work, especially literature. See, e.g., Kontos, "The Dialectics of Domination: An Interpretation of Friedrich Dürrenmatt's *The Visit*." For a discussion that probes a range of genres, see Kariel, *The Desperate Politics of Postmodernism*, esp. the discussion of Maya Ying Lin's *Vietnam Veterans Memorial*, 27–29.

49 Mannheim, *Ideology and Utopia*.

50 Adorno, *Negative Dialectics*, 406.

51 See Wolin, "Political Theory as a Vocation," 1070. Also see Wolin, *Politics and Vision*; Berlin, "Does Political Theory Still Exist?"

52 Bahro, *Building the Green Movement*.

53 Villa, *Arendt and Heidegger*, 4. Arendt's celebration of public life was initially rejected by feminism as hopelessly phallocentric, but recently more diverse, nuanced interpretations have begun to emerge. For an overview, see Dietz, "Feminist Receptions of Hannah Arendt."

54 Arendt, *Between Past and Future*, 137, 153; *The Human Condition*, 206–7.

55 George Kateb, quoted in Kariel, *The Desperate Politics of Postmodernism*, 91.

56 Kariel, *The Promise of Politics*.

57 See Bachrach, *The Theory of Democratic Elitism: A Critique*.

58 Seidel, "Political Discourse Analysis," 45. Cf. Evans, "Ecofeminism and the Politics of the Gendered Self."

59 See Fraser, *Unruly Practices*, chap. 1.

60 Weber, *The Protestant Ethic and the Spirit of Capitalism*, 181; Foucault, *Discipline and Punish*; Habermas, *The Theory of Communicative Action*, 2: 355; Arendt, *The Human Condition*, 38–49. Cf. Lasswell, *World Politics and Personal Insecurity*.

61 See the following by Habermas: "On Systematically Distorted Communication"; "Toward a Theory of Communicative Competence"; "What Is Universal Pragmatics?"; *The Theory of Communicative Action*, 1: chap. 1; "Discourse Ethics". Also see McCarthy, *The Critical Theory of Jürgen Habermas*, chap. 4.2; Benhabib, "Communicative Ethics and Current Controversies in Political Philosophy." What Habermas was trying to get at with his concept of an "ideal speech situation" was perhaps better developed in Karl-Otto Apel's concept of the "ideal communication-community"; see "The Common Presuppositions of Hermeneutics and Ethics," 48, and *Towards a Transformation of Philosophy*, chap. 7.

62 See Habermas, "The Scientization of Politics and Public Opinion" in *Toward a Rational Society*.

63 See Fraser, "Rethinking the Public Sphere"; Young, *Justice and the Politics of Difference*, chaps. 4, 6.

64 Habermas, "Further Reflections on the Public Sphere," 446–52.

65 See Arendt, *The Human Condition*, 38–50, 248–57; Arendt, *The Origins of Totalitarianism*, chaps. 10, 13.

66 Arendt, *The Human Condition*, chap. 3.

67 Ibid., 176, 180, and chap. 5 generally.

68 Villa, 4–12.

69 Arendt, *Between Past and Future*, 220–23, 241–49.

70 Ibid., 241–42, 220–23.

71 Rethinking green political thought in terms of the meaning of politics focuses attention on distinctly human institutions but does not presuppose a homocentric position. Nonetheless, the homocentric inclination of figures like Arendt and Habermas is clear (even if not entirely unequivocal). See, e.g., Macauley, "Hannah Arendt and the Politics of Place"; Whiteside, "Hannah Arendt and Ecological Politics"; Whitebrook, "The Problem of Nature in Habermas"; Eckersley, *Environmentalism and Political Theory*, chap. 5.

72 Norton, *Toward Unity among Environmentalists*, 6.

73 Bahro, 196–211.

74 Cf. Benhabib, *Critique, Norm, and Utopia.*

75 Postmodern interventions, which have more than given pause to such easy notions of coherent identity and purpose, were already anticipated in a Marxian context by the early critical theory of the Frankfurt School, most prominently by Horkheimer and Adorno's *Dialectic of Enlightenment*. Even before that, as the Marxist revolutionary movement was becoming institutionalized in the early Soviet Union, Zamyatin's futuristic *We* set a dystopian pattern that many subsequent theoretical and fictional treatments of social identity have tended, in one way or another, to repeat. See Zamyatin, esp. entries 25–28 of D-503's journal.

76 The green public sphere may involve an ironic paradox. As a distinctively human artifice, the form of the green public sphere seems at odds with the content of much green discourse, which exhibits ecocentric concerns. This issue is considered in chap. 6 below.

2 · STRATEGIC PERPLEXITIES

1 See Polanyi, *The Great Transformation*, chaps. 5–6, 12; Gay, *The Enlightenment*, 2: chap. 7, esp. 319–68; Lefebvre, "Enlightened Despotism," 52.

2 Merchant, *The Death of Nature*, 205, quoting a letter from Descartes to Mersenne of 15 April 1630. Cf. Kontos, "Success and Knowledge in Machiavelli."

3 Weinberg, "Social Institutions and Nuclear Power," 33–34.

4 Orr, *Ecological Literacy*, 61. Cf. Starhawk, "Power, Authority, and Mystery": "I like the definition of magic that says, 'Magic is the art of changing consciousness at will.' I also think that is a very good definition of political change—changing consciousness on a mass scale" (76).

5 See Ferkiss, *The Future of Technological Civilization*, chap. 18.

6 On this slogan, see Goodin, *Green Political Theory*, 156–68.

7 See Damico, *Individuality and Community*, 43, 55–56, 60–65, 78; Torgerson, "Policy Analysis and Public Life," 231–33, 242–43.

8 See Laclau and Mouffe, *Hegemony and Socialist Strategy.*

9 The concept of contextual orientation is derived from the work of Harold Lasswell,

who formulated it with particular reference to Marx and Freud. For the initial formulation, see Lasswell, *World Politics and Personal Insecurity*, chap. 1. On the concept and Lasswell's later development of it in a policy connection, see Torgerson, "Contextual Orientation in Policy Analysis" and "Origins of the Policy Orientation."

10 See Wolin, "Political Theory as a Vocation," 1070.

11 Hjelmar, *The Political Practice of Environmental Organizations*, 43.

12 Dobson, *Green Political Thought*, 124–25, 203.

13 Hjelmar, 136.

14 Richard Bahouth, quoted in Hjelmar, 129 (cf. 68, 58 n. 2), from Scarce, *Eco-Warriors*, 51.

15 Hjelmar, 114. Hjelmar particularly quotes Dave Foreman of Earth First! on the interesting point that radicals improve the image of reformers: "We make them look credible without them having to compromise more" (quoted in Hjelmar, 114 from Scarce, 26).

16 Dobson, *Green Political Thought*, 203, 209–10.

17 A. Carter, "Towards a Green Political Theory," 51.

18 Lewis, *Green Delusions*, 250.

19 See Lindblom, "The Science of 'Muddling Through'" and *The Intelligence of Democracy*. The fundamentally settled and secure world presupposed in these earlier works becomes obvious when Lindblom later poses the prospect of a world "headed for catastrophe" and, guided by a sense of environmental crisis, probes the range of "politico-economic mechanisms" for the explicit purpose of finding ways to protect the quality of life on earth. See Lindblom, *Politics and Markets*, 3. However, he offers no guarantees.

20 Dobson, *Green Political Thought*, 126.

21 Bookchin, *The Ecology of Freedom*, 32; cf. 217.

22 Bookchin, *The Philosophy of Social Ecology*.

23 Bookchin, *Ecology of Freedom*, 179.

24 See, e.g., Eckersley, *Environmentalism and Political Theory*, 55–56; Fox, *Toward a Transpersonal Ecology*, 19–22.

25 Bookchin, *Remaking Society*, 18, 158.

26 Marx, *Early Writings*, 59 (original emphasis). Cf. Marcuse, *Reason and Revolution*, 321–22.

27 Bookchin, *Post-Scarcity Anarchism*, 11, 185–86, 211, 139.

28 Bookchin, *Remaking Society*, 171.

29 Ibid., 168 (original emphasis). Bookchin has also spoken of "new classes" reemerging as "the People" in *The Modern Crisis*, 152. Cf. Hawkins, "The Potential of the Green Movement."

30 Bookchin, *The Modern Crisis*, 172.

31 Naess, "The Deep Ecological Movement," 205.

32 Devall and Sessions, *Deep Ecology*, 154, 132.

33 Devall and Sessions, "The Development of Natural Resources and the Integrity of Nature," 321–22.

34 Devall and Sessions, *Deep Ecology*, chap. 8, esp. 157. Cf. Appendix H.

35 See, e.g., Spretnak, "Ecofeminism"; Starhawk, "Power, Authority and Mystery"; Merchant, "Ecofeminism and Feminist Theory"; Rocheleau, Thomas-Slayter, and Wangari, *Feminist Political Ecology*. Merchant, *Radical Ecology*, suggests "the concept of reproduction construed in its broadest sense" (209) as a point of unity for ecofeminism.

36 "Out of the void comes the spirit that shapes the ends of men." So wrote Chester

Barnard some sixty years ago in the culminating moment of his celebrated administrative classic, *The Functions of the Executive,* 284. To regard this sentence as a mere
rhetorical flourish would be to neglect its deep cultural roots as well as the complexity and sophistication manifest in Barnard's conception of administration as a
creative process. Cf. Torgerson, "Limits of the Administrative Mind," 120–25.

37 Spretnak, *The Spiritual Dimension in Green Politics,* 41, 73.

38 Quinby, "Ecofeminism and the Politics of Resistance," 122–24.

39 Biehl, *Rethinking Ecofeminist Politics,* 90.

40 Quinby, 124.

41 See Fraser, *Unruly Practices,* chap. 1.

42 Warren, "The Power and Promise of Ecological Feminism," 326. Also see Plumwood,
    Feminism and the Mastery of Nature.

43 King, "Healing the Wounds," 118.

44 Cf. Torgerson, "Domination and Liberatory Politics."

45 Salleh, "Nature, Woman, Labor, Capital," 119. Also see Salleh, *Ecofeminism as Poli-
    tics.*

46 Salleh, "Nature, Woman, Labor, Capital," 117.

47 Warren, 336.

48 Salleh, "Nature, Woman, Labor, Capital," 120.

49 Rodman, "Four Forms of Ecological Consciousness Reconsidered." At times, Rodman
    suggests that his dialectical language may just be an analogy, and he even tends to
    apologize for a tendency to create a teleological progression of forms. See Rodman,
    "Four Forms of Ecological Consciousness," 3–4. Indeed, his uncompleted historical
    account is at most suggestive and falls far short of demonstrating any clear-cut pat-
    tern of development. In his conception, nonetheless, there is movement toward the
    final form, and he stresses that the earlier forms are not simply abolished in the
    process: elements of them are also preserved. The entire viewpoint he presents is
    obviously the product of a dialectical manner of thinking.

50 Rodman, introduction, 25. Rodman's theoretical orientation is strongly influenced by
    his studies of the British neo-Hegelian T. H. Green, in terms both of dialectics and of
    the significance of teleology for normative thought. See Rodman, "What Is Living and
    What Is Dead in the Political Philosophy of T. H. Green," 575, 580–81, 583–85. Mar-
    cuse's view of Green is also quite sympathetic (see *Reason and Revolution,* 391–98).

51 Cf. chap. 5 below.

52 Rodman, "Theory and Practice in the Environmental Movement." The key Marx-
    ian objection to idealism is not directly about metaphysical issues but concerns the
    ideological orientation to practice that idealism historically promotes. Cf. Marcuse,
    Reason and Revolution, xiii. The problem, simply put, is that idealism is prone to
    political naïveté.

53 Rodman, "Paradigm Change in Political Science," 114. Resistance by Rodman's ac-
    count does not arise from calculated self-interest or a sense of obligation: "One resists
    because the threat to the land, the river, or the biosphere is perceived also as a threat
    to the self, or rather to the principle of diversity and spontaneity that is the endan-
    gered side of the basic balance that defines and sustains the very nature of things."
    Ecological resistance follows the assumption that "the human personality discovers
    its structure through interaction with the non-human order": "I am what I am at
    least partly in relation to my natural environment, and changes in that environment
    affect my own identity. If I stand by and let it be destroyed, a part of me is also de-
    stroyed or seriously deranged" (Rodman, "Theory and Practice in the Environmental
    Movement," 54, 56).

54 See Rodman, "The Liberation of Nature?" 113–14: "Instead of trying to fabricate a mythology out of the material of contemporary biology, let us instead pay attention to the patterns of metaphor already present in the language of those who protest the exploitation and liquidation of nonhuman nature."

55 Rodman, "The Liberation of Nature?" 118, quoting Thoreau. Cf. Arendt, "Civil Disobedience," in *Crises of the Republic* for a critique of the antipolitical character of Thoreau's resistance.

56 Rodman, "Paradigm Change in Political Science," 115.

57 Rodman, "Theory and Practice in the Environmental Movement," 56.

58 The great refusal in Marcuse is usually recalled in distinctly political terms, as is suggested at the close of *One-Dimensional Man*, 257. Just as, earlier in that book (63–64), the concept has a central aesthetic dimension, so Marcuse had already proclaimed an aesthetic-political "Great Refusal" in the mid-1950s, invoking utopian fantasy and mythic images of Orpheus and Narcissus to recall a dimension of experience that overcomes the opposition between subject and object so that "the things of nature become free to be what they are" (Marcuse, *Eros and Civilization*, 149, 166). Also see Marcuse's discussion of receptivity to nature in *Counterrevolution and Revolt*, 74, which Rodman quotes in the conclusion to "The Liberation of Nature?" 118.

59 See Benhabib, *Critique, Norm, and Utopia*.

60 See Die Grünen, *Programme of the German Green Party*, 7. The translation used here is from Spretnak and Capra, *Green Politics*, 30.

61 Hülsberg, *The German Greens*, 181 (original emphasis). Also see Markovits and Gorski, *The German Left*, chap. 5; Ferris, "Introduction: Political Realism and Green Strategy," 4.

62 See Hülsberg, 145–48. The focus of strategy debates has subsequently shifted to a realist terrain. See Rüdig, "Green Parties: Germany," 325. Also see Markovits and Gorski, chap. 7, conclusion. From André Gorz to Alain Lipietz, the French scene shows a similar tendency. See Whiteside, "French Ecosocialism."

63 Bahro, *Building the Green Movement*, 211.

64 Quoted in Hülsberg, 46.

65 Ibid., 146, 181–82. Cf. Habermas, "The Movement in Germany," in his *Toward a Rational Society*, 49.

66 See Dobson, *Green Political Thought*, 136–39, 149, 159–161.

67 Marx and Engels, *Manifesto of the Communist Party*, in Marx and Engels, *Selected Works*, 1: 136.

68 Bahro, 45.

69 Ibid., 110. An authoritarian tenor to Bahro's thought, though not explicitly discussed here, is clear enough early on and becomes more pronounced later. For a revealing critique, see Biehl, "'Ecology' and the Modernization of Fascism in the German Ultra-right," 48–58.

70 Bahro, 92.

71 Ferris, 19.

72 Wiesenthal, *Realism in Green Politics*, 179.

73 Ferris, 19.

74 Wiesenthal, 217.

75 Hülsberg, 182–85.

76 Marx, *Capital*, 3: 958; 1: 283.

77 Marx, "Preface to *A Contribution to the Critique of Political Economy*," in Marx and Engels, *Selected Works*, 1: 503–4.

78 Engels, *Socialism: Utopian and Scientific*, in Marx and Engels, *Selected Works*, 3: 137–38.

79 Marx, *Capital*, 3: 502, 510–12, 567–72; Engels, *Socialism: Utopian and Scientific*, 143–45, 150–51. Also see Avineri, *The Social and Political Thought of Karl Marx*, chap. 6.

80 See Macpherson, *The Political Theory of Possessive Individualism*.

81 Cf., however, Marx, *Wage Labor and Capital*, in Marx and Engels, *Selected Works*, 1: 163.

82 See, e.g., Marx and Engels, *Manifesto*, 126–27; Marx, preface, 504; Engels, *Socialism: Utopian and Scientific*, 146–51. Also see Avineri, chap. 8.

83 See, e.g., Ophuls, *Ecology and the Politics of Scarcity*.

84 O'Connor, "Captialism, Nature, Socialism," reprinted under the title "The Second Contradiction of Capitalism," in *The Greening of Marxism*. This and other essays by O'Connor have recently been collected in O'Connor, *Natural Causes*.

85 O'Connor, "The Second Contradiction," 201.

86 Enzensberger, "A Critique of Political Ecology," 44.

87 O'Connor, "Is Sustainable Capitalism Possible?" 158.

88 Pepper, *Eco-Socialism*, 95.

89 O'Connor, "Is Sustainable Capitalism Possible?" 155.

90 O'Connor, "The Second Contradiction," 209, 212.

91 Marx viewed capitalism on a dynamic model, drawn primarily from the English experience. England, then the most advanced form of capitalism, held up an image of the future for others (see Avineri, chap. 6). Central to the system's dynamic character, in Marx's model, are its own socializing tendencies, evident particularly in the transition from commercial to industrial capitalism. But the dynamic character of the system obviously raises the issue of boundaries and identity—as when Marx speaks of "the abolition of the capitalist mode of production within the capitalist mode of production itself" (*Capital*, 3: 569). The ambiguity became especially pointed later when neo-Marxist came to identify "state capitalism" as an emerging socioeconomic formation (see, e.g., Pollock, "State Capitalism").

92 O'Connor, "The Second Contradiction," 212.

93 Hegel, *The Phenomenology of Mind*, 105.

94 Hülsberg, 209.

95 Marx, *The Poverty of Philosophy*, 103 (cf. 104–5, 120, 168); Marx and Engels, *The German Ideology* (part 1), in Marx and Engels, *Selected Works*, 1: 41. Cf. Marx and Engels, *Manifesto*, 118. The nineteenth-century emergence of the concept of "social movement" is discussed in Wilkinson, *Social Movement*, chap. 1.

96 See Marcuse, *An Essay on Liberation*, and *Counterrevolution and Revolt*, chap. 4. The idea of a single movement is presupposed, for example, in Habermas's early essay, "The Movement in Germany."

97 Laclau and Mouffe, *Hegemony and Socialist Strategy*.

98 See, e.g., Spretnak and Capra, xxiv–xxvi.

99 See, e.g., Commoner, "Workplace Burden"; Nelson, "The Place of Women in Polluted Places"; Hartley, "Environmental Justice"; Sachs, "Upholding Human Rights and Environmental Justice"; Eckersley, "Green Politics and the New Class."

100 Gramsci, *Selections from the Prison Notebooks*, 171–73, 414.

101 Ibid., 200; cf. 172, 177.

102 Laclau and Mouffe, 142, 48.

103 Ibid., 69–70, 168–69. Note esp. in this connection the way Mouffe draws upon Carl Schmitt's opposition between "friend and enemy" as central to the concept of the political in her *The Return of the Political*, 111. Cf. Carroll, *Organizing Dissent*.

104 Laclau and Mouffe, 190.
105 Lyotard, *The Postmodern Condition*, 15, 33–35, 37.
106 Laclau and Mouffe, 181.
107 See, e.g., Eckersley, "Green Politics," 59.
108 Lipietz, *Green Hopes*, xiii, stresses the limits of any "postmodern cobbling together" of social movements, claiming that "political ecology" offers a "new paradigm" that is "comparable in structure" to Marxism. He instead calls for unity in a "common struggle" (31–34). The "green paradigm" retains something of "historical and dialectical materialism," but has no inexorable direction, only an uncertain direction of hope. Though Lipietz endorses the "autonomous expression" of different social movements, he regards such expression simply as "the precondition of their possible future convergence in a Green paradigm." The green movement, he argues, has the good fortune, coming after Marxism, of being chastened by unhappy historical experience. The green movement, though "in danger of making many mistakes," is thus unlikely to become "one huge monstrous error." Lipietz at times seems tacitly hesitant about the metaphor of movement, and he calls for a "right to dissensus." But he never really ventures beyond that metaphor to address its problems as a guide to action. Lipietz's position would seem to be something of an inversion of Gorz, *Ecology as Politics*: "the ecological movement is not an end in itself, but a stage in the larger struggle" (3; emphasis deleted).

3 · THE GREENING OF PUBLIC DISCOURSE

1 Dryzek, "Strategies of Ecological Democratization," 121. Cf. Dryzek, *The Politics of the Earth*. Also see Myerson and Rydin, *The Language of Environment*. For a relevant, though perhaps overstated, discussion in terms of "postenvironmentalism," see Eder, "The Institutionalisation of Environmentalism."
2 See Meadows et al., *The Limits to Growth*.
3 See, Daly, *Toward a Steady State Economy*.
4 Mill, *Principles of Political Economy*, 3: 752.
5 Meadows et al., *The Limits to Growth*, 179.
6 See Vargish, "Why the Person Sitting Next to You Hates 'Limits to Growth'"; Cole et al., *Thinking about the Future: A Critique of the "Limits to Growth"*; Rosenbluth, "Economists and the Growth Controversy."
7 See Paehlke, "Eco-history."
8 World Commission on Environment and Development (Brundtland Commission), *Our Common Future*, 43, 40 (emphasis added). The commission and the report became popularly known for its chair, Norwegian Prime Minister Gro Harlem Brundtland.
9 See, e.g., Turner, *Sustainable Environmental Management*; Brooks, "The Challenge of Sustainability."
10 Hays, *Beauty, Health, and Permanence*, 393–94.
11 Ibid., 405. This tendency can be seen as a continuation of the technocratic approach to resource management initiated by the early conservation movement. See Hays, *Conservation and the Gospel of Efficiency*.
12 Hays, *Beauty, Health, and Permanence*, 410–15.
13 Cf. World Commission, 211–13.
14 Cf. Bruton and Howlett, "Differences of Opinion"; Davis, *Greening Business*.
15 Roy Aiken, Executive Vice-President of INCO (International Nickel Company), quoted in Collison, "The Greening of the Board Room," 44.

16 Dryzek, *The Politics of the Earth*, 128.

17 Davis, 26.

18 Quoted in Athanasiou, *Divided Planet*, 10–11.

19 Athanasiou, 9–11, 200–3.

20 Ibid., 11–12. On Greenpeace's position on the Earth Summit, see Shaiko, "Greenpeace U.S.A.," 98.

21 Athanasiou, 10, 200. *Agenda 21*, the declaration of the Rio Summit, has been described as "the successor" to Brundtland (Lafferty, "The Politics of Sustainable Development," 194). On the United Nations follow-up after five years, see the "Earth Summit +5" Website (under "environment" at www.un.org/ecosodev/).

22 See Pearce et al., *Blueprint for a Green Economy*, annex; Brooks, 408.

23 Dryzek, *The Politics of the Earth*, 124.

24 Norgaard, *Development Betrayed*, chap. 2.

25 See Gibson, "Respecting Ignorance and Uncertainty."

26 Brooks, 408.

27 Lindblom, *The Intelligence of Democracy*. Also see Weiss and Woodhouse, "Reframing Incrementalism."

28 Lee, *Compass and Gyroscope*, 8.

29 McCaskey, "A Contingency Approach to Planning: Planning with and Planning without Goals."

30 Lee, 199–200.

31 Majone and Wildavsky, "Implementation as Evolution," 168.

32 Ibid. Cf. Hajer, "The Politics of Environmental Performance Review," 30; O'Riordan, "The Politics of Sustainability."

33 Cf. Weiss and Woodhouse.

34 Kennedy, foreword, vii.

35 See Nuu-chah-nulth Tribal Council, *Nuu-chah-nulth Land Question*. Also see Hatch, "The Clayoquot Protests"; Maingon, "Clayoquot."

36 Darling, *In Search of Consensus*, 8.

37 Steering Committee of the District of Tofino and the Tofino–Long Beach Chamber of Commerce, *Sustainable Development Strategy for Clayoquot Sound*, 4.

38 Ibid., 3. Also see Friends of Clayoquot Sound, "The Battle for Clayoquot Sound," 29.

39 Darling, 16, 34.

40 Langer, "It Happened Suddenly," 253.

41 Province of British Columbia, "New Scientific Panel Will Ensure Forest Activities in Clayoquot Sound Stand Up to World Standards," *News Release*, 22 October 1993, quoted in Burney, "Sustainable Development and Civil Disobedience," 151.

42 See Burney. The account here of the Clayoquot case is significantly indebted to the research of Burney, who was a participant-observer in some key events.

43 Friends of Clayoquot Sound, "Statement of Goals" (spring 1993), quoted in ibid., 128.

44 Scientific Panel, *First Nations' Perspectives*. Also see Friends of Clayoquot Sound, "Implementing the Scientific Panel."

45 Porritt, "Sustainable Development," 38.

46 Salsman, "'Corporate Environmentalism' and Other Suicidal Tendencies," 124.

47 Woiceshyn and Woiceshyn, "Commentary: 'Corporate Environmentalism' and Other Suicidal Tendencies," 145.

48 March and Simon, *Organizations*, 164–65.

49 See Hajer, *The Politics of Environmental Discourse*, chap. 6.

50 See Leiss, *Under Technology's Thumb*, chap. 3.

1   On policy professionalism, see Schön, *The Reflective Practitioner*, esp. 338–54; Tribe, "Policy Science." Also see Torgerson, "Between Knowledge and Politics" and the literature cited there. On dissenting social movements, see Carroll, *Organizing Dissent*; Offe, "New Social Movements"; Dalton and Kuechler, *Challenging the Political Order*.

2   See, e.g., Dryzek, "Policy Sciences of Democracy"; Fischer, "Citizen Participation and the Democratization of Policy Expertise."

3   For discussions relevant to agenda setting, problem definition, and epistemology, see Cobb and Elder, "The Politics of Agenda Building"; Dery, *Problem Definition in Policy Analysis*; Kingdon, *Agendas, Alternatives, and Public Policies*; Rochefort and Cobb, "Problem Definition"; Hawkesworth, "Epistemology and Policy Analysis."

4   See Torgerson, "Power and Insight in Policy Discourse" and "Limits of the Administrative Mind."

5   Carson, *Silent Spring*. Also see Graham, *Since Silent Spring*, pt. 1.

6   See, e.g., Szaz, *EcoPopulism*, chap. 8. Szaz stresses antitoxics, feminist, antiracist, and environmental justice interconnections in the "progressive politics" of a larger "environmental populism."

7   See Schlosberg, *Environmental Justice and the New Pluralism*.

8   Hays, *Beauty, Health, and Permanence*, 394, 412. Also see Tribe, "Policy Science," 97–98.

9   See Paehlke and Torgerson, "Environmental Politics and the Administrative State."

10 For an early statement on the fortunes of environmentalism, see Downs, "Up and Down with Ecology—The 'Issue Attention Cycle'"; cf. Schrecker, "Resisting Environmental Regulation."

11 See, e.g., Tribe, "Technology Assessment and the Fourth Discontinuity"; Torgerson, *Industrialization and Assessment*, chap. 7.

12 Bartlett, "Ecological Reason in Administration," 82; 5. Taylor, *Making Bureaucracies Think*.

13 See Commoner, *The Closing Circle*.

14 Weale, *The New Politics of Pollution*, 14, 28.

15 Ibid., 31, 78, 135; cf. Hajer, *The Politics of Environmental Discourse*, 26.

16 Weale, *New Politics*, 100–101.

17 Frosch, "Industrial Ecology," 800–801.

18 Weale, *New Politics*, 29.

19 Cf. Fischer, *Technocracy and the Politics of Expertise*.

20 Weale, *New Politics*, 15.

21 Epstein, Brown, and Pope, *Hazardous Waste in America*, 37. Toxic wastes, strictly speaking, are only the most dramatic form of hazardous wastes, but the distinction is not significant here.

22 Gore, foreword to ibid., x.

23 See Szaz, 4; Williams and Matheny, *Democracy, Dialogue, and Environmental Disputes*, pt. 2, chap. 7. On Love Canal, see Levine, *Love Canal*. Also see Ripley, "Toxic Substances, Hazardous Wastes, and Public Policy." It should be noted that, during the 1970s, environmentally concerned legislators in the United States made some significant early steps with legislation relevant to toxic waste management.

24 On the misadventures of Superfund in the United States, see Williams and Matheny,

101–9; also see Paehlke and Torgerson, "Toxic Waste and the Administrative State"; Cohen and Tipermas, "Superfund."

25 Williams and Matheny, 167. Also see Szaz: "From the point of view of industry, regulators, and most policy scientists, siting opposition was *the problem*" (105; original emphasis). Cf. Rabe, *Beyond Nimby.*

26 Castrilli, "Hazardous Wastes Law in Canada and Ontario," 55. Also see Paehlke and Torgerson, "Toxic Waste and the Administrative State."

27 See Szaz, 144–49; Frosch, 800. Also see Paehlke and Torgerson, "Toxic Waste as Public Business."

28 Szasz, 145. Also see Paehlke and Torgerson, "Toxic Waste and the Administrative State"; Williams and Matheny, chaps. 7–8. On some further issues, see Torgerson, "Policy Professionalism and the Voices of Dissent," 358–59.

29 See Dryzek, *Rational Ecology,* 16–20, and "Complexity and Rationality in Public Life."

30 Quoted in Dryzek, "Complexity and Rationality," 429.

31 Lovins, *Soft Energy Paths.* In this connection, Lovins, "Cost-Risk-Benefit Assessments in Energy Policy," also prefers democratic process to technocratic policy analysis.

32 See Bachrach and Baratz, *Power and Poverty,* pt. 1; Torgerson, "Power and Insight in Policy Discourse," 284–89.

33 Lovins, *Soft Energy Paths,* 24–25.

34 Bosso, "The Contextual Bases of Problem Defintion," 190. Also see Coughlin, "The Tragedy of the Concrete Commons."

35 Carson, 297, 277–78.

36 Hajer, *The Politics of Environmental Discourse,* 281.

37 Ibid., 281–82. Cf. Beck, Giddens, and Lash, *Reflexive Modernization,* esp. chap. 4.

38 Hajer, *The Politics of Environmental Discourse,* 280. Cf. Cristoff, "Ecological Modernisation, Ecological Modernities."

39 Daly, "Electric Power, Employment, and Economic Growth," 276.

40 Mill, *Principles of Political Economy,* 3: 754.

41 Offe, "A Non-Productivist Design for Social Policies," 71. Also see Offe et al., "A Basic Income Guaranteed by the State."

42 See Paehlke, *Environmentalism and the Future of Progressive Politics,* 24–40.

43 Ibid., 104–10.

44 Dobson, editorial comment, in *The Green Reader,* 152.

45 Johnson, "The Guaranteed Income as an Environmental Measure," 179, 188.

46 Ibid., 181–85. A basic income scheme, like other social welfare measures, would serve to support levels of effective demand in the economy. In this respect, a guaranteed basic income would tend to maintain, perhaps to an extent even to expand, total economic activity. However, a systematic loosening of connections between the livelihood of individuals and their uncertain prospects for employment would tend to reduce the scope and intensity of motives for growth—that is, those pressures that often undercut the potential for serious public deliberation about economic alternatives and environmental costs. See Van Parijs, "The Second Marriage of Justice and Efficiency" 215–16; Offe, "A Non-Productivist Design for Social Policies," 70–71.

47 Achterberg, "From Sustainability to Basic Income," 3, 17–18.

48 See Van Parijs, "Competing Justifications of Basic Income."

49 See, e.g., Habermas, *Knowledge and Human Interests,* esp. 4, 67.

50 Galbraith, *The New Industrial State,* 37. Julian Simon rests his Promethean outlook

on a conviction that "solutions are eventually found," at least in a "free society"—that is, one governed by the logic of the market. See Myers and Simon, *Scarcity or Abundance?*, 123, 198.

51 However much "bounded rationality" may be ascribed to intrinsic limitations of human individuals and collectivities, it is characteristically accentuated in administrative organizations, where Herbert Simon first identified it. See his *Administrative Behavior*, esp. xxix–xxx; cf. Dryzek,"Complexity and Rationality in Public Life." Lasswell's stress on contextual orientation and intellectual flexibility may be regarded as an effort to press against such boundaries. See Torgerson, "Contextual Orientation in Policy Analysis."

52 Emery and Trist, "The Causal Texture of Organizational Environments," 254 (original emphasis); also Trist, "A Concept of Organizational Ecology." Also see Hooker and van Hulst, "The Meaning of Environmental Problems for Public Political Institutions," 131–34.

53 For the formulation of this concept, see Weinberg, "Science and Trans-Science." For some striking applications, see Lovins, "Cost-Risk-Benefit Assessments in Energy Policy," 920–27.

54 Gibson, "Respecting Ignorance and Uncertainty," 158, 173. The advent of the "precautionary principle" in environmental policy discourse is significant in this connection. The principle draws attention to the prevailing bias of the administrative mind, for it is a principle that is supposed to come into play when the potential harm of an action has not been proven with scientific certainty. The principle thus exposes what is really remarkable and worthy of investigation: that it ever came to pass that the need for such proof could generally be taken for granted. Once this tenet has been drawn into question, moreover, it becomes possible, in principle, to shift the burden of proof, placing it on those whose actions might threaten harm. However, this is not as straightforward a move as it might immediately appear. It is not only a question of what actions might cause (or prevent) environmental harm, but also (and here is the rub for the usual promotion of the precautionary principle) what kind of *inaction* might cause (or prevent) environmental harm. For a useful survey of the concept and its application, see Cameron and Wade-Gery, "Addressing Uncertainty."

55 Gibson, "Out of Control and Beyond Understanding," 243.

56 Tesh, "Environmentalism, Pre-environmentalism and Public Policy."

57 Williams and Matheny, 96.

58 Tesh, 2–7.

59 Tesh and Williams, "Identity Politics, Disinterested Politics, and Environmental Justice," 297.

60 Tesh, 8–13.

61 Gibson, "Out of Control and Beyond Understanding," 253.

62 Gibson, "Respecting Ignorance and Uncertainty," 167.

63 Williams and Matheny, 193, 196, 200–203, 176–80; cf. Matheny and Williams, "The Crisis of Administrative Legitimacy."

64 See Scöhn, 338–54, and Fischer, *Technocracy and the Politics of Expertise*. Also see Peterse, "The Mobilization of Counter-Expertise."

65 One possibility is a kind of "science court" designed to avoid constraints on participation that might be suggested by conventional legal practice. See Fischer, "Citizen Participation and the Democratization of Policy Expertise." For other possibilities of "discursive design" in an environmental context, see Dryzek, "Designs for Environmental Discourse."

66 Majone, "Technology Assessment and Policy Analysis," 174.

67 Majone, *Evidence, Argument and Persuasion in the Policy Process,* 5–6. Also see Otway, "Public Wisdom, Expert Fallibility."

68 Lovins and Price, *Non-Nuclear Futures,* xix.

69 T. Berger, *Northern Frontier, Northern Homeland,* 1: 161.

70 See Gamble, "The Berger Inquiry"; Torgerson, "Between Knowledge and Politics."

71 Majone, "Technology Assessment and Policy Analysis," 174.

72 See Dryzek, "Policy Analysis and Planning: From Science to Argument." Also see Dryzek, "Discursive Designs."

73 See Fischer, "Participatory Expertise," as well as his *Technocracy and the Politics of Expertise.*

74 Fischer and Forester, *The Argumentative Turn in Policy Analysis and Planning.*

75 Mitroff, "Systemic Problem Solving," 130.

76 See Mason and Mitroff, *Challenging Strategic Planning Assumptions;* Mitroff and Mason, *Creating a Dialectical Social Science.*

77 March and Simon, *Organizations,* 164–65.

78 See Torgerson, "The Paradox of Organizational Rationality."

79 March, "The Technology of Foolishness" and "Footnotes to Organizational Change," 181. Also see Kahn, "Toward an Organizational Sense of Humor."

80 See Torgerson, "Power and Insight in Policy Discourse," 286–88, and "The Paradox of Organizational Rationality."

81 See Bakhtin, *Rabelais and His World:* "All the symbols of the carnival idiom are filled . . . with the sense of the gay relativity of prevailing truths and authorities. We find here a characteristic logic, the peculiar logic of the 'inside out' (*à l'envers*), of the 'turnabout,' of continual shifting from top to bottom, from front to rear, of numerous parodies and travesties, humiliations, profanations, comic crownings and uncrownings" (11).

82 See de Bono, *Lateral Thinking:* "In the reversal method one takes things as they are and then turns them round, inside out, upside down, back to front. Then one sees what happens. It is a provocative rearrangement" (125–26). And de Bono adds: "In some cases reversal may seem utterly ridiculous. This does not matter. It is just as useful to practice being ridiculous as to practice reversal" (129).

5 · COMEDY AND TRAGEDY IN GREEN POLITICS

1 Kariel, *Open Systems,* 114. For his more recent treatment of such themes on an explicitly postmodern terrain, see Kariel, *The Desperate Politics of Postmodernism.* By contrast, to enter politics was, in Max Weber's view, to consort with "diabolical forces." See his "Politics as a Vocation," in *From Max Weber,* 128, 125.

2 Kariel, *The Promise of Politics.*

3 Henri Bergson, *Laughter: An Essay on the Meaning of the Comic,* quoted in Kariel, *Open Systems,* 110.

4 A. N. Whitehead, *Science and the Modern World,* 17, quoted in Hardin, "The Tragedy of the Commons," 20.

5 Hardin, 26–27.

6 See Torgerson, "Obsolescent Leviathan," 18–21.

7 See Ophuls, *Ecology and the Politics of Scarcity;* Heilbroner, *An Inquiry into the Human Prospect.*

8 Ophuls, "Leviathan or Oblivion?" 229.

9   Bookchin, *Post-Scarcity Anarchism*, 33, 41.

10 *Republic* III, 388e; *Laws* VII, 816d–817c.

11 See Curtius, *European Literature and the Latin Middle Ages*, 420–22; Benedict, *The Rule of St. Benedict*, chap. 4 (53, 55); chap. 6, "On Silence."

12 Descartes, *Discourse on Method*, 119; Weber, *The Protestant Ethic and the Spirit of Capitalism*, 118, 108.

13 See Aaron, *Main Currents of Sociological Thought*, 1: chap. 2, "Auguste Comte."

14 For Marx's famous statement on the repetition of "tragedy" as "farce," see *The Eighteenth Brumaire of Louis Bonaparte* in Marx and Engels, *Selected Works*, 1: 398. Marx's apparent fixation on the figure of Prometheus is portrayed (rather bitterly and without acknowledgment of Marx's ironic sensibility) as a "Promethean complex" in Feuer, "The Character and Thought of Karl Marx" Also see Marx, *Early Writings*: "The last stage of a world-historical formation is comedy" (48). Cf. Bakhtin, *Rabelais and His World*, 436.

15 Joseph Wood Krutch, *The Modern Temper*, quoted in Meeker, *The Comedy of Survival* (1974), 92 (all references to Meeker in this chapter are to the 1974 edition).

16 Cf. Kenneth Boulding, "Commons and Community: The Idea of a Public," 286.

17 Meeker, 122.

18 William Faulkner, *The Reivers*, quoted in ibid., 137.

19 See Kerr, *Tragedy and Comedy*, esp. 144. Also see Holman, *A Handbook to Literature*, 107–8, 531.

20 Meeker, 26.

21 It is interesting that Dante found it necessary to give an explicit explanation of his title. See his Letter to Can Grande della Scala, 147–48. Also see Meeker, 163, 182.

22 Meeker, 182, 191.

23 Nietzsche, *On the Genealogy of Morals*, essay 1, section 15. Kaufmann, the editor and translator, indicates (485 n. 1) that Nietzsche's quotation from Aquinas is inexact, but the correction does not alter the substance (49). Augustine wondered whether the torture would be just physical or both physical and spiritual; he expected the latter, but allowed that he would not know for sure until the hereafter. See Augustine, *City of God*, XXI, 9–10.

24 Meeker, 42.

25 Kerr, 64.

26 See Leitch, *Deconstructive Criticism*.

27 Aristotle, *Poetics* 1449b 20–30.

28 Eco, *The Name of the Rose*, 468. Cf. Janko, *Aristotle on Comedy: Towards a Reconstruction of* Poetics II, pt. 4.

29 Eco, 475.

30 P. Berger, *The Sacred Canopy*.

31 Weber, "Science as a Vocation," in *From Max Weber*, 139.

32 See Leiss, *The Domination of Nature*.

33 Weber, *The Protestant Ethic and the Spirit of Capitalism*, 119.

34 See Torgerson, "Limits of the Administrative Mind," 120–21; chap. 1 above.

35 Bahro, *Building the Green Movement*. 45–46, 26.

36 See Eckersley, *Environmentalism and Political Theory*, 163–67.

37 Weber, *The Protestant Ethic and the Spirit of Capitalism*, 181.

38 Kellner, "'To Make Truth Laugh': Eco's *The Name of the Rose*," 29 n. 35. Kellner indicates that St. Benedict's Rule banned laughter, but this is not quite accurate. See n. 11 above.

39 Weber, *The Protestant Ethic and the Spirit of Capitalism*, 118.

40 Bakhtin, *Rabelais and His World*, 5–6.

41 Barry Weisberg, "A One Day Teach-in Is Like an All Day Sucker," *Liberation* (May 1970), cited in Weisberg, *Beyond Repair*, 185 n. 10.

42 Spretnak and Capra, *Green Politics*, 5.

43 The information on EAAAC?! is drawn from Timothy Doyle, *Green Power*, chap. 7. Doyle insists that EAAAC?! exists, that it is no joke (personal communication, 5 October 1997).

44 Horkheimer, *Eclipse of Reason*, 187; Horkheimer and Adorno, *Dialectic of Enlightenment*, 120–67.

45 This is the burden of Habermas's *The Theory of Communicative Action*. Also see, however, Habermas, *Knowledge and Human Interests*, esp. 157, 163, 176, 193, and *On the Logic of the Social Sciences*, chap. 3. Cf. Benhabib, *Critique, Norm, and Utopia*.

46 Denying argumentation through argument would be a form of what Habermas calls "performative contradiction" ("Discourse Ethics," 80, 88–95), drawing upon an idea advanced by Karl-Otto Apel. On the problem of genre, see Habermas, *The Philosophical Discourse of Modernity*, 185–210, where Derrida is described as not being among "those philosophers who like to argue" (193).

47 Bakhtin, "Discourse in the Novel," 275, 288.

48 See, e.g., Habermas, *Legitimation Crisis*, 1–8; J. O'Connor, *The Meaning of Crisis*.

49 Holman, 107, 531.

50 Kerr, 58, 73–74, 64; cf. 78–79.

51 Ibid., 263; Esslin, *The Theatre of the Absurd*, 361.

52 Kerr, 32–33.

53 Ibid., 25. Kerr, 23–25, stresses the fragmentary character of what remains of the ancient plays. The only complete tragic trilogy extant is Aeschylus' *Oresteia*, though there is some information on other trilogies. The only satyr play remaining is Euripides' *Cyclops*. (Sophocles' *Oedipus* cycle, according to Kerr, was conceived in terms of separate plays, not as a trilogy in the sense relevant here.) No complete sequence of trilogy plus satyr play remains.

54 Blake's illustration on the title page has in the foreground two naked human bodies embracing and kissing while other naked bodies rise to heaven through the flames of hell. "The Voice of the Devil" (plate 4) responds accordingly to theological threats of eternal torment: "Energy is Eternal Delight." Blake also indicates that the qualities of Dante as a poet are "infinite" (plate 22), indirectly suggesting that Dante, perhaps even more than Milton, "was a true Poet and of the Devil's party without knowing it" (plate 6). Indeed, despite the dualism of Heaven and Hell in Dante's medieval cosmos, it is the poet Dante who implicitly links Hell, Purgatory, and Paradise by the path of his journey. Only by climbing over Satan's body does Dante reach the exit from Hell on his way to Purgatory and Heaven. And once Dante (with Virgil) is out of Hell, an explicit discussion is needed to explain why this exit does not represent a violation of divine law. Is all hope really to be abandoned? See Dante, *Hell*, canto 34: 69–139; *Purgatory*, canto 1: 39–108. On Blake as a "metaphysical satirist," see Frye, *Fearful Symmetry*, 193–201.

55 Kerr, 33, 262.

56 Dürrenmatt, "Problems of the Theatre," 32–34.

57 Politics can of course be construed in discursive terms as a domain of texts and, to a large extent, in terms of narrative genres. This does not mean that one must accept the curious metaphysical residue lurking in the postmodern predeliction for textualism. See Rorty, "Idealism and Textualism," esp. 154. A prime task of political thought (as Arendt might argue) is to break the spell of such "metaphysical fallacies" for the

sake of a common world, a space for politics. See Arendt, *Thinking*, in *The Life of the Mind*, e.g., 44–45.

58 Merchant, *Radical Ecology*, 74.

59 Eco, 470.

60 Rodman, "The Liberation of Nature?" 112.

61 Rodman, "Paradigm Change in Political Science," 66; cf. Rodman, "Four Forms of Ecological Consciousness Reconsidered."

62 Rodman, "Paradigm Change in Political Science," 66; Rodman, "Four Forms of Ecological Consciousness," 3.

63 Rodman, "Paradigm Change in Political Science," 67.

64 Rodman, "Four Forms of Ecological Consciousness Reconsidered," 88–92.

65 Rodman, "Paradigm Change in Political Science," 67.

66 Rodman, "Four Forms of Ecological Consciousness," 4.

67 Ibid., 1, 3 (emphasis added).

68 Rodman, "Paradigm Change in Political Science," 66.

69 See Goodman, "The Theory of Diversity-Stability Relationships in Ecology," 261; Norton, *Why Preserve Natural Variety?*, chap. 4. Cf. Bookchin, *Post-Scarcity Anarchism*, 57–58, 71; Dobson, *Green Political Thought*, 25.

70 Rodman, "The Liberation of Nature?" 114.

71 Ibid., 115; see Rodman, "Paradigm Change in Political Science," 68.

72 Shepard and McKinley, *The Subversive Science*. McIntosh, *The Background of Ecology*, flatly states: "Ecology was not, and is not a predictive science" (2). McIntosh adds that currently, "even in its limited scientific context," ecology is "a battleground" between reductionism and holism (17).

73 See Merchant, *The Death of Nature*, 293; Commoner, *The Closing Circle*, 33–39; Dryzek, *Rational Ecology*, 20; Worster, *Nature's Economy*.

74 Leopold, "The Land Ethic," in *A Sand Country Almanac*.

75 Spretnak, *The Spiritual Dimension in Green Politics*, 33, quoting Gary Snyder, "Anarchism, Buddhism, and Political Economy," lecture at Fort Mason Center, San Francisco, 27 February 1984.

76 Spretnak, *The Spiritual Dimension*, 33; cf. 32, 63.

77 Kerr, 144.

78 Bakhtin, *Rabelais and His World*, 21.

79 Ibid., 134, 78, 119, 101.

80 Adrados, *Festival, Comedy and Tragedy*, 358, 9.

81 Estes, "Baubo: The Belly Goddess," 338.

82 There are interesting variations to the story of Baubo. See Monaghan, *The Book of Goddesses and Heroines*, entries for "Baubo," "Demeter," "Hecate," "Iambe," "Gaea, Gaia, Ge." Also consult Walker, "Baubo," in *The Woman's Dictionary of Symbols and Sacred Objects*, 235–36. On the historical context, see Gimbutas, "Women and Culture in Goddess-Oriented Old Europe." The "Gaia hypothesis" was formulated by Lovelock, *Gaia*.

83 Rodman's remarkable parodies are noteworthy in this regard. See his "On the Human Question, Being the Report of the Erewhonian High Commission to Evaluate Technological Society" and "The Dolphin Papers."

84 Gibson, "Respecting Ignorance and Uncertainty," 158.

85 Saward, "Green Democracy?" 77.

86 Bentley, "On the Other Side of Despair," 146. Cf. Timmerman, "The Environmentalist as Dark Comedian."

87 See Arendt, *Between Past and Future*, 153, on Machiavelli's *virtù* as virtuosity.

1 B. Taylor, "Environmental Ethics and Political Theory," 567, 576.

2 B. Taylor, "Democracy and Environmental Ethics," 86.

3 Dobson, *Green Political Thought*, 5, 7. Also see Eckersley, *Environmentalism and Political Theory*, chap. 3.

4 See Avineri and de-Shalit, *Communitarianism and Individualism*.

5 The central text is Aristotle's *Nicomachean Ethics* VI. Also see Beiner, *Politial Judgment*; MacIntyre, *Whose Justice? Which Rationality?*, chaps. 6–8; Gadamer, "Practical Philosophy as a Model of the Human Sciences" and *Truth and Method*, esp. 312–24.

6 See, e.g., Livingston, *One Cosmic Instant: A Natural History of Human Arrogance*; Ehrenfeld, *The Arrogance of Humanism*.

7 See Augustine, *City of God* XIV, 11, 28.

8 Norton, *Toward Unity among Environmentalists*, offers an analysis of the place of "moralists" in the green movement. Fox's *Toward a Transpersonal Ecology* promotes an ecocentric understanding of the self that transcends a narrow individualism, avoids moralism, and fully grasps the human character of the ecocentric self, yet does not take any clear political position. In a contrasting, though ironically complementary, way, Goodin in *Green Political Theory* argues that inasmuch as green "personal lifestyle recommendations" are "of an essentially non-political sort" they should be clearly separated from the "more specifically political strands in green thought" (15).

9 See Dryzek, "Green Reason" and "Political and Ecological Communication"; Eckersley, *Environmentalism and Political Theory*, chap. 5; Dobson, "Critical Theory and Green Politics," 197–98. Cf. Whitebrook, "The Problem of Nature in Habermas", 302–7; Habermas, "A Reply to My Critics," 247–50. Also see Habermas, "Remarks on Discourse Ethics," 105–11.

10 On communicative ethics, see the sources cited above, ch. 1, n. 61.

11 See Habermas, *The Structural Transformation of the Public Sphere*; Calhoun, *Habermas and the Public Sphere*.

12 See Rodman, "Four Forms of Ecological Consciousness Reconsidered."

13 Leopold, "The Land Ethic," in *A Sand County Almanac*, 241.

14 Fox in *Toward a Transpersonal Ecology*, 19–22, and Eckersley in *Environmentalism and Political Theory*, 55–56, maintain that it is trivial to point out the inescapably human character of ethical judgment. This may sometimes be so in the context of serious philosophical discussion, but the paradox remains culturally and politically significant: ecocentrism is not only human, but all-too-human. Also see Manes, *Green Rage*, 157–58.

15 See esp. Rodman, "Four Forms of Ecological Consciousness Reconsidered." Eckersley, *Environmentalism and Political Theory*, chap. 2, follows Rodman to a large extent in her account of the "environmental spectrum."

16 See Rodman, "Four Forms of Ecological Consciousness Reconsidered," 82–84, and "Four Forms of Ecological Consciousness."

17 Rodman, "Four Forms of Ecological Consciousness Reconsidered," 84–86; Rodman, "Four Forms of Ecological Consciousness," 72–73.

18 Rodman, "Four Forms of Ecological Consciousness Reconsidered," 86–88; Rodman, "The Liberation of Nature?"; Rodman, "Animal Justice."

19 Rodman, "Four Forms of Ecological Consciousness Reconsidered," 88–92.

20 Cf. Arendt, *Thinking*, in *The Life of the Mind*, 143.

21 See Honig, *Political Theory and the Displacement of Politics*, chap. 2.

22 Cf. Benhabib, *Critique, Norm, and Utopia.*

23 Habermas, "What Is Universal Pragmatics?" 2–4; Apel, "The Common Presupposi- tions of Hermeneutics and Ethics," 47.

24 Horkheimer, "The Latest Attack on Metaphysics," 152.

25 See Scheler, *Man's Place in Nature;* Leiss, *The Domination of Nature.*

26 See, e.g., Horkheimer, *Eclipse of Reason;* Habermas, "Science and Technology as 'Ide- ology'" in his *Toward a Rational Society.*

27 Horkheimer and Adorno, *Dialectic of Enlightenment,* 9.

28 Ibid., 33; also see 43–80.

29 See Habermas, "Toward a Theory of Communicative Competence"; Habermas, *Le- gitimation Crisis,* pt. 3, chaps. 2, 3, 6.

30 See Young, "Impartiality and the Civic Public" and "Communication and the Other"; Benhabib, "Communicative Ethics and Current Controversies in Political Philoso- phy"; Warnke, "Communicative Rationality and Cultural Values."

31 Habermas, *Legitimation Crisis,* 142.

32 Peters, *Reason and Compassion,* 54.

33 Apel, "Types of Rationality Today: The Continuum of Reason between Science and Ethics," 142.

34 See Peters, 33–35; C. Taylor, "Neutrality in Political Science"; Berlin, "Rationality of Value Judgement."

35 Cf. Dallmayr, "Reason and Emancipation: Notes on Habermas," 96.

36 See Apel, "The Conflicts of Our Time and the Problem of Political Ethics."

37 Cf. Whitebrook, "The Problem of Nature in Habermas," 302–7.

38 Dryzek, "Green Reason," 205.

39 Freud, "A Difficulty in the Path of Psycho-Analysis," 140.

40 Cf. Habermas, *Knowledge and Human Interests.*

41 Manes, "Nature and Silence," 339.

42 Ibid. Also see Manes, *Green Rage,* 156–58. Cf. Lukács, *History and Class Conscious- ness,* 234; Leiss, *Domination of Nature,* 23.

43 See Bernstein, *Beyond Objectivism and Relativism.*

44 Leopold, 137.

45 Dryzek, "Green Reason," 199.

46 Seed et al., *Thinking Like a Mountain: Toward a Council of All Beings.*

47 Bakhtin, *Rabelais and His World,* 121–22.

48 See above, chap. 5, nn. 80–82.

49 King, "Healing the Wounds," 120–21.

50 Cf. Kushner, "Interpretations of Life and Prohibitions against Killing," 148; Heming- way, *The Old Man and the Sea,* 105.

51 Cf. Arendt, *Between Past and Future,* 220–24.

52 Cf. Leiss, *The Domination of Nature,* 33–35, 55–57.

53 Leopold, 240.

54 Lovelock, *Gaia,* 145. Cf. Dryzek, "Green Reason," 205.

55 Hay, "The Politics of Tasmania's World Heritage Area."

56 Weale, "The Limits of Ecocentrism," 342.

7 · THE GREEN PUBLIC SPHERE

1 Sagoff, *The Economy of the Earth,* 53.

2 Arendt, *Between Past and Future,* 219–24.

3 See Dryzek, *Discursive Democracy*; Benhabib, "Toward a Deliberative Model of Democratic Legitimacy."

4 See Macpherson, *Democratic Theory*, chaps. 10, 14.

5 Myerson and Rydin, *The Language of Environment*, chap. 1.

6 Cf. Tokar, *Earth for Sale*.

7 Dryzek, *The Politics of the Earth*, 95.

8 See Macpherson, *The Political Theory of Possessive Individualism*.

9 See Tawney, *Religion and the Rise of Capitalism*, chaps. 1.ii, 4.iii.

10 See McFie, *The Individual and Society*, chap. 6.

11 This phrase concludes the discussion of Locke in Strauss, *Natural Right and History*, 251. In a radically different vein, see the critique of the "performance principle" in Marcuse, *Eros and Civilization*, 44–45, 157.

12 Suggestive in this regard is Gundersen's *The Environmental Promise of Democratic Deliberation*.

13 Arendt, *Between Past and Future*, 241.

14 These three aspects correspond to Arendt's tripartite scheme of the active life in *The Human Condition*, as discussed above in chap. 1.

15 Arendt, *Between Past and Future*, 222–23.

16 For this contrast between antiquity and modernity in Arendt, compare *The Human Condition* with *On Revolution*.

17 Arendt, *The Origins of Totalitarianism*, chaps. 10, 13. Cf. Arendt, *Between Past and Future*, 93.

18 See Arendt, *On Revolution*, chap. 2.

19 Arendt, *The Human Condition*, 180.

20 Arendt, *On Revolution*, chaps. 3, 6.

21 Arendt, *Between Past and Future*, 263.

22 Arendt, *Crises of the Republic*, 203.

23 See ibid., 6, 12, 18–20, 233; Arendt, "On Hannah Arendt," 317; Arendt, *Between Past and Future*, 20, 249–50, 252–57. On the question of the opportunity for political participation in Arendt, see Richard J. Bernstein, *Beyond Objectivism and Relativism*, 213–14. Also see Arendt, "Public Rights and Private Interests," 107–8.

24 Arendt, *The Human Condition*, 125.

25 See Arendt, *Between Past and Future*, 109–12, and *The Human Condition*, 194–95.

26 Arendt, *Between Past and Future*, 153; cf. 137.

27 Arendt, *On Revolution*, 28–32.

28 For Mary McCarthy's question, see Arendt, "On Hannah Arendt," 313–14.

29 Ibid, 318–19.

30 See Torgerson, "Limits of the Administrative Mind," 122–23.

31 See Dryzek, "Complexity and Rationality in Public Life."

32 See Simon, *Administrative Behavior*, 82.

33 See, e.g., Mesthene, *Technological Change*, 80–81, 91 n. 1.

34 Dryzek, "Complexity and Rationality in Public Life," 429–30.

35 See Torgerson, "Policy Analysis and Public Life," 227–28, 231–40, 242–43.

36 See March, "The Technology of Foolishness." Cf. Kahn, "Toward an Organizational Sense of Humor."

37 See, e.g., Fischer and Forester, *The Argumentative Turn in Policy Analysis and Planning*.

38 Dryzek, "Complexity and Rationality in Public Life," 435.

39 This is a "peculiarly forceless force," according to Habermas, "Hannah Arendt's Com-

munications Concept of Power," 6. Also see McCarthy, *The Critical Theory of Jürgen Habermas*, 304-10.

40 Dryzek, "Political and Ecological Communication," 20.

41 Habermas, "Further Reflections on the Public Sphere," 451-56. See chap. 1 above.

42 Dryzek, *Democracy in Capitalist Times*, 13; also see 47-53. Dryzek points as well to the importance of workplace democracy and community politics, 58-64.

43 Habermas, "Further Reflections on the Public Sphere," 452.

44 Dryzek, *Democracy in Capitalist Times*, 32; also 10, 24. In addition, see Dryzek, "Democracy and Environmental Policy Instruments," 294, 307.

45 Dryzek, *Democracy in Capitalist Times*, 42-44. It is thus that he allows for some structural "indeterminacy" and contradictory cross-pressures (see 13-14, 36, 40, 149).

46 Dryzek, "Ecology and Discursive Democracy," 188.

47 Cf. chap. 1, n. 43 above.

48 Bachrach and Baratz, *Power and Poverty*, 57.

49 Ibid., 8, 43, 58. The term "mobilization of bias" is drawn from Schattscheinder, *The Semisovereign People*, 69. The concept is employed in the context of environmental policy by Schrecker, *Political Economy of Environmental Hazards*.

50 March, "The Technology of Foolishness"; cf. March and Simon, *Organizations*, 36-47. Also see Morgan, "Cybernetics and Organization Theory: Epistemology or Technique?"

51 See Lindblom, "The Science of 'Muddling Through'"; Weiss and Woodhouse, "Reframing Incrementalism."

52 See, e.g., Dente, *Environmental Policy in Search of New Instruments*. Also see Dryzek, "Democracy and Environmental Policy Instruments," 61. Cf. Dryzek, *The Politics of the Earth*, chap. 8; Christoff, "Ecological Modernisation, Ecological Modernities."

53 On the externalization of costs as an intrinsic feature of market dynamics, see Meadows, "Equity, the Free Market, and the Sustainable State," 143.

54 Dryzek, *The Politics of the Earth*, 137-41.

55 See Hajer, *The Politics of Environmental Discourse*, 280-81. Also see Cristoff, "Ecological Modernisation," 491-97.

56 See chap. 2 above.

57 Plant, "Green Business in a Gray World," 3.

58 See Laclau and Mouffe, *Hegemony and Socialist Strategy*.

59 Schlosberg, *Environmental Justice and the New Pluralism*, 111-12, 117.

60 Ibid., 135-36.

61 See Moore and Head, "Building a Net That Works."

62 Schlosberg, 137.

63 Szasz, *Ecopopulism*, 164.

64 Grossman, "The People of Color Environmental Summit," 272.

65 Schlosberg, 113.

66 Quoted in ibid., 112, n. 5.

67 Quoted in Grossman, 274, 272.

68 See Dryzek, *The Politics of the Earth*, chap. 6; Eckersley, "Markets, the State and the Environment"; Sagoff, *The Economy of the Earth*, chap. 8.

69 Cf. Pickel, "Authoritarianism or Democracy?" Also see Pickel, "Neoliberalism, Gradualism and Some Typical Ambiguities and Confusions in the Transformation Debate."

70 Gramsci, *Selections from the Prison Notebooks*, 177.

71 On the historical and cultural construction of the economic actor as an anonymous and abstract action type of central significance, see Macpherson, *Democratic Theory*, chap. 14, and *The Political Theory of Possessive Individualism*, along with Schutz, *The Phenomenology of the Social World*, 242–46, and Machlup, "Homo Oeconomicus and His Class Mates."

72 Johnson, "The Guaranteed Income as an Environmental Measure," 179. Cf. chap. 4 above. Green discourse exhibits some ambivalence on the issue of work. The labor intensity of certain environmental measures is often heralded as promoting employment, and work is even celebrated as intrinsically valuable. See, e.g., Dobson, *Green Political Thought*, 104–12; Gorz, *Paths to Paradise*, chap. 4. The enthusiasm for work reaches its pinnacle in ecomonasticism, to the extent of neglecting the continuing role of the work ethic in disciplining the population of advanced industrial society.

73 Paehlke, "Work in a Sustainable Society," 272. For an instructive discussion of the relationship between economic and environmental concerns in the Canadian context, see Harrison, *Passing the Buck*, 116–20.

74 The significance of Foucault's treatment of specific discursive practices in this regard is particularly evident in his "Governmentality."

75 Lyndon Johnson once remarked that Gerald Ford was the only man he ever met who couldn't walk and chew gum at the same time, a comment widely recalled at the time of Ford's ascendance to the presidency.

76 See the discussion of deep ecology in chap. 2 above.

77 See n. 17 above.

78 Cf. Arendt, *Crises of the Republic*, 233; Habermas, "Further Reflections on the Public Sphere," 451–57.

79 Meeker, *The Comedy of Survival* (3d ed.).

80 Ibid., 17–18; cf. 10.

81 Kariel, *Open Systems*, 53–55.

82 Ibid., 114. Also see Kariel, *The Promise of Politics*.

83 Lakoff and Johnson, *Metaphors We Live By*, 5.

84 Arendt, *The Human Condition*, 194–95.

85 See ibid., 199–207.

86 See Arendt, *On Revolution*, 207, and *Between Past and Future*, 110–13.

87 Arendt, *Crises of the Republic*, 93–94. Also see Arendt, *The Human Condition*, 237, 243–47.

88 See Arendt, *On Revolution*, 214–15. Also see Arendt, *The Human Condition*, 206.

89 Myerson and Rydin, *The Language of Environment*, 32.

90 Cf. Kenny, "Paradoxes of Community."

8 · GREEN POLITICS AND PUBLIC LIFE

1 Cf. Martin Nicolas, Remarks at the American Sociological Association Convention, 1968, quoted in Yurick, "The Politics of the Imagination," 501.

2 The phrase "conserver society" gained currency in Canada in the mid-1970s and received quasi-official endorsement. See Science Council of Canada, *Canada as a Conserver Society*.

3 See *Adbusters: Journal of the Mental Environment* (www. adbusters.org).

4 Myerson and Rydin, *The Language of Environment*, 7–9.

5 See Wapner, *Environmental Activism and World Civic Politics*; Dryzek, "Global Ecological Democracy." Also see Christoff, "Ecological Citizens and Ecologically Guided Democracy."

6   Gundersen, *The Environmental Promise of Democratic Deliberation*, 247 n. 1.

7   Arendt, *The Human Condition*, 198.

8   Arendt, *Crises of the Republic*, 233.

9   Eckersley, *Environmentalism and Political Theory*, 185 (emphasis deleted).

10 Roderick Nash, "Do Rocks Have Rights?" *The Center Magazine* (1997), cited and discussed in Merchant, *Radical Ecology*, 76, 248 n. 33.

11 Arendt, *On Revolution*, 215; cf. 169–70, 174–75.

12 Kostede, "The Greens and the Intellectuals," 133.

13 Young, "Impartiality and the Civic Public," 75.

14 Adorno, *Negative Dialectics*, esp. 150, 406; Derrida, *Of Grammatology*, esp. 10–11, 158.

15 Bakhtin, "Discourse in the Novel," 278. The term "textual carnivals" is from Susan Miller, *Textual Carnivals: The Politics of Composition*, quoted in Myerson and Rydin, 7.

16 Bakhtin, *Rabelais and His World*, 121.

17 Myerson and Rydin, 7.

18 Doyle, "Green Politics in Grey Times," 7–8.

19 Quoted in Doyle, *Green Power*, chap. 7 (emphasis deleted). Cf. Brown, *Life Against Death: The Psychoanalytical Meaning of History*.

20 Doyle, "Green Politics in Grey Times," 9.

21 Scarce, *Eco-Warriors*, 57.

22 Quoted in ibid., 58. Cf. Abbey, *The Monkey Wrench Gang*. It should be noted, though, that Abbey explicitly disavows misanthropy and defends the preservation of wilderness for the sake of civilization itself. See his *Desert Solitaire*, esp. 148, 192, 274–77.

23 Scarce, 57.

24 Ibid., 91–94.

25 R. Carter, *Becoming Bamboo*, 188. Cf. R. Carter, *The Nothingness Beyond God*.

26 Cf. Benjamin, "Theses on the Philosophy of History," 257.

27 See Rowell, *Green Backlash*, esp. chaps. 10 (on France) and 11 (on Nigeria). On the American scene, see Helvarg, *The War Against the Greens*.

28 Nietzsche, *Beyond Good and Evil*, pt. 4, section 146.

29 Cf. Adorno, *Minima Moralia*: "In the end, glorification of splendid underdogs is nothing other than glorification of the splendid system that makes them so" (28). Salleh, "Nature, Woman, Labor, Capital," understates this difficulty with her rather affirmative reading of negative dialectics.

Aaron, Raymond. 1969. *Main Currents of Sociological Thought,* vol. 1. Garden City, NY: Anchor Books.

Abbey, Edward. 1976. *The Monkey Wrench Gang.* New York: Avon Books.

———. 1971. *Desert Solitaire: A Season in the Wilderness.* New York: Ballantine Books.

Achterberg, Wouter. 1995. "From Sustainability to Basic Income: A Seamless Web of Justice," paper presented to the Conference on Planning for Sustainability, University of Sheffield, 8–10 September.

Adorno, Theodor W. 1974. *Minima Moralia: Reflections from Damaged Life.* Trans. E. F. N. Jephcott. London: Verso.

———. 1987. *Negative Dialectics.* Trans. E. B. Ashton. New York: Continuum Publishing.

Adrados, Francisco R. 1975. *Festival, Comedy and Tragedy: The Greek Origins of Theatre.* Trans. Christopher Holme. Leiden, Netherlands: E. J. Brill.

Alford, Robert R., and Roger Friedland. 1985. *Powers of Theory: Capitalism, the State, and Democracy.* Cambridge: Cambridge University Press.

Apel, Karl-Otto. 1978. "The Conflicts of Our Time and the Problem of Political Ethics," in *From the Contract to Community,* ed. Fred R. Dallmayr. New York: Marcel Dekker.

———. 1979. "The Common Presuppositions of Hermeneutics and Ethics: Types of Rationality Beyond Science and Technology," *Research in Phenomenology,* 9: 35–53.

———. 1979. "Types of Rationality Today: The Continuum of Reason between Science and Ethics," in *Rationality Today,* ed. Theodore F. Geraets. Ottawa: Ottawa University Press.

———. 1980. *Towards a Transformation of Philosophy.* Trans. Glyn Adey and David Frisby. London: Routledge and Kegan Paul.

Arendt, Hannah. 1958. *The Human Condition.* Chicago: University of Chicago Press.

———. 1965. *On Revolution.* New York: Viking Press.

———. 1968. *Between Past and Future: Eight Exercises in Political Thought.* New York: Viking Press.

———. 1972. *Crises of the Republic.* New York: Harcourt Brace Jovanovich.

———. 1977. "Public Rights and Private Interests," in *Small Comforts for Hard Times: Humanists on Public Policy,* ed. Michael Mooney and Floria Stuber. New York: Columbia University Press.

———. 1978. *The Life of the Mind,* 1 vol. ed. San Diego: Harcourt Brace Jovanovich.

———. 1979. "On Hannah Arendt," in *Hannah Arendt: The Recovery of the Public World,* ed. Melvyn Hill. New York: St. Martin's Press.

——. 1979. *The Origins of Totalitarianism,* new ed. San Diego: Harcourt Brace Jovanovich.

Athanasiou, Tom. 1996. *Divided Planet: The Ecology of Rich and Poor.* Boston: Little, Brown.

Avineri, Shlomo. 1968. *The Social and Political Thought of Karl Marx.* Cambridge: Cambridge University Press.

Avineri, Shlomo, and Avner de-Shalit, eds. 1992. *Communitarianism and Individualism.* Oxford: Oxford University Press.

Bachrach, Peter. 1967. *The Theory of Democratic Elitism: A Critique.* Boston: Little, Brown.

Bachrach, Peter, and Morton S. Baratz. 1970. *Power and Poverty: Theory and Practice.* New York: Oxford University Press.

Bahro, Rudolph. 1986. *Building the Green Movement.* Trans. Mary Tyler. London: GMP Publishers.

Bakhtin, Mikhail. 1968. *Rabelais and His World.* Trans. Hélène Iswolsky. Cambridge, MA: MIT Press.

——. 1981. "Discourse in the Novel," in *The Dialogical Imagination.* Trans. Caryl Emerson and Michael Holquist. Austin: University of Texas Press.

Barnard, Chester. 1968. *The Functions of the Executive,* 30th anniversary ed. Cambridge, MA: Harvard University Press.

Bartlett, Robert V. 1990. "Ecological Reason in Administration: Environmental Impact Assessment and Administrative Theory," in *Managing Leviathan,* ed. Paehlke and Torgerson.

Bateson, Gregory. 1974. "Conscious Purpose versus Nature," in *Steps to an Ecology of Mind.* New York: Ballantine Books.

Beck, Ulrich, Anthony Giddens, and Scott Lash. 1994. *Reflexive Modernization: Politics, Tradition and Aesthetics in the Modern Social Order.* Cambridge, MA: Polity Press.

Beiner, Ronald. 1983. *Political Judgment.* London: Metheun.

Benedict. 1966. *The Rule of St. Benedict* (ca. 528). Trans. Cardinal Gasquet. New York: Cooper Square Publishers.

Benhabib, Seyla. 1986. *Critique, Norm, and Utopia: A Study of the Foundations of Critical Theory.* New York: Columbia University Press.

——. 1990. "Communicative Ethics and Current Controversies in Political Philosophy," in *The Communicative Ethics Controversy,* ed. Seyla Benhabib and Fred Dallmayr. Cambridge, MA: MIT Press.

——. 1996. "Toward a Deliberative Model of Democratic Legitimacy," in *Democracy and Difference: Contesting the Boundaries of the Political,* ed. Seyla Benhabib. Princeton: Princeton University Press.

Benjamin, Walter. 1969. "Theses on the Philosophy of History," in *Illuminations.* Trans. Harry Zohn. New York: Schocken Books.

Bentley, Eric. 1984. "On the Other Side of Despair," in *Comedy: Developments in Criticism,* ed. D. J. Palmer. New York: Macmillan.

Berger, Peter L. 1969. *The Sacred Canopy: Elements of a Sociological Theory of Religion.* Garden City, NY: Anchor Books.

Berger, Thomas. 1977. *Northern Frontier, Northern Homeland: The Report of the Mackenzie Valley Pipeline Inquiry,* 2 vols. Ottawa: Supply and Services Canada.

Berlin, Isaiah. 1962. "Does Political Theory Still Exist?" in *Philosophy, Politics and Society,* 2d series, ed. Peter Laslett and W. G. Runcimann. Oxford: Basil Blackwell.

——. 1964. "Rationality of Value Judgement" in *Rational Decision,* ed. Carl J. Friedrich. New York: Atherton Press.

Bernstein, Richard. 1985. *Beyond Objectivism and Relativism: Science, Hermeneutics and Praxis.* Philadelphia: University of Pennsylvania Press.

Biehl, Janet. 1991. *Rethinking Ecofeminist Politics.* Boston: South End Press.

——. 1995. "'Ecology' and the Modernization of Fascism in the German Ultra-right," in *Ecofascism: Lessons from the German Experience,* ed. Janet Biehl and Peter Staudenmaier. Edinburgh: AK Press.

Blake, William. 1975. *The Marriage of Heaven and Hell.* London: Oxford University Press.

Bookchin, Murray. 1971. *Post-Scarcity Anarchism.* San Francisco: Ramparts Press.

——. 1982. *The Ecology of Freedom: The Emergence and Dissolution of Hierarchy.* Palo Alto, CA: Cheshire Books.

——. 1987. *The Modern Crisis,* 2d ed. Montreal: Black Rose Books.

——. 1990. *Remaking Society: Pathways to a Green Future.* Boston: South End Press.

——. 1995. *The Philosophy of Social Ecology: Essays on Dialectical Naturalism,* 2d ed. Montreal: Black Rose Books.

Bosso, Christopher. 1994. "The Contextual Bases of Problem Defintion," in *The Politics of Problem Definition: Shaping the Policy Agenda,* ed. David A. Rochefort and Roger W. Cobb. Lawrence: University Press of Kansas.

Boulding, Kenneth. 1977. "Commons and Community: The Idea of a Public," in *Managing the Commons,* ed. Garrett Hardin and John Baden. San Francisco: W. H. Freeman.

Brooks, David B. 1992. "The Challenge of Sustainability: Is Integrating Environment and Economy Enough?" *Policy Sciences* 26: 401–8.

Brown, Norman O. 1959. *Life Against Death: The Psychoanalytical Meaning of History.* London: Routledge and Kegan Paul.

Bruton, Jim, and Michael Howlett. 1992. "Differences of Opinion: Round Tables, Policy Networks, and the Failure of Canadian Environmental Strategy." *Alternatives: Perspectives on Society, Technology and Environment* 19, no. 1: 25–28, 31–33.

Burney, Leanne. 1996. "Sustainable Development and Civil Disobedience: The Politics of Environmental Discourse in Clayoquot Sound." Master's thesis, Trent University, Peterborough, Ontario.

Calhoun, Craig, ed. 1992. *Habermas and the Public Sphere.* Cambridge, MA: MIT Press.

Cameron, James, and Will Wade-Gery. 1995. "Addressing Uncertainty: Law, Policy and the Development of the Precautionary Principle," in *Environmental Policy in Search of New Instruments,* ed. Bruno Dente. Dordrecht: Kluwer Academic Publishers.

Carroll, William K., ed. 1992. *Organizing Dissent: Contemporary Social Movements in Theory and Practice.* Toronto: Garamond Press.

Carson, Rachel. 1962. *Silent Spring.* Boston: Houghton Mifflin.

Carter, Alan. 1993. "Towards a Green Political Theory," in *The Politics of Nature: Explorations in Green Political Theory,* ed. Andrew Dobson and Paul Lucardie. London: Routledge.

Carter, Robert E. 1989. *The Nothingness Beyond God: An Introduction to the Philosophy of Nishida Kitaro.* New York: Paragon Books.

——. 1992. *Becoming Bamboo: Western and Eastern Explorations on the Meaning of Life.* Montreal and Kingston: McGill-Queen's University Press.

Castrilli, Joe. 1982. "Hazardous Wastes Law in Canada and Ontario," *Alternatives: Perspectives on Society and Environment* 10, nos. 2–3: 50–58.

Christoff, Peter. 1996. "Ecological Citizens and Ecologically Guided Democracy," in *Democracy and Green Political Thought,* ed. Brian Doherty and Marius de Geus. London: Routledge.

——. 1996. "Ecological Modernisation, Ecological Modernities." *Environmental Politics* 5: 476–500.

Cobb, Robert W., and Charles D. Elder. 1971. "The Politics of Agenda Building: An Alternative Perspective for Modern Democratic Theory." *Journal of Politics* 33: 892–915.

Cohen, Jean L. 1985. "Strategy or Identity: New Theoretical Paradigms and Contemporary Social Movements." *Social Research* 52: 663–716.

Cohen, Steven, and Marc Tipermas. 1983. "Superfund: Preimplementation Planning and Bureaucratic Politics," in *The Politics of Hazardous Waste Management*, ed. James P. Lester and Ann O'M. Bowman. Durham, NC: Duke University Press.

Cole, H. S. D., et al. 1973. *Thinking about the Future: A Critique of the "Limits to Growth."* London: Chatto and Windus.

Collison, Robert. 1989. "The Greening of the Board Room." *Report on Business Magazine, The Globe and Mail* (Toronto), 6 July: 42–55.

Commoner, Barry. 1971. *The Closing Circle.* New York: Alfred A. Knopf.

———. 1973. "Workplace Burden." *Environment* 15 (July–August): 15–33.

Coughlin, Joseph. 1994. "The Tragedy of the Concrete Commons: Defining Traffic Congestion as a Public Problem," in *The Politics of Problem Definition: Shaping the Policy Agenda*, ed. David A. Rochefort and Roger W. Cobb. Lawrence: University Press of Kansas.

Crozier, Michel, Samuel P. Huntington, and Joji Watanuki. 1975. *The Crisis of Democracy: Report on the Governability of Democracies to the Trilateral Commission.* New York: New York University Press.

Curtius, E. R. 1953. *European Literature and the Latin Middle Ages.* Trans. Willard R. Trask. Princeton: Princeton University Press.

Dallmayr, Fred R. 1992. "Reason and Emancipation: Notes on Habermas." *Man and World* 5: 79–109.

Dalton, Russell J. 1994. *The Green Rainbow: Environmental Groups in Western Europe.* New Haven: Yale University Press.

Dalton, Russell J., and Manfred Kuechler, eds. 1990. *Challenging the Political Order: New Social and Political Movements in Western Democracies.* Oxford: Oxford University Press.

Daly, Herman E. 1973. "Electric Power, Employment, and Economic Growth: A Case Study in Growthmania," in *Toward a Steady-State Economy*, ed. Daly.

———. ed. 1973. *Toward a Steady State Economy.* San Francisco: W. H. Freeman.

Damico, Alfonso J. 1978. *Individuality and Community: The Social and Political Thought of John Dewey.* Gainesville: The University Presses of Florida.

Dante. 1951. Letter to Can Grande della Scala (Epistola 10, ca. 1318), in *The Great Critics*, 3d ed., ed. James H. Smith and Edd W. Parks. New York: W. W. Norton.

Darling, Craig R. n.d. *In Search of Consensus: An Evaluation of the Clayoquot Sound Sustainable Development Task Force Process.* Victoria, BC: UVic Institute for Dispute Resolution, University of Victoria.

Davis, John. 1991. *Greening Business: Managing for Sustainable Development.* Oxford: Basil Blackwell.

de Bono, Edward. 1977. *Lateral Thinking: A Textbook of Creativity.* Harmondsworth: Penguin Books.

Dente, Bruno, ed. 1995. *Environmental Policy in Search of New Instruments.* Dordrecht: Kluwer Academic Publishers.

Derrida, Jacques. 1976. *Of Grammatology.* Trans. Gayatri Chakravorty Spivak. Baltimore: Johns Hopkins University Press.

Dery, David. 1985. *Problem Definition in Policy Analysis.* Lawrence: University Press of Kansas.

Descartes, René. 1975. *Discourse on Method* (1637), in *The Philosophical Works of Descartes*, vol. 1. Trans. Elizabeth S. Haldane and G. R. T. Ross. Cambridge: Cambridge University Press.

Devall, Bill, and George Sessions. 1984. "The Development of Natural Resources and the Integrity of Nature." *Environmental Ethics* 6: 293-322.

———. 1985. *Deep Ecology: Living as if Nature Mattered.* Salt Lake City: Peregrine Smith Books.

Diamond, Irene, and Gloria Feman Orenstein, eds. 1990. *Reweaving the World: The Emergence of Ecofeminism.* San Francisco: Sierra Club Books.

Die Grünen. 1983. *Programme of the German Green Party.* Trans. Hans Fernbach. London: Heretic Books.

Dietz, Mary G. 1995. "Feminist Receptions of Hannah Arendt," in *Feminist Interpretations of Hannah Arendt,* ed. Bonnie Honig. University Park: Pennsylvania State University Press.

Dobson, Andrew. 1993. "Critical Theory and Green Politics," in *The Politics of Nature: Explorations in Green Political Theory,* ed. Andrew Dobson and Paul Lucardie. London: Routledge.

———. 1995. *Green Political Thought,* 2d ed. London: Routledge.

———. 1996. "Democratising Green Theory: Preconditions and Principles," in *Democracy and Green Political Thought,* ed. Brian Doherty and Marius de Geus. London: Routledge.

———. ed. 1991. *The Green Reader: Essays Toward a Sustainable Society.* San Francisco: Mercury House.

Downs, Anthony. 1972. "Up and Down with Ecology—The 'Issue Attention Cycle.'" *The Public Interest* 28: 38-50.

Doyle, Timothy. 1997. "Green Politics in Grey Times: The Dynamics of Political Resiliance," Phil Tighe Memorial Lecture, Ecopolitics XI Conference, University of Melbourne, Australia, 4 October.

———. Forthcoming. *Green Power: The Environmental Movement in Australia.* Sydney: University of New South Wales Press.

Dryzek, John S. 1983. "Ecological Rationality." *International Journal of Environmental Studies* 21: 5-10.

———. 1987. "Complexity and Rationality in Public Life." *Political Studies* 35: 424-42.

———. 1987. "Discursive Designs: Critical Theory and Political Institutions." *American Journal of Political Science* 31: 656-79.

———. 1987. *Rational Ecology: Environment and Political Economy.* London: Basil Blackwell.

———. 1989. "Policy Sciences of Democracy." *Polity* 22: 97-118.

———. 1990. "Designs for Environmental Discourse," in *Managing Leviathan,* ed. Paehlke and Torgerson.

———. 1990. *Discursive Democracy: Politics, Policy and Political Science.* Cambridge: Cambridge University Press.

———. 1990. "Green Reason: Communicative Ethics for the Biosphere." *Environmental Ethics* 12: 195-210.

———. 1993. "Policy Analysis and Planning: From Science to Argument," in *The Argumentative Turn in Policy Analysis and Planning,* ed. Fischer and Forester.

———. 1994. "Ecology and Discursive Democracy: Beyond Liberal Capitalism and the Administrative State," in *Is Capitalism Sustainable? Political Economy and the Politics of Ecology,* ed. Martin O'Connor. New York: Guilford Press.

———. 1996. *Democracy in Capitalist Times.* Oxford: Oxford University Press.

———. 1996. "Democracy and Environmental Policy Instruments," in *Markets, the State and the Environment,* ed. Robyn Eckersley. London: Macmillan.

——. 1996. "Political and Ecological Communication," in *Ecology and Democracy,* ed. Freya Mathews. London: Frank Cass.

——. 1996. "Strategies of Ecological Democratization," in *Democracy and the Environment,* ed. William M. Lafferty and James Meadowcroft. Cheltenham, UK: Edward Elgar.

——. 1997. "Global Ecological Democracy," paper presented at the International Conference on Environmental Justice, University of Melbourne, Australia, 1–3 October.

——. 1997. *The Politics of the Earth: Environmental Discourses.* Oxford: Oxford University Press.

Dürrenmatt, Friedrich. 1964. "Problems of the Theatre," in *Four Plays.* London: Jonathan Cape.

Eckersley, Robyn. 1988. "Green Politics: A Practice in Search of a Theory?" *Alternatives: Perspectives on Society, Technology and Environment* 15, no. 4: 52–61.

——. 1989. "Green Politics and the New Class: Selfishness or Virtue?" *Political Studies* 37: 205–23.

——. 1992. *Environmentalism and Political Theory: Toward an Ecocentric Approach.* Albany: State University of New York Press.

——. 1996. "Greening Liberal Democracy: The Rights Discourse Revisited," in *Democracy and Green Political Thought,* ed. Brian Doherty and Marius de Geus. London: Routledge.

——. 1996. "Markets, the State and the Environment: An Overview," in *Markets, the State and the Environment,* ed. Robyn Eckersley. London: Macmillan.

——. 1997. "Green Justice, the State and Democracy," paper presented at the International Conference on Environmental Justice, University of Melbourne, 1–3 October.

——. Forthcoming. "Green Political Thought," in *A Companion to Environmental Philosophy,* ed. Dale Jamieson. Oxford: Blackwell.

Eco, Umberto. 1983. *The Name of the Rose.* Trans. William Weaver. San Diego: Harcourt Brace Jovanovich.

Eder, Klaus. 1996. "The Institutionalisation of Environmentalism: Ecological Discourse and the Second Transformation of the Public Sphere," in *Risk, Environment and Modernity: Towards a New Ecology,* ed. Scott Lash, Bronislaw Szerszynski, and Brian Wynne. London: Sage Publications.

Ehrenfeld, David. 1978. *The Arrogance of Humanism.* New York: Oxford University Press.

Emery, F. E., and Eric Trist. 1981. "The Causal Texture of Organizational Environments" (1965) in *Systems Thinking,* vol. 1, rev. ed., ed. F. E. Emery. Harmondsworth: Penguin Books

Enzensberger, Hans Magnus. 1996. "A Critique of Political Ecology" (1974) in *The Greening of Marxism,* ed. Ted Benton. New York: Guilford Press.

Epstein, Samuel S., Lester O. Brown, and Carl Pope. 1982. *Hazardous Waste in America.* San Francisco: Sierra Club Books.

Esslin, Martin. 1969. *The Theatre of the Absurd,* rev. ed. Garden City, NY: Anchor Books.

Estes, Clarissa Pinkola. 1995. "Baubo: The Belly Goddess," in *Women Who Run with the Wolves: Myths and Stories of the Wild Woman Archetype.* New York: Random House.

Evans, Judy. 1993. "Ecofeminism and the Politics of the Gendered Self," in *The Politics of Nature: Explorations in Green Political Theory,* ed. Andrew Dobson and Paul Lucardie. London: Routledge.

Ferkiss, Victor. 1974. *The Future of Technological Civilization.* New York: George Braziller.

Ferris, John. 1993. "Introduction: Political Realism and Green Strategy," in *Realism in Green Politics,* by Wiesenthal.

Feuer, Lewis. 1969. "The Character and Thought of Karl Marx: The Promethean Complex and Historical Materialism," in *Marx and the Intellectuals: A Set of Post-Ideological Essays.* New York: Anchor Books, 1969.

Fischer, Frank. 1992. "Participatory Expertise: Toward the Democratization of Policy Science," in *Advances in Policy Studies since 1950,* ed. William N. Dunn and Rita M. Kelly. New Brunswick, NJ: Transaction Publishers.

——. 1993. "Citizen Participation and the Democratization of Policy Expertise: From Political Theory to Practical Cases." *Policy Sciences* 26: 165–87.

——. 1993. *Technocracy and the Politics of Expertise.* Newbury Park, CA: Sage Publications.

Fischer, Frank, and John Forester, eds. 1993. *The Argumentative Turn in Policy Analysis and Planning.* Durham, NC: Duke University Press.

Foucault, Michel. 1979, "The Eye of Power," in *Power/Knowledge,* ed. Colin Gordon. New York: Pantheon Books.

——. 1980. *Discipline and Punish: The Birth of the Prison.* Trans. Alain Sheridan. New York: Vintage Books.

——. 1991. "Governmentality," in *The Foucault Effect: Studies in Governmentality,* ed. Graham Burchell et al. Chicago: University of Chicago Press.

Fox, Warwick. 1990. *Toward a Transpersonal Ecology: Developmenting New Foundations for Environmentalism.* Boston: Shambhala.

Fraser, Nancy. 1989. *Unruly Practices: Power, Discourse, and Gender in Contemporary Social Theory.* Minneapolis: University of Minnesota Press.

——. 1992. "Rethinking the Public Sphere: A Contribution to the Critique of Actually Existing Democracy," in *Habermas and the Public Sphere,* ed. Calhoun.

Freud, Sigmund. 1955. "A Difficulty in the Path of Psycho-Analysis," in *The Standard Edition of the Complete Psychological Works of Sigmund Freud,* vol. 17. Trans. James Strachey. London: Hogarth Press.

Friends of Clayoquot Sound. 1989. "The Battle for Clayoquot Sound." *Canadian Dimension* 23, no. 5: 25–27.

——. 1998. "Implementing the Scientific Panel: Three Years and Counting." Tofino, BC (www.island.net/~focs).

Frosch, Robert A. 1992. "Industrial Ecology: A Philosophical Introduction." *Proceedings of the National Academy of Sciences U.S.A.* 89: 800–803.

Frye, Northrop. 1962. *Fearful Symmetry: A Study of William Blake.* Boston: Beacon Press.

Gadamer, Hans-Georg. 1979. "Practical Philosophy as a Model of the Human Sciences." *Research in Phenomenology* 9: 74–85.

——. 1989. *Truth and Method,* 2d ed. Trans. Joel Weinsheimer and Donald G. Marshall. New York: Crossroad.

Galbraith, John Kenneth. 1972. *The New Industrial State,* 2d ed. New York: Mentor Books.

Gallon, Gary. 1992. "The Green Product Endorsement Controversy: Lessons from the Pollution Probe/Loblaws Experience." *Alternatives: Perspectives on Society, Technology and Environment* 18, no. 3: 16–25.

Gamble, D. J. 1979. "The Berger Inquiry: An Impact Assessment Process." *Science* 199: 946–52.

Gay, Peter. 1969. *The Enlightenment: An Interpretation,* vol. 2. New York: Alfred Knopf.

Gibson, Robert B. 1990. "Out of Control and Beyond Understanding: Acid Rain as a Political Dilemma." in *Managing Leviathan,* ed. Paehlke and Torgerson.

——. 1992. "Respecting Ignorance and Uncertainty," in *Achieving Environmental Goals: The Concept and Practice of Environmental Performance Review,* ed. E. Lykke. London: Belhaven Press.

Gimbutas, Marija. 1982. "Women and Culture in Goddess-Oriented Old Europe," in *The Politics of Women's Spirituality*, ed. Charlene Spretnak. New York: Doubleday.

Goodin, Robert E. 1992. *Green Political Theory*. Cambridge: Polity Press.

Goodman, Daniel. 1975. "The Theory of Diversity-Stability Relationships in Ecology." *The Quarterly Review of Biology* 50, no. 3: 237–66.

Gore, Albert, Jr. 1982. Foreword to *Hazardous Waste in America*, by Epstein, Brown, and Pope.

Gorz, André. 1980. *Ecology as Politics*. Trans. Patsy Vigderman and Jonathan Cloud. Montreal: Black Rose Books.

——. 1985. *Paths to Paradise: On the Liberation from Work*. Trans. Malcolm Imrie. London: Pluto Press.

Graham, Frank, Jr. 1970. *Since Silent Spring*. Greenwich, CT: Fawcett Publications.

Gramsci, Antonio. 1971. *Selections from the Prison Notebooks*. Trans. Quintin Hoare and Geoffrey Nowell Smith. New York: International Publishers.

Grossman, Karl. 1994. "The People of Color Environmental Summit," in *Unequal Protection: Environmental Justice and Communities of Color*, ed. Robert Bullard. San Francisco: Sierra Club Books.

Gundersen, Adolf G. 1995. *The Environmental Promise of Democratic Deliberation*. Madison: University of Wisconsin Press.

Habermas, Jürgen. 1970. "On Systematically Distorted Communication." *Inquiry* 13: 205–18.

——. 1970. "Toward a Theory of Communicative Competence." *Inquiry* 13: 360–75.

——. 1971. *Knowledge and Human Interests*. Trans. Jeremy J. Shapiro. Boston: Beacon Press.

——. 1971. *Toward a Rational Society*. Trans. Jeremy J. Shapiro. Boston: Beacon Press.

——. 1975. *Legitimation Crisis*. Trans. Thomas McCarthy. Boston: Beacon Press.

——. 1977. "Hannah Arendt's Communications Concept of Power." *Social Research* 44: 3–24.

——. 1979. "What Is Universal Pragmatics?" in *Communication and the Evolution of Society*. Trans. Thomas McCarthy. Boston: Beacon Press.

——. 1982. "A Reply to My Critics," in *Habermas: Critical Debates*, ed. John B. Thompson and David Held. London: Macmillan.

——. 1984/87. *The Theory of Communicative Action*, 2 vols. Trans. Thomas McCarthy. Boston: Beacon Press.

——. 1987. *The Philosophical Discourse of Modernity*. Trans. Frederick Lawrence. Cambridge, MA: MIT Press.

——. 1988. *On the Logic of the Social Sciences*. Trans. Shierry Weber Nicholsen and Jerry A. Stark. Cambridge, MA: MIT Press.

——. 1989. *The Structural Transformation of the Public Sphere: An Inquiry into a Category of Bourgeois Society*. Trans. Thomas Burger. Cambridge, MA: MIT Press.

——. 1990. "Discourse Ethics: Notes on a Program of Philosophical Justification," in *Moral Consciousness and Communicative Action*. Trans. Christian Lenhardt and Shierry Weber Nicholsen. Cambridge, MA: MIT Press.

——. 1992. "Further Reflections on the Public Sphere," in *Habermas and the Public Sphere*, ed. Calhoun.

——. 1993. "Remarks on Discourse Ethics," in *Justification and Application*. Trans. Ciaran P. Cronin. Boston: MIT Press.

——. 1996. *Between Facts and Norms: Contributions to a Discourse Theory of Law and Democracy*. Trans. William Rehg. Boston: MIT Press.

Hajer, Maarten. 1992. "The Politics of Environmental Performance Review: Choices in Design," in *Achieving Environmental Goals: The Concept and Practice of Environmental Performance Review*, ed. E. Lykke. London: Belhaven Press.

——. 1995. *The Politics of Environmental Discourse: Ecological Modernization and the Policy Process*. Oxford: Oxford University Press.

Hardin, Garrett. 1977. "The Tragedy of the Commons" (1968) in *Managing the Commons*, ed. Garrett Hardin and John Baden. San Francisco: W. H. Freeman.

Harrison, Kathryn. 1996. *Passing the Buck: Federalism and Canadian Environmental Policy*. Vancouver: University of British Columbia Press.

Hartley, Troy W. 1995. "Environmental Justice." *Environmental Ethics* 17: 277–82.

Hatch, Christopher. 1994. "The Clayoquot Protests: Taking Stock One Year Later," in *Clayoquot Mass Trials: Defending the Rainforest*, ed. Anne Champagne and Ron MacIssac. Gabriola Island, British Columbia: New Society Publishers.

Hawkesworth, Mary. 1995. "Epistemology and Policy Analysis," in *Advances in Policy Studies since 1950*, ed. William N. Dunn and Rita M. Kelly. New Brunswick, NJ: Transaction Publishers.

Hawkins, Howard. 1988. "The Potential of the Green Movement." *New Politics* 3: 85–105.

Hay, P. R. 1994. "The Politics of Tasmania's World Heritage Area: Contesting the Democratic Subject." *Environmental Politics* 3: 1–21.

Hays, Samuel P. 1975. *Conservation and the Gospel of Efficiency: The Progressive Conservation Movement, 1890–1920*. New York: Antheneum, 1975.

——. 1989. *Beauty, Health, and Permanence: Environmental Politics in the United States, 1955–1985*. Cambridge: Cambridge University Press.

Hegel, G. W. F. 1967. *The Phenomenology of Mind*. Trans. J. B. Baille. New York: Harper & Row.

Heilbroner, Robert H. 1980. *An Inquiry into the Human Prospect*, updated ed. New York: W.W. Norton. (1st ed., 1974.)

Helvarg, David. 1994. *The War Against the Greens: The 'Wise-Use' Movement, the New Right, and Anti-Environmental Violence*. San Francisco: Sierra Club Books.

Hemingway, Ernest. 1952. *The Old Man and the Sea*. New York: Charles Scribner's Sons.

Hjelmar, Ulf. 1996. *The Political Practice of Environmental Organizations*. Aldershot, UK: Averbury.

Holman, Hugh C. 1972. *A Handbook to Literature*, 3d ed. New York: Bobbs-Merrill.

Honig, Bonnie. 1993. *Political Theory and the Displacement of Politics*. Ithaca, NY: Cornell University Press.

Hooker, C. A., and R. van Hulst. 1979. "The Meaning of Environmental Problems for Public Political Institutions," in *Ecology versus Politics in Canada*, ed. William Leiss. Toronto: University of Toronto Press.

Horkheimer, Max. 1972. "The Latest Attack on Metaphysics," in *Critical Theory*. Trans. Matthew J. Connell et al. New York: Seabury Press.

——. 1974. *Eclipse of Reason* (1947). New York: Seabury Press.

Horkheimer, Max, and Theodor W. Adorno. 1977. *Dialectic of Enlightenment* (1944). Trans. John Cumming. New York: Seabury Press.

Hülsberg, Werner. 1988. *The German Greens: A Social and Political Profile*. Trans. Gus Fagan. London: Verso.

Jänicke, Martin. 1996. "Democracy as a Condition for Environmental Policy Success: The Importance of Non-institutional Factors," in *Democracy and the Environment*, ed. William M. Lafferty and James Meadowcroft. Cheltenham, UK: Edward Elgar.

Janko, Richard. 1984. *Aristotle on Comedy: Towards a Reconstruction of Poetics II*. Berkeley: University of California Press.

Johnson, Warren A. 1973. "The Guaranteed Income as an Environmental Measure," in *Toward a Steady-State Economy*, ed. Daly.

Kahn, William A. 1989. "Toward an Organizational Sense of Humor: Implications for Organizational Diagnosis and Change." *Journal of Applied Behavioral Science* 25: 45–63.

Kariel, Henry S. 1966. *The Promise of Politics*. Englewood Cliffs, NJ: Prentice-Hall.

——. 1969. *Open Systems: Arenas for Political Action*. Itasca, IL: F. E. Peacock Publishers.

——. 1989. *The Desperate Politics of Postmodernism*. Amherst: University of Massachusetts Press.

Kellner, Hans. 1988. " 'To Make Truth Laugh': Eco's *The Name of the Rose*," in *Naming the Rose: Essays on Eco's* The Name of the Rose, ed. M. Thomas Inge. Jackson: University Press of Mississippi.

Kennedy, Robert, Jr. 1994. Foreword to *Clayoquot Mass Trials: Defending the Rainforest*, ed. Ron MacIssac and Anne Champagne. Philadelphia and Gabriola Island, BC: New Society Publishers.

Kenny, Michael. 1996. "Paradoxes of Community," in *Democracy and Green Political Thought*, ed. Brian Doherty and Marius de Geus. London: Routledge.

Kerr, Walter. 1985. *Tragedy and Comedy*. New York: Plenum Publishing.

King, Ynestra. 1990. "Healing the Wounds: Feminism, Ecology, and the Nature/Culture Dualism," in *Reweaving the World*, ed. Diamond and Orenstein.

Kingdon, John W. 1994. *Agendas, Alternatives, and Public Policies*. Boston: Little, Brown.

Kontos, Alkis. 1972. "Success and Knowledge in Machiavelli," in *The Political Calculus: Essays on Machiavelli's Philosophy*, ed. Anthony Parel. Toronto: University of Toronto Press.

——. 1979. "The Dialectics of Domination: An Interpretation of Friedrich Dürrenmatt's *The Visit*," in *Powers, Possessions and Freedom: Essays in Honour of C. B. Macpherson*, ed. Alkis Kontos. Toronto: University of Toronto Press.

Kostede, Norbert. 1989. "The Greens and the Intellectuals," in *The Greens in West Germany*, ed. Eva Kolinsky. Oxford: Berg Publishers.

Kushner, Thomasine. 1981. "Interpretations of Life and Prohibitions against Killing." *Environmental Ethics* 3: 147–54.

Laclau, Ernesto, and Chantal Mouffe. 1985. *Hegemony and Socialist Strategy: Towards a Radical Democratic Politics*. London: Verso.

Lafferty, William M. 1996. "The Politics of Sustainable Development: Global Norms for National Implementation." *Environmental Politics* 5: 183–208.

Lakoff, George, and Mark Johnson. 1980. *Metaphors We Live By*. Chicago: University of Chicago Press.

Langer, Valerie. 1994. "It Happened Suddenly (Over a Long Period of Time): A Clayoquot History," in *Witness to Wilderness: The Clayoquot Sound Anthology*, ed. Howard Breen-Needham et al. Vancouver: Arsenal Pulp Press.

Lasswell, Harold D. 1935. *World Politics and Personal Insecurity*. New York: McGraw-Hill.

——. 1971. *Propaganda Technique in World War I* (1926). Cambridge, MA: MIT Press.

Lee, Kai N. 1993. *Compass and Gyroscope: Integrating Science and Politics for the Environment*. Washington, DC: Island Press.

Lefebvre, Georges. 1964. "Enlightened Despotism," in *The Development of the Modern State*, ed. Heinz Lubasz. New York: Macmillan.

Leiss, William. 1974. *The Domination of Nature*. Boston: Beacon Press.

——. 1990. *Under Technology's Thumb*. Montreal and Kingston: McGill-Queen's University Press.

Leitch, Vincent B. 1983. *Deconstructive Criticism*. New York: Columbia University Press.

Leopold, Aldo. 1970. *A Sand County Almanac* (1949). New York: Ballantine Books.

Levine, Adeline Gordon. 1982. *Love Canal: Science, Politics, and People.* Lexington, MA: Lexington Books.

Lewis, Martin W. 1992. *Green Delusions: An Environmentalist Critique of Radical Environmentalism.* Durham, NC: Duke University Press.

Lindblom, Charles E. 1959. "The Science of 'Muddling Through.'" *Public Administration Review* 19: 79–88.

———. 1965. *The Intelligence of Democracy: Decision Making through Mutual Adjustment.* New York: Free Press.

———. 1968. *The Policy-Making Process.* Englewood Cliffs, NJ: Prentice-Hall.

———. 1977. *Politics and Markets: The World's Political-Economic Systems.* New York: Basic Books.

———. 1982. "Another State of Mind." *American Political Science Review* 76: 9–21.

Lipietz, Alain. 1995. *Green Hopes: The Future of Political Ecology.* Trans. Malcolm Slater. Cambridge: Polity Press.

Livingston, John A. 1973. *One Cosmic Instant: A Natural History of Human Arrogance.* Toronto: McClelland and Stewart.

Lovelock, James. 1979. *Gaia: A New Look at Life on Earth.* Oxford: Oxford University Press.

Lovins, Amory B. 1977. "Cost-Risk-Benefit Assessments in Energy Policy." *George Washington Law Review* 45: 911–43.

———. 1977. *Soft Energy Paths.* Cambridge, MA: Ballinger Publishing.

Lovins, Amory B., and John H. Price. 1975. *Non-Nuclear Futures: The Case for an Ethical Energy Strategy.* Cambridge, MA: Ballinger Publishing.

Lukács, Georg. 1971. *History and Class Consciousness.* Trans. Rodney Livingstone. London: Merlin Press.

Lyotard, Jean-François. 1984. *The Postmodern Condition: A Report on Knowledge.* Trans. Geoff Bennington and Brian Massumi. Minneapolis: University of Minnesota Press.

Macauley, David. 1996. "Hannah Arendt and the Politics of Place: From Earth Alienation to *Oikos*," in *Minding Nature: The Philosophers of Ecology*, ed. David Macauley. New York: Guilford Press.

Machlup, Fritz. 1970. "Homo Oeconomicus and His Class Mates," in *Phenomenology and Social Reality: Essays in Memory of Alfred Schutz*, ed. Maurice Natanson. The Hague: Martinus Nijhoff.

MacIntyre, Alasdair. 1988. *Whose Justice? Which Rationality?* Notre Dame, IN: University of Notre Dame Press.

Macpherson, C. B. 1964. *The Political Theory of Possessive Individualism: Hobbes to Locke.* Oxford: Oxford University Press.

———. 1965. *The Real World of Democracy.* Toronto: CBC Publications.

———. 1973. *Democratic Theory: Essays in Retrieval.* Oxford: Clarendon Press.

———. 1977. *The Life and Times of Liberal Democracy.* Oxford: Oxford University Press.

Maingon, Loÿs. 1994. "Clayoquot: Recovering from Cultural Rape," in *Clayoquot and Dissent*, ed. Tzeporah Berman et al. Vancouver, BC: Ronsdale Press.

Majone, Giandomenico. 1977. "Technology Assessment and Policy Analysis." *Policy Sciences* 8: 173–75.

———. 1989. *Evidence, Argument and Persuasion in the Policy Process.* New Haven: Yale University Press.

Majone, Giandomenico, and Aaron Wildavsky. 1984. "Implementation as Evolution," in *Implementation*, 3d ed., ed. Jeffrey Pressman and Aaron Wildavsky. Berkeley: University of California Press.

Manes, Christopher. 1990. *Green Rage: Radical Environmentalism and the Unmaking of Civilization.* Boston: Little, Brown.

———. 1992. "Nature and Silence." *Environmental Ethics* 14: 339–50.

Mannheim, Karl. 1936. *Ideology and Utopia.* Trans. Louis Wirth and Edward Shils. New York: Harcourt, Brace and World.

March, James G. 1989. "Footnotes to Organizational Change," in *Decisions and Organizations.* Oxford: Basil Blackwell.

———. 1989. "The Technology of Foolishness," in *Decisions and Organizations.* Oxford: Basil Blackwell.

March, James G., and Herbert A. Simon. 1958. *Organizations.* New York: John Wiley and Sons.

Marcuse, Herbert. 1960. *Reason and Revolution: Hegel and the Rise of Social Theory.* Boston: Beacon Press.

———. 1964. *One-Dimensional Man: Studies in the Ideology of Advanced Industrial Society.* Boston: Beacon Press.

———. 1966. *Eros and Civilization: A Philosophical Inquiry into Freud.* Boston: Beacon Press.

———. 1969. *An Essay on Liberation.* Boston: Beacon Press.

———. 1972. *Counterrevolution and Revolt.* Boston: Beacon Press.

Markovits, Andrei S., and Philip S. Gorski. 1993. *The German Left: Red, Green and Beyond.* New York: Oxford University Press.

Marx, Karl. 1964. *Early Writings.* Trans. T. B. Bottomore. New York: McGraw Hill.

———. 1976. *Capital,* vol. 1. Trans. Ben Fowkes. Harmondsworth: Penguin.

———. 1981. *Capital,* vol. 3. Trans. David Fernbach. Harmondsworth: Penguin.

———. n.d. *The Poverty of Philosophy.* Moscow: Foreign Languages Publishing House.

Marx, Karl, and Frederick Engels. 1969. *Selected Works,* 3 vols. Moscow: Progress Publishers.

Mason, Richard O., and Ian I. Mitroff. 1981. *Challenging Strategic Planning Assumptions.* New York: John Wiley and Sons.

Matheny, Albert R., and Bruce A. Williams. 1990. "The Crisis of Administrative Legitimacy: Regulatory Politics and the Right To Know," in *Managing Leviathan,* ed. Paehlke and Torgerson.

McCarthy, Thomas. 1978. *The Critical Theory of Jürgen Habermas.* Cambridge, MA: MIT Press.

McCaskey, Michael B. 1974. "A Contingency Approach to Planning: Planning with and Planning without Goals." *Academy of Management Journal* 17: 281–91.

McFie, A. L. 1967. *The Individual and Society: Papers on Adam Smith.* London: Allen and Unwin.

McIntosh, Robert. 1986. *The Background of Ecology.* Cambridge: Cambridge University Press.

Meadows, Donella. 1977. "Equity, the Free Market, and the Sustainable State," in *Alternatives to Growth, I: Toward a Sustainable Future,* ed. Dennis Meadows. Cambridge, MA: Ballinger.

Meadows, Donella H., et al. 1972. *The Limits to Growth: A Report for the Club of Rome's Project on the Predicament of Mankind.* New York: Universe Books.

Meeker, Joseph W. 1974. *The Comedy of Survival: Studies in Literary Ecology.* New York: Charles Scribner's Sons.

———. 1997. *The Comedy of Survival: Literary Ecology and a Play Ethic,* 3d ed. Tucson: University of Arizona Press.

Merchant, Carolyn. 1983. *The Death of Nature: Women, Ecology and the Scientific Revolution.* New York: Harper & Row.

———. 1990. "Ecofeminism and Feminist Theory," in *Reweaving the World,* ed. Diamond and Orenstein.

———. 1992. *Radical Ecology.* London: Routledge.

Mesthene, Emmanuel G. 1970. *Technological Change.* New York: Mentor Books.

Mill, John Stuart. 1965. *Considerations on Representative Government,* 3d ed. Indianapolis: Bobbs-Merrill.

———. 1965. *Principles of Political Economy* (1848), in *The Collected Works of John Stuart Mill,* vols. 2–3. Toronto: University of Toronto Press.

Mitroff, Ian I. 1978. "Systemic Problem Solving," in *Leadership,* ed. Morgan W. McCall and Michael M. Lombardo. Durham, NC: Duke University Press.

Mitroff, Ian I., and Richard D. Mason. 1981. *Creating a Dialectical Social Science.* Dordrecht: D. Reidel Publishing.

Monaghan, Patrica. 1981. *The Book of Goddesses and Heroines.* New York: E. P. Dutton.

Moore, Richard, and Louis Head. 1994. "Building a Net That Works: SWOP," in *Unequal Protection: Environmental Justice and Communities of Color,* ed. Robert Bullard. San Francisco: Sierra Club Books.

Morgan, Gareth. 1982. "Cybernetics and Organization Theory: Epistemology or Technique?" *Human Relations* 35: 521–38.

Mouffe, Chantal. 1993. *The Return of the Political.* London: Verso.

Myers, Norman, and Julian Simon. 1994. *Scarcity or Abundance? A Debate on the Environment.* New York: W. W. Norton.

Myerson, George, and Yvonne Rydin. 1996. *The Language of Environment: A New Rhetoric.* London: UCL Press.

Naess, Arne. 1993. "The Deep Ecological Movement: Some Philosophical Aspects" (1986) in *Environmental Philosophy,* ed. Michael Zimmerman et al. Englewood Cliffs, NJ: Prentice-Hall.

Nelson, Lin. 1990. "The Place of Women in Polluted Places," in *Reweaving the World,* ed. Diamond and Orenstein.

Nietzsche, Friedrich. 1968. *Beyond Good and Evil,* in *The Basic Writings of Nietzsche.* Trans. Walter Kaufmann. New York: Modern Library.

———. 1968. *On the Genealogy of Morals,* in *The Basic Writings of Nietzsche.* Trans. Walter Kaufmann. New York: Modern Library.

Norgaard, Richard B. 1994. *Development Betrayed: The End of Progress and a Coevolutionary Revisioning of the Future.* London: Routledge.

Norton, Bryan G. 1987. *Why Preserve Natural Variety?* Princeton, NJ: Princeton University Press.

———. 1991. *Toward Unity among Environmentalists.* Oxford: Oxford University Press.

Nuu-chah-nulth Tribal Council. 1990. *Nuu-chah-nulth Land Question: Land Sea and Resources.* Port Alberni, BC, September.

O'Connor, James. 1987. *The Meaning of Crisis: A Theoretical Introduction.* New York: Basil Blackwell.

———. 1988. "Capitalism, Nature, Socialism: A Theoretical Introduction." *Capitalism, Nature, Socialism* 1: 11–38.

———. 1994. "Is Sustainable Capitalism Possible?" in *Is Capitalism Sustainable? Political Economy and the Politics of Ecology,* ed. Martin O'Connor. New York: Guilford Press.

———. 1996. "The Second Contradiction of Capitalism," in *The Greening of Marxism,* ed. Ted Benton. New York: Guilford Press.

———. 1998. *Natural Causes: Essays in Ecological Marxism.* New York: Guilford Press.

O'Riordan, Timothy. 1988. "The Politics of Sustainability," in *Sustainable Environmental Management,* ed. Turner.

Offe, Claus. 1980. "The Separation of Form and Content in Liberal Democratic Politics." *Studies in Political Economy* 3: 5–16.

——. 1985. "New Social Movements: Challenging the Boundaries of Institutional Politics." *Social Research* 52: 817–68.

——. 1992. "A Non-Productivist Design for Social Policies," in *Arguing for Basic Income: Ethical Foundations for a Radical Reform*, ed. Philippe Van Parijs. London: Verso.

Offe, Claus, et al. 1996. "A Basic Income Guaranteed by the State: A Need of the Moment in Social Policy," in *Modernity and the State*. Cambridge, MA: MIT Press.

Ophuls, William. 1973. "Leviathan or Oblivion?" in *Toward a Steady-State Economy*, ed. Daly.

——. 1977. *Ecology and the Politics of Scarcity*. San Francisco: W. H. Freeman.

Orr, David W. 1992. *Ecological Literacy*. Albany: State University of New York Press.

Otway, Harry. 1992. "Public Wisdom, Expert Fallibility: Toward a Contextual Theory of Risk," in *Social Theories of Risk*, ed. Sheldon Krimsky and Dominic Golding. Westport, CT: Praeger.

Paehlke, Robert. 1989. *Environmentalism and the Future of Progressive Politics*. New Haven: Yale University Press.

——. 1992. "Eco-history: Two Waves in the Evolution of Environmentalism." *Alternatives: Perspectives on Society, Technology and Environment* 19, no. 1: 18–23.

——. 1998. "Work in a Sustainable Society," in *Political Ecology: Local and Global*, ed. David V. Bell, Leesa Fawcett, Robert Keil, and Peter Penz. London: Routledge.

Paehlke, Robert, and Douglas Torgerson. 1990. "Environmental Politics and the Administrative State," in *Managing Leviathan*, ed. Paehlke and Torgerson.

——. 1990. "Toxic Waste and the Administrative State: NIMBY Syndrome or Participatory Management?" in *Managing Leviathan*, ed. Paehlke and Torgerson.

——. 1992. "Toxic Waste as Public Business." *Canadian Public Administration* 35: 339–62.

Paehlke, Robert, and Douglas Torgerson, eds. 1990. *Managing Leviathan: Environmental Politics and the Administrative State*. Peterborough, Ontario: Broadview Press.

Pateman, Carole. 1971. *Participation and Democratic Theory*. Cambridge: Cambridge University Press.

Pearce, David, et al. 1989. *Blueprint for a Green Economy*. London: Earthscan.

Pepper, David. 1993. *Eco-Socialism: From Deep Ecology to Social Justice*. London: Routledge.

Peters, R. S. 1973. *Reason and Compassion*. London: Routledge and Kegan Paul.

Peterse, Aat. 1995. "The Mobilization of Counter-Expertise: Using Fischer's Model of Policy Inquiry." *Policy Sciences* 28: 369–73.

Pickel, Andreas. 1993. "Authoritarianism or Democracy? Marketization as a Political Problem." *Policy Sciences* 26: 139–63.

——. 1997. "Neoliberalism, Gradualism and Some Typical Ambiguities and Confusions in the Transformation Debate." *New Political Economy* 2: 221–35.

Plant, Christopher. 1991. "Green Business in a Gray World—Can It Be Done?" in *Green Business: Hope or Hoax? Toward an Authentic Strategy for Restoring the Earth*, ed. Christopher Plant and Judith Plant. Philadelphia: New Society Publishers.

Plumwood, Val. 1993. *Feminism and the Mastery of Nature*. London: Routledge.

Polanyi, Karl. 1957. *The Great Transformation: The Political and Economic Origins of Our Times*. Boston: Beacon Press.

Pollock, Frederick. 1978. "State Capitalism: Its Possibilities and Limitations" (1941), in *The Essential Frankfurt School Reader*, ed. Andrew Arato and Eike Gebhardt. New York: Urizen Books.

Porritt, Jonathan. 1993. "Sustainable Development: Panacea, Platitude, or Downright Deception?" in *Energy and the Environment*, ed. Bryan Cartledge. Oxford: Oxford University Press.

Press, Daniel. 1994. *Democratic Dilemmas in the Age of Ecology: Trees and Toxics in the American West*. Durham, NC: Duke University Press.

Quinby, Lee. 1990. "Ecofeminism and the Politics of Resistance," in *Reweaving the World*, ed. Diamond and Orenstein.

Rabe, Barry. 1994. *Beyond Nimby: Hazardous Waste Siting in Canada and the United States*. Washington, DC: Brookings Institution.

Reich, Charles A. 1970. *The Greening of America*. New York: Random House.

Ripley, Richard. 1983. "Toxic Substances, Hazardous Wastes, and Public Policy: Problems in Implementation," in *The Politics of Hazardous Waste Management*, ed. James P. Lester and Ann O'M. Bowman. Durham, NC: Duke University Press.

Rochefort, David A., and Roger W. Cobb. 1994. "Problem Definition: An Emerging Perspective," in *The Politics of Problem Definition: Shaping the Policy Agenda*, ed. David A. Rochefort and Roger W. Cobb. Lawrence: University Press of Kansas.

Rocheleau, Dianne, Barbara Thomas-Slayter, and Esther Wangari, eds. 1996. *Feminist Political Ecology: Global Issues and Local Experiences*. London: Routledge.

Rodman, John. 1964. Introduction to *The Political Theory of T. H. Green*, ed. John Rodman. New York: Meredith Publishing.

——. 1973. "What Is Living and What Is Dead in the Political Philosophy of T. H. Green." *Western Political Quarterly* 26: 566–86.

——. 1974. "The Dolphin Papers." *North American Review* 259: 13–26.

——. 1975. "On the Human Question, Being the Report of the Erewhonian High Commission to Evaluate Technological Society." *Inquiry* 18: 127–66.

——. 1976. "Four Forms of Ecological Consciousness, Part 1: Resource Conservation," paper presented to the Annual Meeting of the American Political Science Association, Chicago, 2–5 September.

——. 1977. "The Liberation of Nature?" *Inquiry* 20: 83–145.

——. 1978. "Theory and Practice in the Environmental Movement: Notes Toward an Ecology of Experience," in *The Search for Absolute Values in a Changing World: Proceedings of the Sixth International Conference on the Unity of the Sciences*, vol. 1. New York: International Cultural Foundation Press.

——. 1979. "Animal Justice: The Counter-revolution in Natural Right and Law." *Inquiry* 22: 3–22.

——. 1980. "Paradigm Change in Political Science: An Ecological Perspective." *American Behavioral Scientist* 24: 49–78.

——. 1983. "Four Forms of Ecological Consciousness Reconsidered," in *Ethics and the Environment*, ed. Donald Scherer and Thomas Attig. Englewood Cliffs, NJ: Prentice-Hall.

Rorty, Richard. 1982. "Idealism and Textualism," in *Consequences of Pragmatism*. Minneapolis: University of Minnesota Press.

Rosenbluth, Gideon. 1976. "Economists and the Growth Controversy." *Canadian Public Policy* 11: 225–39.

Rowell, Andrew. 1996. *Green Backlash: Global Subversion of the Environmental Movement*. New York: Routledge.

Rüdig, Wolfgang. 1995. "Green Parties: Germany," in *Conservation and Environmentalism: An Encyclopedia*, ed. Robert Paehlke. New York: Garland Publishing.

Sachs, Aaron. 1996. "Upholding Human Rights and Environmental Justice," in *State of the World 1996*, ed. Lester R. Brown et al. New York: W. W. Norton.

Sagoff, Mark. 1988. *The Economy of the Earth: Philosophy, Law, and the Environment*. Cambridge: Cambridge University Press.

Salleh, Ariel. 1994. "Nature, Woman, Labor, Capital: Living the Deepest Contradiction," in

Is Capitalism Sustainable? Political Economy and the Politics of Ecology, ed. Martin O'Connor. New York: Guilford Press.

———. 1997. *Ecofeminism as Politics: Nature, Marx and the Postmodern*. London: Zed Books.

Salsman, Richard M. 1993. "'Corporate Environmentalism' and Other Suicidal Tendencies," in *Environmentalism: What Does It Mean for Business?*, ed. Jaana Woiceshyn. Calgary: University of Calgary, Faculty of Management.

Saward, Michael. 1993. "Green Democracy?" in *The Politics of Nature: Explorations in Green Political Theory*, ed. Andrew Dobson and Paul Lucardie. London: Routledge.

Scarce, Rik. 1990. *Eco-Warriors: Understanding the Radical Environmental Movement*. Chicago: Noble Press.

Schattscheinder, E. E. 1975. *The Semisovereign People*. Hinsdale, IL: Dryden Press.

Scheler, Max. 1961. *Man's Place in Nature*. Trans. Hans Meyeroff. Boston: Beacon Press.

Schlosberg, David. 1999. *Environmental Justice and the New Pluralism: The Challenge of Difference for Environmentalism*. Oxford: Oxford University Press.

Schön, Donald A. 1983. *The Reflective Practitioner: How Professionals Think in Action*. New York: Basic Books.

Schrecker, Ted. 1984. *Political Economy of Environmental Hazards*. Ottawa: Law Reform Commission of Canada.

———. 1990. "Resisting Environmental Regulation: The Cryptic Pattern of Business-Government Relations," in *Managing Leviathan*, ed. Paehlke and Torgerson.

Schutz, Alfred. 1967. *The Phenomenology of the Social World*. Trans. George Walsh and Frederick Lehnert. Evanston, IL: Northwestern University Press.

Science Council of Canada. 1977. *Canada as a Conserver Society*. Ottawa: Science Council of Canada, Report no. 27.

Scientific Panel for Sustainable Forest Practices in Clayoquot Sound. 1995. *First Nations' Perspectives Relating to Forest Practice Standards in Clayoquot Sound*. Report 3. Victoria, BC: Cortex Consultants, Inc.

Seed, John, et al., eds. 1988. *Thinking Like a Mountain: Toward a Council of All Beings*. Philadelphia: New Society Publishers.

Seidel, Gill. 1985. "Political Discourse Analysis," in *Handbook of Discourse Analysis*, vol. 4, ed. Teun A. van Dijk. London: Academic Press.

Shaiko, Ronald G. 1993. "Greenpeace U.S.A.: Something Old, New, Borrowed." *The Annals of the American Academy of Political and Social Science* 528: 88–100.

Shepard, Paul, and Daniel McKinley, eds. 1969. *The Subversive Science*. Boston: Houghton Mifflin.

Simon, Herbert A. 1976. *Administrative Behavior: A Study of Decision-Making in Administrative Organization*, 3d ed. New York: Free Press.

Spretnak, Charlene. 1986. *The Spiritual Dimension in Green Politics*. Santa Fe, NM: Bear and Company.

———. 1990. "Ecofeminism: Our Roots and Our Flowering," in *Reweaving the World*, ed. Diamond and Orenstein.

Spretnak, Charlene, and Fritjof Capra. 1986. *Green Politics: The Global Promise*. Santa Fe, NM: Bear and Company.

Starhawk. 1990. "Power, Authority, and Mystery: Ecofeminism and Earth-based Spirituality," in *Reweaving the World*, ed. Diamond and Orenstein.

Steering Committee of the District of Tofino and the Tofino–Long Beach Chamber of Commerce. 1989. *Sustainable Development Strategy for Clayoquot Sound: A Project Proposal*. Tofino, BC, May.

Strauss, Leo. 1953. *Natural Right and History*. Chicago: University of Chicago Press.

Szaz, Andrew. 1994. *Ecopopulism: Toxic Waste and the Movement for Environmental Justice*. Minneapolis: University of Minnesota Press.

Tawney, R. H. 1984. *Religion and the Rise of Capitalism*. Harmondsworth: Penguin.

Taylor, Bob Pepperman. 1991. "Environmental Ethics and Political Theory." *Polity* 23: 567–83.

———. 1996. "Democracy and Environmental Ethics," in *Democracy and the Environment*, ed. William M. Lafferty and James Meadowcroft. Cheltenham, UK: Edward Elgar.

Taylor, Charles. 1973. "Neutrality in Political Science," *The Philosophy of Social Explanation*, ed. Alan Ryan. Oxford: Oxford University Press.

Taylor, Serge. 1984. *Making Bureaucracies Think: The Environmental Impact Statement Strategy of Administrative Reform*. Stanford: Stanford University Press.

Tesh, Sylvia N. 1993. "Environmentalism, Pre-environmentalism and Public Policy." *Policy Sciences* 26: 1–20.

Tesh, Sylvia N., and Bruce A. Williams. 1996. "Identity Politics, Disinterested Politics, and Environmental Justice." *Polity* 28: 285–305.

Timmerman, Peter. 1989. "The Environmentalist as Dark Comedian," *Alternatives: Perspectives on Society, Technology and Environment* 16, no. 2: 24–27.

Tokar, Brian. 1997. *Earth for Sale: Reclaiming Ecology in the Age of Corporate Greenwashing*. Boston: South End Press.

Torgerson, Douglas. 1978. "Domination and Liberatory Politics." *Canadian Journal of Political and Social Theory* 2: 137–57.

———. 1980. *Industrialization and Assessment: Social Impact Assessment as a Social Phenomenon*. Toronto: York University.

———. 1985. "Contextual Orientation in Policy Analysis: The Contribution of Harold D. Lasswell." *Policy Sciences* 18: 241–61.

———. 1986. "Between Knowledge and Politics: Three Faces of Policy Analysis." *Policy Sciences* 19: 33–59.

———. 1990. "Limits of the Administrative Mind: The Problem of Defining Environmental Problems," in *Managing Leviathan*, ed. Paehlke and Torgerson.

———. 1990. "Obsolescent Leviathan: Problems of Order in Administrative Thought," in *Managing Leviathan*, ed. Paehlke and Torgerson.

———. 1990. "Origins of the Policy Orientation: The Aesthetic Dimension in Lasswell's Political Vision." *History of Political Thought* 11: 211–24.

———. 1993. "The Paradox of Organizational Rationality: Uncertainty Absorption and the Technology of Foolishness," paper presented at the School of Business, Queen's University, Kingston, Ontario.

———. 1995. "Policy Analysis and Public Life: The Restoration of *Phronēsis?*" in *Political Science in History: Research Programs and Political Traditions*, ed. James Farr, John S. Dryzek, and Stephen T. Leonard. Cambridge: Cambridge University Press.

———. 1996. "Power and Insight in Policy Discourse: Postpositivism and Problem Definition," in *Policy Studies in Canada: The State of the Art*, ed. Laurent Dobuzinskis, Michael Howlett, and David Laycock. Toronto: University of Toronto Press.

———. 1997. "Policy Professionalism and the Voices of Dissent: The Case of Environmentalism." *Polity* 29: 358–59.

Tribe, Laurence H. 1972. "Policy Science: Analysis or Ideology?" *Philosophy and Public Affairs* 2: 66–110.

———. 1972–73. "Technology Assessment and the Fourth Discontinuity: The Limits of Instrumental Rationality." *Southern California Law Review* 46: 617–60.

Trist, Eric. 1977. "A Concept of Organizational Ecology." *Australian Journal of Management* 2: 161–75.

Turner, R. K., ed. 1988. *Sustainable Environmental Management*. London: Belhaven Press.

Van Parijs, Philippe. 1992. "Competing Justifications of Basic Income," in *Arguing for Basic Income: Ethical Foundations for a Radical Reform*, ed. Philippe Van Parijs. London: Verso.

——. 1992. "The Second Marriage of Justice and Efficiency," in *Arguing for Basic Income: Ethical Foundations for a Radical Reform*, ed. Philippe Van Parijs. London: Verso.

Vargish, Thomas. 1980. "Why the Person Sitting Next to You Hates 'Limits to Growth.'" *Technological Forecasting and Social Change* 16: 179–89.

Villa, Dana R. 1996. *Arendt and Heidegger: The Fate of the Political*. Princeton: Princeton University Press.

Walker, Barbara G. 1988. *The Woman's Dictionary of Symbols and Sacred Objects*. San Francisco: Harper Collins.

Wapner, Paul. 1996. *Environmental Activism and World Civic Politics* Albany: State University of New York Press.

Warnke, Georgia. 1995. "Communicative Rationality and Cultural Values," *The Cambridge Companion to Habermas*, ed. Stephen K. White. Cambridge: Cambridge University Press.

Warren, Karren J. 1993. "The Power and Promise of Ecological Feminism," in *Environmental Philosophy*, ed. Michael E. Zimmerman. Englewood Cliffs, NJ: Prentice-Hall.

Weale, Albert. 1992. *The New Politics of Pollution*. Manchester, UK: University of Manchester Press.

——. 1993. "The Limits of Ecocentrism." *Environmental Politics* 2: 340–43.

Weber, Max. 1958. *From Max Weber: Essays in Sociology*. Trans. H. H. Gerth and C. Wright Mills. New York: Oxford University Press.

——. 1958. *The Protestant Ethic and the Spirit of Capitalism*. Trans. Talcott Parsons. New York: Charles Schriber's Sons.

Weinberg, Alvin M. 1972. "Science and Trans-Science." *Minerva* 10: 209–22.

——. 1972. "Social Institutions and Nuclear Power," *Science* 177: 27–34.

Weisberg, Barry. 1971. *Beyond Repair: The Ecology of Capitalism*. Boston: Beacon Press.

Weiss, Andrew, and Edward Woodhouse. 1992. "Reframing Incrementalism: A Constructive Response to the Critics." *Policy Sciences* 25: 255–74.

Whitebrook, Joel. 1996. "The Problem of Nature in Habermas," in *Minding Nature: The Philosophers of Ecology*, ed. David Macauley. New York: Guilford Press.

Whitehead, A. N. 1948. *Science and the Modern World*. New York: Mentor.

Whiteside, Kerry. 1994. "Hannah Arendt and Ecological Politics." *Environmental Ethics* 16: 339–58.

——. 1997. "French Ecosocialism: From Utopia to Contract." *Environmental Politics* 6: 99–124.

Wiesenthal, Helmut. 1993. *Realism in Green Politics: Social Movements and Ecological Reform in Germany*. Manchester, UK: Manchester University Press.

Wilkinson, Paul. 1971. *Social Movement*. New York: Praeger Publishers.

Williams, Bruce A., and Albert R. Matheny. 1995. *Democracy, Dialogue, and Environmental Disputes: The Contested Languages of Social Regulation*. New Haven: Yale University Press.

Woiceshyn, Glen, and Jaana Woiceshyn. 1993. "Commentary: 'Corporate Environmentalism' and Other Suicidal Tendencies," in *Environmentalism: What Does It Mean for Business?*, ed. Jaana Woiceshyn. Calgary: University of Calgary, Faculty of Management.

Wolin, Sheldon S. 1960. *Politics and Vision: Continuity and Innovation in Western Political Thought*. Boston: Little, Brown.

———. 1969. "Political Theory as a Vocation." *American Political Science Review* 63: 1062–82.

World Commission on Environment and Development. 1987. *Our Common Future.* Oxford: Oxford University Press.

Worster, Donald. 1979. *Nature's Economy: The Roots of Ecology.* Garden City, NY: Anchor Books.

Young, Iris Marion. 1987. "Impartiality and the Civic Public," in *Feminism as Critique*, ed. Seyla Benhabib and Drucilla Cornell. Minneapolis: University of Minnesota Press.

———. 1990. *Justice and the Politics of Difference.* Princeton: Princeton University Press.

———. 1996. "Communication and the Other: Beyond Deliberative Democracy," in *Democracy and Difference*, ed. Seyla Behabib. Princeton: Princeton University Press.

Yurick, Sol. 1972. "The Politics of the Imagination," in *Literature in Revolution*, ed. George Abbott White and Charles Newman. New York: Holt, Rinehart and Winston.

Zamyatin, Yevgeny. 1972. *We* (1925). Trans. Mirra Ginsberg. New York: Bantam Books.

Heilbroner, Robert, 84
Historical agency, 2, 23, 26, 28, 32–34, 39, 49, 71
Hjelmar, Ulf, 24–25, 37, 173 n.15
Hobbes, Thomas, 84, 130, 155
Holism, 100, 102
Homocentrism, x, 5, 22, 28, 98, 108–111, 119, 125, 172 n.71
Horkheimer, Max, xiv, 112–14, 164, 172 n.75
Hülsberg, Werner, 40, 45
Human/nature, ix, 2, 6, 64, 105, 107–8, 110–12, 120, 123–24, 127, 130, 135, 138–39, 146, 167. *See also* Domination of nature

Idealism, 22, 34–35, 174 n.52
Identity, x–xii, 1, 4, 12, 17, 19, 33–34, 44, 48–49, 66, 75, 81, 95, 106, 109, 113, 153, 157–58, 167–68, 172 n.75
Ideology, 12–13, 169 n.3
Ignorance, 57, 77, 79, 102, 138, 143
Incrementalism, 27, 58–59, 69, 137, 143, 146–48. *See also* Strategic thought
Incremental radicalism, 147–48, 151. *See also* Incrementalism; Radicalism; Radical reform; Reformism
Industrial ecology, 69, 74
Industrialism, x, xi, 2, 4, 20–21, 27, 31, 38–39, 44, 52–53, 55–56, 62–66, 71–73, 75, 85, 95, 97–98, 130, 135–36, 138, 143–44, 148, 151, 153–54, 159, 160–63, 168. *See also* Administrative mind; Dysfunctions of industrialism; Pre-environmentalism; Scientism; Technocratic orientation
Instrumental rationality, 81–82, 113–14
Instrumentalism, x–xii, 4, 6–7, 15–16, 19, 21, 25, 112, 131–32, 149, 151, 155, 160
Intrinsic value: of nature, 110; of political action, 15, 17, 133–34, 149, 154–57, 162, 168

Jacobson, Norman, xiv
Johnson, Lyndon, 190 n.75
Johnson, Mark, 156

Kant, Immanuel, 115
Kantianism, 112, 118
Kariel, Henry, xiv, 15, 83, 156, 171 n.48, 182 n.1

Kaufmann, Walter, 183 n.23
Kellner, Hans, 183 n.38
Kerr, Walter, 95–96, 101, 183 n.38, 184 n.53
King, Ynestra, 33, 123
Kontos, Alkis, xiv, 171 n.48
Kostede, Norbert, 163
Krutch, Joseph Wood, 86, 88

Laclau, Ernesto, 45–48
Lakoff, George, 156
Land ethic, 100, 111
Language of environment, 51, 130, 160–61. *See also* Environmental discourse; Green discourse
Lasswell, Harold, 137, 172 n.9, 181 n.51
Laughter, xiii–xiv, 1, 83, 90, 92, 94–95, 101–2, 123, 165, 167, 183 n.38
Lee, Kai, 58–59
Leiss, William, xv, 12
Leopold, Aldo, 100, 108, 111, 121–22, 124
Liberal democracy, xi, 8–10, 27, 69, 130, 138, 170 n.25, 170 n.33, 170 n.38
Lilliput strategy, 149, 155
Limits to Growth, The (Donella Meadows et al.), 51–53
Lindblom, Charles, 27, 58, 137, 173 n.19
Lipietz, Alain, 175 n.62, 177 n.108
Locke, John, 130, 188 n.11
Logocentrism, 164
Love Canal, 70
Lovelock, James, 121
Lovins, Amory, 72–73, 80, 180 n.31
Lukács, Georg, 120
Lyotard, Jean-François, xiv, 48

Machiavelli, Niccolo, 15, 21, 46–47, 135
Macpherson, C. B., xiv
Majone, Giandomenico, 80–81
Manes, Christopher, 120
Mannheim, Karl, 13, 169 n.3
March, James, 81–82, 137, 142
Marcuse, Herbert, xiv, 36–37, 45, 174 n.50, 175 n.58
Market, 8, 21–22, 55, 143–44, 152, 171 n.43
Marx, Karl, 34, 37–47, 173 n.9, 183 n.14
Marxism, 19, 22, 28, 34–36, 37–47, 142, 146, 172 n.75, 174 n.52, 177 n.108. *See also* Ecomarxism; Hegelian Marxism; Post-Marxism
Materialism, 22, 28, 39, 45

Douglas Torgerson is Professor and Chair, Department of
Political Studies, and a member of the Environmental and
Resource Studies Program at Trent University in
Peterborough, Ontario, Canada. He is author of
*Industrialization and Assessment: Social Impact
Assessment as a Social Phenomenon* and editor (with
Robert Paehlke) of *Managing Leviathan: Environmental
Politics and the Administrative State.*
Library of Congress Cataloging-in-Publication Data
Torgerson, Douglas
The promise of green politics : environmentalism and
the public sphere / Douglas Torgerson.
Includes bibliographical references and index.
ISBN 0-8223-2337-0 (cloth : alk. paper).
ISBN 0-8223-2370-2 (paper : alk. paper)
1. Political ecology. 2. Green movement. 3. Human
ecology. 4. Environmentalism. I. Title.
JA75.8.T67 1999 304.2—dc21 98-56543 CIP